AF735336

Dynamics and Issues of Local Autonomy

Dynamics and Issues of Local Autonomy

A Comparative Study

Andreas Ladner

Nicolas Keuffer

Alexander Bastianen

Harald Baldersheim

Nikos Hlepas

Carmen Navarro

Kristof Steyvers

Paweł Swianiewicz

Edward Elgar PUBLISHING

Cheltenham, UK • Northampton, MA, USA

© Andreas Ladner, Nicolas Keuffer, Alexander Bastianen, Harald Baldersheim, Nikos Hlepas, Carmen Navarro, Kristof Steyvers and Paweł Swianiewicz 2025

BY NC ND

This is an open access work distributed under the Creative Commons Attribution-NonCommercial-NoDerivatives 4.0 International (https://creativecommons.org/licenses/by-nc-nd/4.0/) license.

Published by
Edward Elgar Publishing Limited
The Lypiatts
15 Lansdown Road
Cheltenham
Glos GL50 2JA
UK

Edward Elgar Publishing, Inc.
William Pratt House
9 Dewey Court
Northampton
Massachusetts 01060
USA

Authorised representative in the EU for GPSR queries only: Easy Access System Europe – Mustamäe tee 50, 10621 Tallinn, Estonia, gpsr.requests@easproject.com

A catalogue record for this book
is available from the British Library

Library of Congress Control Number: 2024952795

This book is available electronically in the **Elgar**online
Political Science and Public Policy subject collection
https://doi.org/10.4337/9781035337958

MIX
Paper | Supporting responsible forestry
FSC® C013604
FSC www.fsc.org

ISBN 978 1 0353 3794 1 (cased)
ISBN 978 1 0353 3795 8 (eBook)

Printed and bound by CPI Group (UK) Ltd, Croydon, CR0 4YY

Contents

Figures

Authors

Andreas Ladner, formerly Professor of Political Institutions and Public Administration, Swiss Graduate Institute of Public Administration (IDHEAP), University of Lausanne, Switzerland.

Nicolas Keuffer, Senior Research Fellow, Swiss Graduate Institute of Public Administration (IDHEAP), University of Lausanne, Switzerland.

Alexander Bastianen, Research Assistant and PhD Candidate, Swiss Graduate Institute of Public Administration (IDHEAP), University of Lausanne, Switzerland.

Harald Baldersheim, Professor Emeritus, Department of Political Science, University of Oslo, Norway.

Nikos Hlepas, Professor of Regional Administration and Self Government, Department of Political Science and Public Administration, National and Kapodistrian University of Athens, Greece.

Carmen Navarro, Professor, Department of Political Science and International Relations, Universidad Autónoma de Madrid, Spain.

Kristof Steyvers, Professor, Department of Political Science, Ghent University, Belgium.

Paweł Swianiewicz, Professor of Local Government and Urban Economics, Wroclaw University of Environmental and Life Sciences, Poland.

Preface

The Local Autonomy Index (LAI) is a multi-dimensional conceptualization and measurement of local autonomy initially developed in 2015. The first volume on the LAI was published in 2019, focusing on the construction of the index, its application to the European context to highlight various patterns of local autonomy and the study of its causes and consequences. In this second book, the Local Autonomy Index 2.0 ('the LAI 2.0') refines our measurement and extends it to countries on six continents. The LAI 2.0 proposes an analysis of the dynamics of local autonomy and related issues over 30 years (1990–2020) in a comparative perspective. We hope that it will serve as a reference in the active academic and practical fields on questions related to the territorial organization of states, decentralization, public administration, local governance and intergovernmental relations.

This book is the fruit of a collaborative endeavour. The diversity of territorial and institutional models in Europe and beyond means that a project like the LAI 2.0 has to be organized on a decentralized basis.

As the approach taken in the first study has proved to be relevant, valid and usable (Harguindéguy et al. 2021), we have used a similar organization and methodology, relying on national experts of local government who are as close as possible to the reality of local autonomy in their respective countries. We would like to take this opportunity to express our great gratitude to them, because without their expertise in the subject and their meticulous work in researching sources and justifications, this study would not have been feasible (a full list of country experts is found in Chapter 1). We, the co-authors of this book, have contributed to gathering the most accurate data possible as country group coordinators. Given the heterogeneity of local-government systems even within the same geographical region, exchanges with national experts on the government structures to be taken into account, the scores attributed to each variable and the reforms that have taken place at a given time represented an enormous enrichment. Every discussion and decision contributed to the realization of this project. During the writing of this book, the meeting of different normative visions of local autonomy or of the various challenges encountered in one region or another enabled us to balance our conception of the concept and to present issues faced in many contexts.

Mobilizing a network of local-government experts to set up this collaborative study would not have been possible without the financial support of the European Commission. The updating and refinement of the existing data up to 2020, the increase in the number of countries covered (now including all European Union (EU) member states as well as those of the Council of Europe (CoE) and of the Organisation for Economic Co-operation and Development (OECD)) and the inclusion of additional variables have been done in accordance with the European Commission's call for tender 2019CE16BAT176 (Ladner et al. 2021). The coordination of this project and the writing of this book have been centrally coordinated (to benefit from economies of scale) by the leading house, the Graduate Institute of Public Administration (IDHEAP) at the University of Lausanne. We are grateful for financial support in the coordination of this publication to Katia Horber-Papazian, Honorary Professor at the IDHEAP, as well as the IDHEAP's reserve fund for additional expenses related to the overall project.

As mentioned above, the text of the book is the result of the collective effort of all the authors. However, for each individual chapter, the names responsible for preparing and serving as their (lead) authors are as follows:

1. The LAI 2.0: project scope, conceptualization of local autonomy, methodology and contributions: Nicolas Keuffer and Alexander Bastianen
2. Main results and dynamics of local autonomy: Nicolas Keuffer and Alexander Bastianen
3. Self-rule versus interactive rule: towards a cross-national empirical typology of local autonomy: Kristof Steyvers and Paweł Swianiewicz
4. Asymmetric decentralization at the subnational level: varied arrangements of local autonomy: Kristof Steyvers
5. Organizational autonomy: Carmen Navarro, Nikos Hlepas and Alexander Bastianen
6. Financial autonomy as local democratic space: Harald Baldersheim and Paweł Swianiewicz
7. Assigned tasks and tasks delivered: Nikos Hlepas
8. Legal regimes and local autonomy: the interaction of administrative supervision and legal protection: Harald Baldersheim
9. Regional and local autonomy: comparing measurements of decentralization: Nicolas Keuffer and Carmen Navarro
10. Pathways of access: configurations of formal and informal channels: Kristof Steyvers
11. The impact of global crises on local autonomy: Carmen Navarro and Nikos Hlepas

12. The European Charter of Local Self-Government and its impact on local autonomy: Nikos Hlepas and Paweł Swianiewicz
13. Rapid changes in local autonomy: a race away from the bottom or a fall from a great height?: Paweł Swianiewicz and Kristof Steyvers
14. The potential influences of local autonomy on local-government legitimacy: Alexander Bastianen and Nicolas Keuffer

The LAI 2.0 project and this book were initiated by the late Prof Dr Andreas Ladner. His immense accumulated knowledge and recognized work on territorial organization, political institutions, public administration, decentralization, federalism, local-government systems and municipalities, from a national (Swiss) as well as a cross-national comparative perspective, made him the right person to develop the LAI. To our great sadness, our friend and colleague Andreas passed away on 7 February 2023, while this book was being written.

In Switzerland and beyond, Andreas had a great interest in diversity and was keen to enable exchanges between different cultures, organizations and forms of knowledge. The decentralized organization of the local autonomy projects described above is a fine illustration of this. Always pragmatic, Andreas was also committed to forging links between disciplines. At a time where there was no consensus on any theory of local autonomy, he had the brilliant idea of taking into account the different approaches, theoretical paradigms and conceptualizations of the many disciplines and studies that deal with the concept in order to develop our own approach and measurement of local autonomy. In addition, Andreas always endeavoured to ensure that the results of his research were useful and shared with a wider audience. The use of our index to shed light on the dynamics and issues related to local autonomy faced by countries in recent years is not only addressed to scholars but also to practitioners, and is in line with his vision. But, above all, we miss Andreas' passionate, brilliant, inspiring, caring and accessible personality. This book is dedicated to him.

The co-authors of this book: Nicolas Keuffer, Alexander Bastianen, Harald Baldersheim, Nikos Hlepas, Carmen Navarro, Kristof Steyvers and Paweł Swianiewicz

IDHEAP, 30 July 2024

PART I

ASSESSING AND MEASURING LOCAL AUTONOMY

1. The LAI 2.0: project scope, conceptualization of local autonomy, methodology, and contributions

INTRODUCTION

The Local Autonomy Index (LAI), an overall multi-dimensional measurement of the degree of autonomy enjoyed by local governments, has brought a measure of theoretical convergence regarding the core components of local autonomy. The LAI is an accurate, recognized indicator enabling an understanding of the territorial organization of states, public administration, decentralization, local governance and intergovernmental relations. This book draws upon updated and expanded data from the refined Local Autonomy Index 2.0, hereafter referred to as 'the LAI 2.0'. It extends the coverage to additional countries (57 in total) and years (1990 to 2020), and incorporates new variables to measure the effects of local autonomy and related issues.

Considered as the most robust decentralization index available at the local level based on multiple criteria (Harguindéguy et al. 2021), the LAI has been extensively used and cited by many scholars to compare public-administration traditions (e.g. Kuhlmann and Wollmann 2019), develop typologies of local-government systems (e.g. Heinelt et al. 2018b), test the effects of local autonomy on local democracy and efficiency (e.g. Däubler et al. 2018; Gendźwiłł 2021), measure decentralization (e.g. Teles 2023) or serve as a conceptual model to assess local autonomy at subnational levels (e.g. Bolgherini et al. 2021). Policymakers in international multilateral and national organizations have also shown interest in the results of the previous project and have advocated the values associated with the concept. For example, the Organisation for Economic Co-operation and Development (OECD) report on multilevel governance uses the fiscal-decentralization dataset and institutional databases such as the LAI to constitute a solid foundation on which recommendations for policymakers to make decentralization work are based (OECD 2019). Also, the eighth cohesion report of the European Commission affirms the importance of local and regional autonomy in promoting locally tailored policies (European Commission 2022). The LAI has been a useful resource for practical lessons on local governance (Ladner 2017) and some national organizations have also shown an interest in using existing data for benchmarking or requesting more targeted information (e.g. Baldersheim et al. 2019).

The original Local Autonomy Index 1.0 (LAI 1.0) measured local autonomy between 1990 and 2014 in 39 countries (Ladner et al. 2019). As the methodology of the LAI 1.0 has been proved to be relevant, valid and usable, we have used a similar methodology and decentralized organization, relying on country group coordinators and national experts of local autonomy. Mobilizing a network of local-government experts to set up this collaborative study would not have been possible without the call for tenders from the European Commission. The mandate from the European Commission lasted from the end of November 2020 to the end of December 2021. It requested an update of the existing data, from 1990 up to 2020, an increase in the number of countries covered and the inclusion of additional variables, and led to the delivery of a final report (Ladner et al. 2021).

In this LAI 2.0 project, we have updated and expanded the existing data for 1990 to 2020 and increased the number of countries covered, namely the countries from the European Union (EU) as well as those of the Council of Europe (CoE) and the OECD. Table 1.1 provides information on the countries included in the LAI 2.0, their affiliation in multilateral organizations, the units of analysis and the experts responsible for coding. We now cover 57 countries, located on six continents, including all 27 EU member states, 44 CoE member states (missing are Azerbaijan, Monaco and San Marino), and 36 OECD member states (New Zealand is missing, as is Costa Rica which joined the OECD in May 2021 when the project was already in progress). Additionally, Argentina, Belarus, Kosovo and South Africa have been included. For all these countries we now have data from 1990 to 2020. All the data, methodological explanations and country profiles can also be downloaded from our website.[1]

The rest of this first chapter provides information on the conceptualization and definition of local autonomy, on the seven dimensions of local autonomy and the construction of the index, on the codebook used in the project and the organization of data collection and control, as well as on the contributions of the LAI 2.0 project on democratic theory.

1 See http://local-autonomy.andreasladner.ch/.

Table 1.1 *Countries covered, membership affiliations, units of aggregation and analysis, coding experts and geographical location*

Country	Membership	Unit of aggregation	Units of analysis	Country expert	Country group coordinator	Continent
Denmark	EU, CoE, OECD	Country level	Municipalities (Kommuner)	Kurt Houlberg	Harald Baldersheim	Europe
Finland	EU, CoE, OECD	Country level	Municipalities (Kunta)	Pekka Kettunen	Harald Baldersheim	Europe
Iceland	CoE, OECD	Country level	Municipalities (Sveitarfélag)	Eva Hlynsdottir	Harald Baldersheim	Europe
Norway	CoE, OECD	Country level	Municipalities (Kommune)	Harald Baldersheim	Harald Baldersheim	Europe
Sweden	EU, CoE, OECD	Country level	Municipalities (Kommuner)	Anders Lidström	Harald Baldersheim	Europe
Cyprus	EU, CoE	Country level	Communities (Koinotites) Municipalities (Dimoi)	Andreas Kirlappos	Nikolaos Hlepas	Europe
Greece	EU, CoE, OECD	Country level	Municipalities (Dimos)	Nikos Hlepas	Nikolaos Hlepas	Europe
Malta	EU, CoE	Country level	Local Councils (Kunsill Lokali)	Natalino Caruana de Brincat	Nikolaos Hlepas	Europe

Country	Membership	Unit of aggregation	Units of analysis	Country expert	Country group coordinator	Continent
Turkey	CoE, OECD	Country level	Municipalities (Belediye) Metropolitan cities Special Provincial Administrations	Ali Cenap Yologlu	Nikolaos Hlepas	Europe
Russian Federation	CoE (at the time of the study)	Country level	Settlements Urban okrugs Federal cities	Emil Markwart and Alexander Larichev	Nikolaos Hlepas	Europe
Italy	EU, CoE, OECD	Country level	Municipalities (Comuni)	Annick Magnier	Carmen Navarro	Europe
Spain	EU, CoE, OECD	Country level	Municipalities below/above 20000 inhabitants (Municipios)	Carmen Navarro	Carmen Navarro	Europe
Portugal	EU, CoE, OECD	Country level	Municipalities (Municípios)	Miguel Angelo Rodriguez	Carmen Navarro	Europe
Andorra	CoE	Country level	Municipalities (Paroisses)	Lluis Medir	Carmen Navarro	Europe
Belgium	EU, CoE, OECD	Federal (3 Regions, Brussels-Capital, Flanders and Wallonia)	Municipalities (Gemeenten, Gemeinde or Communes)	Kristof Steyvers	Kristof Steyvers	Europe
Netherlands	EU, CoE, OECD	Country level	Municipalities (Gemeenten)	Bas Denters	Kristof Steyvers	Europe

Country	Membership	Unit of aggregation	Units of analysis	Country expert	Country group coordinator	Continent
Luxembourg	EU, CoE, OECD	Country level	Municipalities (Commune, Gemeng, Gemeinde)	Raphaël Kies and Dan Schmidt	Kristof Steyvers	Europe
Switzerland	CoE, OECD	Federal (26 cantons)	Municipalities (Gemeinden, Communes, Comune)	Nicolas Keuffer and Alexander Bastianen	Andreas Ladner	Europe
Liechtenstein	CoE	Country level	Municipalities (Gemeinden)	Andreas Ladner and Alexander Bastianen	Andreas Ladner	Europe
United Kingdom	CoE, OECD	England, Wales, Scotland and Northern Ireland	Local authorities	Michael Goldsmith	Andreas Ladner	Europe
Ireland	EU, CoE, OECD	Country level	Municipalities	Gerard Turley	Andreas Ladner	Europe
Estonia	EU, CoE, OECD	Country level	Municipalities (Parishes and Urban municipalities)	Georg Sottla	Pawel Swianiewicz	Europe
Latvia	EU, CoE, OECD	Country level	Municipalities (Novads)	Iveta Reinholde	Pawel Swianiewicz	Europe
Lithuania	EU, CoE, OECD	Country level	Municipalities (Savivaldybė)	Jurga Bucaite-Vilke	Pawel Swianiewicz	Europe
Czech Republic	EU, CoE, OECD	Country level	Municipalities (Obec)	Jakyb Lysek	Pawel Swianiewicz	Europe

Country	Membership	Unit of aggregation	Units of analysis	Country expert	Country group coordinator	Continent
Poland	EU, CoE, OECD	Country level	Municipalities (Gminy) Cities (Powiat)	Pawel Swianiewicz	Pawel Swianiewicz	Europe
Slovakia	EU, CoE, OECD	Country level	Municipalities (Ocbe)	Jan Bucek	Pawel Swianiewicz	Europe
Slovenia	EU, CoE, OECD	Country level	Municipalities (Občin) Cities (Mestna občina)	Irena Baclija	Pawel Swianiewicz	Europe
Hungary	EU, CoE, OECD	Country level	Municipalities (Települések)	Gábor Dobos	Pawel Swianiewicz	Europe
Romania	EU, CoE	Country level	Municipalities (Comune)	Cristina Stanus	Pawel Swianiewicz	Europe
Bulgaria	EU, CoE	Country level	Municipalities (Obshtina)	Desislava Kalcheva	Pawel Swianiewicz	Europe
Croatia	EU, CoE	Country level	Municipalities (Općina) Cities (Grad)	Mihovil Skarica	Pawel Swianiewicz	Europe
Serbia	CoE	Country level	Municipalities (Opštine) Cities (Gradovi) Belgrade City	Dusan Vasiljevic	Pawel Swianiewicz	Europe

Country	Membership	Unit of aggregation	Units of analysis	Country expert	Country group coordinator	Continent
Bosnia and Herzegovina	CoE	3 subjects (Republika Srpska, District Brcko and Federation of Bosnia and Herzegovina which includes 10 cantons)	Municipalities (opština)	Zdravko Miovcic and Marijana Galic	Pawel Swianiewicz	Europe
Albania	CoE	Country level	Municipalities (Bashkia)	Orsiola Kurti	Pawel Swianiewicz	Europe
Moldova	CoE	Country level	Districts (Raion)	Alexandru Osadci	Pawel Swianiewicz	Europe
Georgia	CoE	Country level	Municipalities (Minucipaliteti)	Natia Daghelishvili	Pawel Swianiewicz	Europe
Ukraine	CoE	Country level	Villages (Sela) Towns (Selyshcha) Amalgamated Hromadas Cities (Mista)	Markiyan Dacyshyn	Pawel Swianiewicz	Europe
Montenegro	CoE	Country level	Municipalities (Opština)	Ana Đurnić	Pawel Swianiewicz	Europe
North Macedonia	CoE	Country level	Municipalities (Opštini)	Veli Kreci	Pawel Swianiewicz	Europe

Country	Membership	Unit of aggregation	Units of analysis	Country expert	Country group coordinator	Continent
Armenia	CoE	Country level	Communities (hamaynk) Yerevan capital	Arpi Sargsyan	Pawel Swianiewicz	Europe
Belarus		Country level	Municipalities (Raion) Cities (Oblast)	Dmitry Sokol	Pawel Swianiewicz	Europe
Kosovo		Country level	Municipalities (Komuna, Opština)	Memet Memeti	Pawel Swianiewicz	Europe
Austria	EU, CoE, OECD	Federal (9 Länder)	Municipalities (Gemeinden)	Franz Fallend and Armin Mühlböck	Sabine Kuhlmann	Europe
Germany	EU, CoE, OECD	Federal (16 Länder)	Municipalities (Gemeinden) Cities (Städte)	Angelika Vetter	Sabine Kuhlmann	Europe
France	EU, CoE, OECD	Country level	Municipalities (communes) Cities (Paris, Marseille, Lyon)	William Gilles	Sabine Kuhlmann	Europe
Canada	OECD	Federal (10 provinces and 3 territories)	Municipalities	Zack Taylor and Martin Horak	Nicolas Keuffer	North-America
United States of America	OECD	Federal (50 states)	Local governments	Harold L. Wolman and Jamie Boex	Nicolas Keuffer	North-America
Argentina		Federal (23 Provincias)	Municipalities (Municipio)	Daniel Cravacuore	Carmen Navarro	South America

Country	Membership	Unit of aggregation	Units of analysis	Country expert	Country group coordinator	Continent
Chile	OECD	Country level	Municipalities (Municipio)	Daniel Cravacuore	Carmen Navarro	South America
Colombia	OECD	Country level	Municipalities (Municipio)	Pablo Sanabria	Carmen Navarro	South America
Mexico	OECD	Federal (32 Estados)	Municipalities (Municipio)	Ady Patricia Carrera	Carmen Navarro	South America
Israel	OECD	Country level	Municipalities	Eran Razin	Nikolaos Hlepas	Asia
Japan	OECD	Country level	Towns/villages (Chō/ Mura) Cities (Shi)	Masao Kikuchi	Alexander Bastianen	Asia
Republic of Korea	OECD	Country level	Municipalities	Kwang-Hoon Lee	Alexander Bastianen	Asia
Australia	OECD	Federal (6 states)	Municipalities	Roberta Ryan	Kristof Steyvers	Oceania
South Africa		Federal (9 provinces)	Municipalities	Tinashe Chigwata	Andreas Ladner	Africa
57 countries	**27 EU, 44 CoE, 36 OECD member states**	**12 non-unitary countries**	**14 countries with asymmetrical arrangements at the local level**	**63 local experts**	**9 country group coordinators**	**6 continents**

Source: Authors' own.

LOCAL AUTONOMY, A MULTIFACETED CONCEPT DIFFERENTLY APPREHENDED

Local autonomy affirms the freedom of management and decision-making of public authorities, called local because they are distinct from the state, and sub-national from a geographical or legal standpoint (Guérard 2016). It is a central current principle related to the way a state organizes its territory and provides services to its population. Since the emergence of the modern nation-state, local autonomy has been at the centre of debates between those who favour a strong centre and subordinate state entities and those who insist on power sharing between different levels of state. It is also a highly valued feature of local government and good governance. Many international and European institutions, such as the World Bank, the International Monetary Fund, the OECD, the CoE and the EU have promoted decentralization reforms and the transfer of political responsibilities to the levels of government closest to the citizen (Ivanyna and Shah 2014; UCLG 2008; OECD 2004). Local autonomy has long been advocated by traditional political philosophers as a necessary condition for strong citizen participation in political decisions, greater accountability of decision-makers, increased attachment to the community, improved economic efficiency, the encouragement of healthy local competition and innovation in certain public policies (Mill 1975 [1859]; Tocqueville 1994 [1835]; Smith 1951 [1851]).

Despite the importance of the concept, there was little theoretical convergence regarding the definition and the core elements of local autonomy. In their identification of future research avenues for comparative studies on local public-sector reforms, Bouckaert and Kuhlmann (2016) identified local autonomy as one of the priority research areas for gaining a better understanding of the challenges faced by local governments and local governance, whether through quantitative or qualitative methods. This gap to be filled in the academic field can largely be explained by the conceptual issues underlying the study of local autonomy, which we group into three main points.

First, as the references above suggest, local autonomy has a strong normative component. It is often considered as the cornerstone of a genuine democracy, where decisions meet citizens' needs, demands and problems, or as the condition under which local government can deliver public services more efficiently through proximity. However, local autonomy should not be seen as a positive value in itself – which was too often the case in the literature according to King and Stoker (1996) – but rather as a means of achieving desirable effects from a democratic or functional perspective. These expected effects must, however, be tested empirically.

Second, difficulties have been pointed out in the literature on local autonomy with regard to comparative studies. These relate in particular to the terminology of the concept (meaning different things in different contexts), the heterogeneity of territorial models, leading to different notions of the local (Page and Goldsmith 1987a, 1987b), the lack of comparable data relating to the local level (Kuhlmann and Wollmann 2019) or the need to take the sectoral dimension of public policies into account (Marcou 2010).

Third, there was a consensus in the literature that there was no single established theory or definition of local autonomy (Clark 1984; Pierre 1990). On the one hand, this heterogeneity of views of local autonomy stems from 'formal', 'dynamic', 'functional' and 'governance' analytical approaches (Fleurke and Willemse 2004) and different theoretical insights: 'freedom from', 'freedom to' and 'reflection of local identity' (Pratchett 2004). On the other hand, it results from the multi-dimensional and transdisciplinary nature of the concept (Keuffer 2016). As a result, the literature is not unanimous on the subject of operationalizing the various components of local autonomy (Hansen and Klausen 2002; Vetter 2007).

The thorough review of the literature in our previous book highlighted the fact that local autonomy lies at the crossroads of different disciplines that approach the concept through specific dimensions or by combining them very differently. We relied on these various approaches and disciplines to propose a multi-dimensional theory-based concept of local autonomy (Ladner et al. 2019). The theoretical conception of local autonomy is the same in the present book. We primarily apprehend local autonomy as a relative concept that expresses the formal (vertical) modes of intergovernmental relationships. This corresponds to the traditional approach to local autonomy, the 'freedom from' higher levels of government (Pratchett 2004), without considering the horizontal relations between local government and social or economic interests (Gurr and King 1987). Our conception relies on law, with a focus on the legislative framework that stipulates the status and means of protection of local government; on economics, dealing with the financial resources local government can independently dispose of and the expenses of delivering public services; on political science, which mainly highlights intergovernmental relations between levels of government in the sense of control, influence and discretion over decisions; and on public administration, which emphasizes how local authorities decide on their political and administrative organization and fulfil their tasks.

Considering local autonomy as the constituent element of the 'two faces of democratic self-determination' (Scharpf 1970) which guarantees political legitimacy, we define it as a policy space for local democracy (Ladner et al. 2016). In this sense, our conceptualization and definition are very close to the European Charter of Local Self-Government (hereafter: the European

Charter), which sets standards for national legislation to guarantee 'the right and the ability of local authorities, within the limits of the law, to regulate and manage a substantial share of public affairs under their own responsibility and in the interests of the local population' (CoE 1985, art. 3).[2] We have also relied on this international instrument to define the dimensions of local autonomy.

THE SEVEN DIMENSIONS OF LOCAL AUTONOMY AND THE CONSTRUCTION OF THE LAI

In accordance with our theory-based conceptualization, we apprehend local autonomy as a multi-dimensional phenomenon. Relying on the literature and various disciplines, we have identified legal, functional, political and organizational aspects of local autonomy as its important components. This operationalization is in keeping with substantial elements set out in the European Charter, which 'commits the parties to applying basic rules guaranteeing the political, administrative and financial independence of local authorities'. The European Charter was adopted by the CoE in 1985 to maintain and promote local autonomy in its member states. Its 18 articles set the standards for national legislation on local government on issues such as the constitutional and legal foundation of local authorities, their right to associate, the scope of their tasks, the conditions under which their responsibilities are exercised, their financial resources, appropriate administrative structures and resources, and administrative supervision of their activities. By laying out the conditions necessary both for the right of local authorities to resist constraint from higher levels of government and for their ability to satisfy local interests, the European Charter constitutes a pivotal shift towards a more positive conception of local autonomy and a big step towards an objectively measurable concept (Ladner et al. 2019).

In the LAI 1.0, we followed a more inductive approach. We argued that empirical aspects covered the different approaches to local autonomy and

2 www.coe.int, Treaty No. 122. The idea of 'local self-government' as employed in the European Charter means 'local autonomy' since the French version of the treaty is called 'Charte européenne de l'autonomie locale' (see also the preamble). By 2023, 46 member states of the CoE have signed and ratified the European Charter (the Russian Federation being no longer a member of the CoE). Furthermore, the European Charter has served as a model for the development of a draft text of a worldwide charter for local self-government by the United Nations Centre for Human Settlements (UNCHS Habitat) and the World Associations of Cities and Local Authorities Coordination (WACLAC). The United Cities and Local Governments (UCLG) declared in 2004 that the adoption of a World Charter for Local Self-Government remains one of its key objectives.

appeared in dimensions that were then weighted based on theoretical arguments. In the LAI 2.0, the logic is more deductive, as we rely on our theory-based concept of local autonomy to develop the dimensions of local autonomy (Ladner et al. 2023). We distinguish between the following seven dimensions of local autonomy:

1. Legal autonomy: the legal status and protection of local authorities within the state
2. Access: the degree of influence that local authorities exert on political decisions at higher levels of government
3. Policy scope: the range of functions for which local authorities are responsible
4. Political discretion: the range of functions over which local authorities have a say and whether they enjoy a general competence clause
5. Financial autonomy: the financial resources of local authorities and the ability to decide on their sources
6. Organizational autonomy: the free organization of local political systems and administrations
7. Noninterference: the degree of liberty left by higher levels of government in their control of local authorities.

In our prior research on the development of the LAI, we addressed issues pertaining to dimensionality and weighting (Ladner and Keuffer 2021). The literature on local autonomy does not present a unanimous consensus on the significance of any of its various facets. If we were to simply sum up these dimensions to derive an overarching measure of local autonomy, they would carry equal weight in the assessment. However, depending on the various theoretical approaches, certain dimensions may be awarded greater importance (Ladner et al. 2019). From our perspective on local autonomy, the functional and financial aspects are more important than the legal dimension, and we thus award higher weights to them. Nevertheless, it is worth noting that, depending on distinct purposes, the weighting may be adjusted accordingly.

For the LAI 2.0, we maintain similarities to the construction of the LAI 1.0, deeming political discretion and financial autonomy as the most prominent dimensions (weighted triple). Just below, we find policy scope, closely linked to political discretion, and organizational autonomy (weighted double). At the pinnacle, we address access to higher-level decisions, noninterference by higher levels and legal autonomy (weighted single). The dimensions of legal autonomy, financial autonomy and political discretion constitute the three foundational pillars and cornerstones of local autonomy. This 'triangle of local autonomy' also summarizes the construction of the overall LAI, which is assembled by adding the seven dimensions of local autonomy and their relative significance (Ladner and Keuffer 2021: 224).

The weighted overall LAI can be presented as follows: LAI = (legal autonomy + access + 2*policy scope + 3*political discretion + 3*financial autonomy + 2*organizational autonomy +noninterference)/13.

THE MEASUREMENT OF LOCAL AUTONOMY THROUGH A CODING SCHEME OF 11 VARIABLES

The seven dimensions of local autonomy are measured through 11 variables, which more precisely capture specific characteristics of the concept. Here, inspiration also comes from earlier endeavours on measuring regional authority. Drawing on studies on federalism, decentralization and regionalization (e.g. Hooghe et al. 2016), some variables are more closely related to governments' capacity to organize themselves and provide services independently (self-rule) and others to intergovernmental relationships (shared-rule). We decided to favour the term "interactive rule" rather than shared-rule since local government may enjoy shared-rule with higher levels of government and access to higher decision-making, but their performance is more likely to be influenced through innate procedures of control (Ladner et al. 2016).

Self-rule

1. Institutional depth: the extent to which local government is formally autonomous and can choose the tasks it wants to perform
2. Policy scope: the range of functions (tasks) where local government assumes responsibility for the delivery of services (whether provided by municipal personnel or through other arrangements)
3. Effective political discretion: the extent to which local government can make final decisions over the functions listed under policy scope
4. Fiscal autonomy: the extent to which local government can independently tax its population
5. Financial transfer system: the proportion of unconditional financial transfers to total financial transfers received by local government
6. Financial self-reliance: the proportion of local government revenues derived from own/local sources (taxes, fees, charges over which local government has influence)
7. Borrowing autonomy: the extent to which local government can borrow
8. Organizational autonomy: the extent to which local government is free to decide about its own organization and electoral system

Interactive Rule

9. Legal protection: the existence of constitutional or legal means to assert local autonomy
10. Administrative supervision: the extent to which administrative supervision of local government is (un)obtrusive
11. Central or regional access: the extent to which local authorities have channels to influence higher level governments' policy-making.

When dealing with variables that delve into the finer nuances of the concept and are encapsulated in various dimensions, the issue of weighting comes also into play. For example, consider the four financial variables, each of which captures vital aspects of local autonomy. The challenge lies in orchestrating them in a way that collectively measures an aspect of autonomy holistically and in establishing relationships that assign varying degrees of importance to these characteristics in the most justifiable way possible. Furthermore, with values ranging from 0 to 3 or 0 to 4, to render them comparable, we opted to standardize them on a scale ranging from 0 to 100, mirroring the dimensions.

A threefold process had to be undertaken: transforming variables for equal comparability, verifying relations between variables to determine whether they measure different parts of local autonomy or whether a combination is needed and, if so, properly combining and weighting them (Ladner et al. 2019). Factor-analysis outcomes and theoretical considerations led us to amalgamate institutional depth with effective political discretion in the political-discretion dimension, with a heightened emphasis on the latter variable due to its more tangible implications for local authorities' autonomy in assuming new functions. Simultaneously, we disentangled policy scope from effective political discretion, and grouped fiscal autonomy with financial self-reliance and borrowing autonomy. In the realm of financial autonomy, we posited that fiscal autonomy and financial self-reliance held greater significance than borrowing autonomy, while in the domain of noninterference, we regarded both variables – administrative supervision and financial transfer system – as equally important (Ladner and Keuffer 2021).

It is essential to note that the allocation of weights to these variables is essentially arbitrary and reflects our perception of the relative importance of various elements within the sphere of local autonomy, albeit it based on a broad landscape of literature and multiple series of empirical tests. The variables employed for the different dimensions (in bold) along with their assigned importance weights (numbers) are the following:

- **Legal autonomy:** YEAR=100/3*legal protection_YEAR

- **Access:** YEAR=100/3*central or regionalaccess_YEAR
- **Policy scope:** YEAR=100/4*policy scope_Total_YEAR
- **Political discretion:** YEAR=100/16*(institutionaldepth_YEAR + 3*effective political discretion_Total_YEAR)
- **Financial autonomy:** YEAR=100/25*(3*fiscal autonomy_YEAR + 3*financial selfreliance_YEAR + borrowing autonomy_YEAR)
- **Organizational autonomy:** YEAR=100/4*organizationalautonomy_YEAR
- **Noninterference:**_YEAR=100/7*(financial-transfer system_YEAR + administrative supervision_YEAR)

The coding framework for the LAI 2.0 closely resembles that of the LAI 1.0, with only a few minor adjustments to yield more detailed information, based on updated theoretical debates and empirical hindsight. The adjustments were made to ensure continuity in the time series, facilitating the analysis of trends and developments. This was also done in the context of the mandate of the European Commission, where a more detailed codebook was presented to ensure more precise scores in accordance with the updated state of knowledge on local autonomy in the various countries under scrutiny.

The codebook continues to include 11 variables, drawing on various types of rights and abilities as outlined in the literature, as well as coding instructions (see Appendix). While the codebook for the LAI 2.0 differs slightly from that of the LAI 1.0, most changes revolve around criteria adjustments and minor phrasing alterations that do not substantially affect scoring. These changes are aimed at collecting more precise information on various aspects of local autonomy while ensuring comparability with the initial results. Modifications involved policy scope, effective political discretion, organizational autonomy and central or regional access. In some instances, these changes impacted scoring, prompting adjustments. However, in most cases, scores remained unaffected. For instance, alterations in scores for specific service categories within the policy-scope and effective-political-discretion variables typically do not result in changes at the aggregated variable level. Significant changes in the aspects will be discussed in subsequent chapters.

To maintain a consistent time series spanning from 1990 to 2020 across all 57 countries at the aggregated 11-variable level, variable scores from the LAI 1.0 release were adapted to align with the updated LAI 2.0 codebook (Ladner et al. 2023). This ensured compatibility between the scoring for countries included in the first release (1990–2014) and newly added countries, covering the period from 2015 to 2020. The interpretation process was backed by a meticulous review of situations during the LAI 1.0 and LAI 2.0 research process. Scores from the previous release were adapted in the best way possible to reflect the detail of the LAI 2.0 codebook, whenever necessary. Country experts, coordinators and the leading house assessed these scores, considering the coding sheets and country profiles from both releases. Some scores were also recalibrated based on the most recent country profiles or external reports to better align with the current codebook. These adaptations serve the purpose of enhancing the updated and expanded LAI 2.0, which should be evaluated independently and not in direct comparison with the previous coding scheme.

As previously mentioned, the LAI 2.0 project involves the incorporation of additional variables aimed at assessing the factors influencing and the consequences of local autonomy. This approach aligns with the concept of 'freedom to' local autonomy as proposed by Pratchett (2004). In this project, we took the opportunity to collaborate with country experts, providing us with access to supplementary data at the local level. They were tasked with providing information on the number and size of local governments spanning the years from 1990 to 2020 (see Appendix). Furthermore, to gain deeper insights into how external shocks, such as the COVID-19 pandemic, may influence local autonomy in a given country, we inquired about the pandemic's implications. Regarding the effects of local autonomy, we made additional inquiries to these experts to gather primary data on two critical aspects among others: the quality of democracy and the efficiency of local government. These encompass various dimensions, including satisfaction with local-government service delivery, the significance of local government for citizens, satisfaction levels with local democracy, voter turnout in local elections and the trustworthiness of local politicians (see Appendix).

THE ORGANIZATION OF THE DATA-COLLECTION AND -CONTROL PROCESS

In the LAI 2.0 project, our methodology was similar to that used in the initial project, relying on the same terminology, units of analysis and aggregation, and control process (Ladner et al. 2019).

In this book we are still using the term 'local autonomy', following the criteria outlined by Lidström (1998), to indicate local government based on a defined territory, sufficient self-government for public-policy provision, authoritative power and elected decision-makers or assemblies. To gather data, we have focused on one level of local government, typically the lowest and most impactful one, where local autonomy is most effective. We aimed to cover the entire territory of each country, except for rare and less significant exceptions. In some newly included countries we consulted with country experts and coordinators to determine the appropriate unit of analysis (see Table 1.1). To aggregate the coding of the different variables measured according to the following rules:

- In unitary countries where all local governments have equal autonomy, the country serves as the unit of aggregation.
- In unitary countries with asymmetrical arrangements across local governments, different units of aggregation may exist and are therefore considered (e.g. 'general municipalities' and 'cities with special competencies').
- In federal countries with uniform local autonomy across subunits, the country is the unit of aggregation.
- In federal countries with varying autonomy across subunits (cantons, states), the subunits serve as the units of aggregation.

Our method for measuring local autonomy involved expert assessments and enabled us to amass an impressive volume of comparable data. To address the reliability and validity concerns associated with expert judgements, as highlighted in the literature (e.g. Steenbergen and Marks 2007), we conducted multiple coordination meetings with experts. An online workshop on 30 and 31 January 2020 was attended by all country group coordinators and the experts involved in coding the countries of their respective groups. The aim was to present the renewed project, goals and expected outputs, and to respond to any questions about the coding process and instructions.

As was the case during the LAI 1.0 process, we reviewed the coding of countries internally while compiling the data. We cross-checked the information using existing datasets covering fiscal decentralization, local-government expenditures and local-government employees. Our approach involved three levels of consistency checks:

- At the country level, we assessed whether there were variables where the coded values deviated from the overall country pattern.
- Within country groups, we looked for countries with coded variables that did not align with the overall pattern of the group.
- Across all countries compared, we identified outliers for each variable and for the total value to ensure consistency.

We also carried out an external control of our initial outputs, which were the country profiles, coding sheets and variables, and first results. The international experts Prof Dr Anders Lidström (Umeå University, Sweden) and Isabelle Chatry (Unit on Decentralization, Public Investment and Subnational Finance at the OECD) carefully reviewed our results and outputs and stated their respective agreements and disagreements with the coding scheme.

LOCAL AUTONOMY AND GOOD DEMOCRATIC GOVERNANCE: CONSEQUENCES, PRECONDITIONS AND PATHS FOR FUTURE RESEARCH

Democratic governance is under pressure in many parts of the world. Understanding the dynamics of democratic progress, and of backsliding, is a central issue for academic research and democratic reforms today. A series of data banks present various indicators and interpretations of good democratic governance. Unfortunately most of them neglect local government and local autonomy, at least in any systematic fashion. We think that studies of local autonomy could make significant contributions in this regard. The literature on political-administrative decentralization often voices expectations about positive outcomes of decentralization, such as higher rates of political participation or better adaptation of public goods to local needs, although some negative aspects are also sometimes pointed out. In Chapter 14, these expectations or predictions are sorted into input-, throughput- and output-related consequences of decentralization and tested as far as available data permit. Arguably, the LAI 2.0 measure is a better operationalization of decentralization than many of the indicators used in previous studies, which should lend extra weight to the results reported in this last chapter of our book.

We emphasize, furthermore, that analyses of consequences of local autonomy do not only yield insights relevant to the organization of local or regional government. Such studies are also of interest for the wider study of good democratic governance in general. In the majority of countries covered in this project, local government is the largest branch of government and also the branch closest to the people; therefore, studies of good governance that neglect local government do not really capture the totality of government, nor do they provide insights into governance that really matter to people. Local autonomy may in fact be a vital component of the overall democratic quality of nations, as argued for instance by Vetter (2007). Such a claim can be examined more precisely using LAI 2.0 indicators. These also allow for a better study of decentralization. As argued in Chapter 9, when decentralization is viewed as a static state, the degree of decentralization becomes a characteristic of the politico-administrative system and implies more or less autonomy enjoyed by the various tiers of the state. The chapter combines the LAI with other decentralization indexes focused on levels of government other than local to assess the distribution of power and responsibilities among multiple tiers. Indeed, this book emphasizes the importance of the variety of existing subnational arrangements, in both a vertical and a horizontal dimension. Chapter 4 scrutinizes asymmetric decentralization at the subnational level by probing into varied arrangements of local autonomy within states.

As the LAI 2.0 data covers a span of 30 years, the dynamics of local autonomy are also brought to the forefront. For example, Chapter 9 not only studies the territorial organization of countries in a static, formal perspective, but also looks at the developments that have occurred in decentralization over the past three decades, in a dynamic perspective. To better understand the evolution of local autonomy and the triggers of local-government reforms, Chapter 13 describes where, when and how rapid changes occurred in the 57 countries covered. Chapters 11 and 12, in turn, focus more on the consequences for local autonomy arising from two particular significant challenges, the COVID-19 pandemic and the adoption of the European Charter. Chapter 2 presents the main results of the LAI 2.0 project, by also taking a diachronic outlook.

If local autonomy is of relevance to, or a driver of, good democratic governance, then investigating the preconditions for local autonomy is also of great interest. Is it possible to identify any levers that reformers may push in order to obtain efficient local autonomy? Or any traps or blind alleys that they should avoid? This issue is followed up in Chapter 6, which concentrates mainly on the financial dimension of local autonomy. Other chapters address issues related to local autonomy with a particular focus on a specific dimension of the concept: Chapter 8, legal autonomy and noninterference; Chapter 10, access; Chapter 7, political discretion and policy scope; and Chapter 5, organizational autonomy. After providing an overview of existing typologies of intergovernmental relations in Europe with a focus on local autonomy, Chapter 3 undertakes the challenging endeavour of empirically grouping the 57 countries covered in this book, situated on six different continents, into ideal types of local autonomy.

While the LAI 2.0 project yielded insightful findings, it is important to acknowledge certain limitations. First, the analysis focused exclusively on the lowest and most effective tier of local government, thus omitting intermediate local governments and intermunicipal cooperation bodies. Furthermore, it serves cross-national rather than cross-municipal purposes. Second, we mainly assessed potential rather than effective autonomy, which may imply that local autonomy in practice differs from local autonomy as conceived here. Thirdly, we relied on codebook-based expert judgement. While efforts were made to improve coding instructions, in future research the introduction of additional opinions and objective indicators to back up experts' claims will be very welcome.

Nevertheless, external experts affirmed the robustness of our methodology and the significance of the extensive set of dimensions and variables for measuring local autonomy. The LAI now encompasses countries on six continents over a 30-year span, making it a valuable resource for policymakers and scholars of comparative public administration, decentralization or local governance. As suggested by Bouckaert and Kuhlmann (2016), it constitutes a good starting point for a more qualitative understanding of local autonomy, apprehending the concept as a 'reflection of local identity' (Pratchett 2004) in a 'bottom-up' approach, and also provides a comprehensive, quantitative, empirically grounded perspective on local autonomy and its evolution for a better understanding of issues faced by local governments around the world.

2. Main results and dynamics of local autonomy

INTRODUCTION

This book, as suggested by its title, provides an overview of the dynamics and issues of local autonomy. The previous chapter (see Chapter 1) covered the overall organization of the project and the detailed construction of the index and its measurements. In this chapter, we visualize the dynamics of local autonomy through the presentation of the main results taken from the Local Autonomy Index 2.0 (LAI 2.0). We will begin with the presentation of the 11 variables, followed by the seven dimensions, and then finally the overall index (LAI). When presenting the dimensions and the LAI, we will also highlight differences depending on the 57 countries' affiliations to the EU (European Union), CoE (Council of Europe) and OECD (Organisation for Economic Co-operation and Development), and whether the countries are federal states or not. This will allow us to present varying dynamics among the broad set of countries assessed by the LAI 2.0. The results presented are shown by country or affiliation group, or in some cases represented by all 57 countries together.

The timespan covered goes from 1990 to 2020, except for the following ten countries where the time series starts at a later point (indicated in parentheses): Latvia (1991), Ukraine (1991), Albania (1992), Romania (1992), Andorra (1993), Malta (1993), South Africa (1994), Armenia (1996), Bosnia and Herzegovina (1996) and Kosovo (2000).

To reduce space and complexity in the tables and figures, and to present broader time-related developments, we have combined the dates into five-year means, except for the final period under scrutiny, which goes from 2015 to 2020 and therefore six years long. Since the final period is one of general stability, this does not alter the means over time too much.

All scores (variables, dimensions and the LAI) have been standardized to a 100-point scale, as it allows for easier comparability and visualization. The remainder of the chapter will therefore describe the dynamics in percentages. Only data aggregated at the country level will be presented; subnational variations in federal states or states with asymmetrical solutions are left out of this chapter but will be mentioned in subsequent chapters (see Chapter 4). All detailed scoring, justifications and records of reforms or other situations that lead to coding changes are provided in the coding sheets and country profiles of the LAI 2.0.[1]

VARIABILITY AMONG INDICATORS: RESULTS AND DYNAMICS AT THE VARIABLE LEVEL

Looking at the variable level first, considering all 57 studied countries altogether, we observe a general increase across the board, but also high variation in how the trends developed over time, and their relative degree of improvement among the different variables. For this chapter, this is the lowest level of aggregated measurements. We do not delve deeper into sub-variable indicators, some of which are treated in their respective later chapters. All details on coding and indicators are provided in the Appendix.

The scores of all variables increase over time. The biggest climbs are to be observed in the variables of institutional depth and of central or regional access, which have increased by around 14 and 17 per cent respectively between the periods of 1990–94 and 2015–20 (see Figure 2.1). Looking at relative values, institutional depth went from the third-highest-scoring to highest-scoring variable. Among the other remaining variables, the next highest increase is attributable to legal protection (9 per cent) and the lowest one to the financial-transfer-system variable (3 per cent), over the 30-year period. An alternative angle shows that variables that are part of interactive rule (those that measure vertical relations of local governments with higher state levels) have generally increased more than those that measure self-rule (the capacity of local governments to organize themselves and their task/service execution independently). The variables of legal protection, administrative supervision and central or regional access have all increased by at least 8 per cent, whereas the self-rule variables (except for institutional depth) have only increased by between 3 per cent and 7 per cent. This seems to indicate a stronger emphasis on strengthening the position of local governments vis-à-vis higher levels of government and influencing them than on the rights and capacities of local governments. Overall, eight out of 11 variables have only shown increasing trends, whereas policy scope, effective political discretion and fiscal autonomy have shown a slight decrease during the final two studied periods of 2010–14 and 2015–20. They also share the commonality of being the lowest globally scoring variables, in relative values.

---

[1] https://ec.europa.eu/regional_policy/en/information/publications/studies/2021/self-rule-index-for-local-authorities-in-the-eu-council-of-europe-and-oecd-countries-1990–2020.

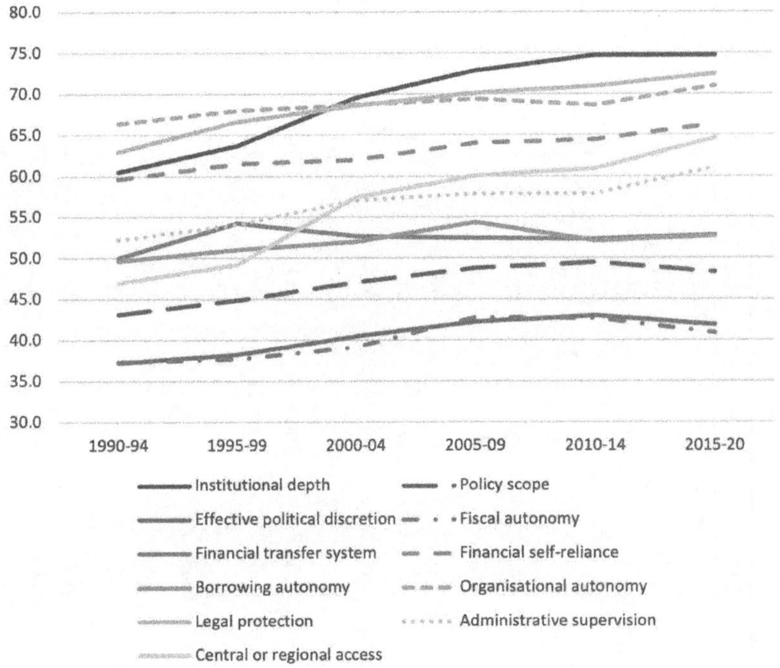

Note: Five-year means for the 11 variables of the LAI 2.0 over time (1990–2020), N=57 (N=54 for 90–94, N=56 for 95–99), standardized.
Source: Authors' own.

Figure 2.1 Longitudinal development of the LAI 2.0 variables (1990–2020)

COUNTRY-SPECIFIC DEVELOPMENT AND DYNAMICS ACROSS THE SEVEN DIMENSIONS OF THE LAI

Compared to the variable level where only the means for all 57 countries aggregated together were shown, this section will go deeper into more country-specific dynamics, examining the development over every dimension over time for every country, grouping the scores by five-year means as mentioned earlier. This choice aligns with the more deductive logic followed in the LAI 2.0 project (see Chapter 1). Tables 2.1 to 2.7 provide the full detail of the scores standardized to a 100-point scale as was done for all results in this chapter.

Starting with legal autonomy, 20 countries of the 57 under scrutiny present the maximum value of 100 points on the standardized scale, ranging

Table 2.1 *Legal autonomy, five-year means per country (N=57), standardized*

Country	1990–94	1995–99	2000–04	2005–09	2010–14	2015–20	Diff. 90–20
Albania	33	53	67	67	67	67	33
Andorra	100	100	100	100	100	100	0
Argentina	77	79	79	81	82	82	4
Armenia	-	50	50	50	50	67	17
Australia	33	33	33	33	33	33	0
Austria	67	67	67	67	67	67	0
Belarus	67	40	33	33	33	33	–33
Belgium	100	100	100	100	100	100	0
Bosnia and Herzegovina	-	55	55	67	67	67	12
Bulgaria	87	100	100	100	100	100	13
Canada	0	0	0	0	0	0	0
Chile	80	100	100	100	100	100	20
Colombia	87	100	100	100	100	100	13
Croatia	83	83	83	83	83	83	0
Cyprus	67	67	67	67	67	67	0
Czech Republic	100	100	100	100	100	100	0
Denmark	33	33	33	33	33	33	0
Estonia	80	100	100	100	100	100	20
Finland	100	100	100	100	100	100	0
France	67	67	80	100	100	100	33

Country	1990–94	1995–99	2000–04	2005–09	2010–14	2015–20	Diff. 90–20
Georgia	0	13	33	67	67	50	50
Germany	67	67	67	67	67	67	0
Greece	83	83	83	83	83	83	0
Hungary	67	67	67	67	67	67	0
Iceland	67	67	67	67	67	67	0
Ireland	0	7	33	33	33	33	33
Israel	17	17	17	17	17	17	0
Italy	67	67	67	67	67	78	11
Japan	67	67	67	67	67	67	0
Kosovo	-	-	0	27	67	67	67
Latvia	42	67	67	67	67	67	25
Liechtenstein	100	100	100	100	100	100	0
Lithuania	33	40	67	67	67	78	44
Luxembourg	67	67	67	67	67	100	33
Macedonia	100	100	100	100	100	100	0
Malta	67	67	67	67	67	67	0
Mexico	60	60	61	61	61	65	5
Moldova	13	7	33	33	33	39	26
Montenegro	67	67	67	87	100	100	33
Netherlands	67	67	67	67	67	67	0
Norway	0	0	0	0	0	39	39

Country	1990–94	1995–99	2000–04	2005–09	2010–14	2015–20	Diff. 90–20
Poland	67	67	67	67	67	53	−14
Portugal	100	100	100	100	100	100	0
Republic of Korea	100	100	100	100	100	100	0
Romania	100	100	100	100	100	100	0
Russian Federation	60	100	100	100	100	100	40
Serbia	83	83	83	83	83	83	0
Slovakia	100	100	100	100	100	100	0
Slovenia	47	100	100	73	67	67	20
South Africa	100	100	100	100	100	100	0
Spain	50	50	100	100	100	100	50
Sweden	33	33	33	33	33	33	0
Switzerland	94	94	94	94	94	94	0
Turkey	33	33	33	33	33	33	0
Ukraine	33	60	67	67	67	61	28
United Kingdom	33	33	33	33	33	33	0
United States of America	57	57	57	57	57	57	0
MEANS	63	67	69	70	71	72	11

Source: Authors' own.

from Andorra to Spain, including South American states such as Chile and Colombia, but also South Africa and the Republic of Korea among the non-European states (see Table 2.1). Inside Europe, the maximum-scoring countries include more continentally centrally situated countries such as Belgium, Luxembourg and Liechtenstein, as well as Eastern and South-Eastern countries, among them North Macedonia and Slovakia.

Trend-wise, the biggest increases by far are observed in Kosovo, Georgia and Spain (66 per cent for Kosovo, 50 per cent for the latter two). Many countries have shown stability, where scores did not change on average over time. This includes countries that have maintained a maximum score over time (e.g. Andorra, North Macedonia, Republic of Korea and South Africa), but also others who have stayed at a stable lower value (e.g. Israel, Japan, Sweden and Turkey). A handful of countries have known a certain decrease, either recently as was the case for Poland, or steadily over time (e.g. Belarus). This suggests tightened legal restrictions that might be the result of legal reforms towards stricter central control. These possible shifts in legal frameworks are detailed more explicitly in Chapter 8. Overall, legal autonomy has increased by around 10 per cent over 30 years across all countries in a steady fashion.

Moving to the access dimension, as we have already seen at the central- or regional-access variable level, we can observe more drastic changes among the 57 countries (see Table 2.2). Here also, many countries have remained stable or have only shown minor improvements over 30 years (e.g. Colombia, Cyprus and Germany) a certain number of them even maintaining the highest possible score of 100 (e.g. Australia, Austria and Spain). Many countries have shown an increase of over 50 per cent over 30 years, among which Bulgaria started at 0 to finish at 100 during the early 2000s, and countries such as Albania, Italy and Slovakia have all increased by over 66 per cent. However, we also see a few countries that have decreased along the access dimension, the most notable examples being Hungary, Estonia and Denmark (showing respectively decreases of 66, 42 and 33 per cent). Overall, the access dimension has shown the biggest growth over 30 years – 18 per cent – with a stable upward tendency across time. This suggests an overall trend towards better access for municipalities to their higher tiers of government, thus reinforcing the possibility of strong, efficient multilevel governance. The issues related to the various pathways municipalities have at their disposal are addressed in greater detail in Chapter 10.

For policy scope, although the average increase is not as remarkable, the amount of variation across all 57 countries is more widespread. This is notably due to the fact that policy-scope scores are sourced from a wide variety of services in different policy fields (see Appendix). Only a handful of countries have displayed no change over 30 years, among them Australia, Chile and Israel. Some countries have shown impressive progress in expanding policy

Table 2.2 *Access, five-year means per country (N=57), standardized*

Country	1990–94	1995–99	2000–04	2005–09	2010–14	2015–20	Diff. 90–20
Albania	0	0	67	67	67	67	67
Andorra	33	33	33	33	33	33	0
Argentina	33	33	36	37	37	37	4
Armenia	-	33	33	33	33	33	0
Australia	100	100	100	100	100	100	0
Austria	100	100	100	100	100	100	0
Belarus	33	33	33	33	33	33	0
Belgium	33	33	33	33	33	33	0
Bosnia and Herzegovina	-	64	88	88	89	89	24
Bulgaria	0	30	100	100	100	100	100
Canada	35	36	36	36	36	36	0
Chile	33	33	33	33	33	61	28
Colombia	33	33	33	33	33	33	0
Croatia	33	33	33	33	33	33	0
Cyprus	67	67	67	67	67	67	0
Czech Republic	0	13	33	33	33	67	67
Denmark	83	83	83	83	83	50	−33
Estonia	83	83	67	42	42	42	−42
Finland	67	67	67	67	67	67	0
France	67	67	67	67	67	67	0

Country	1990–94	1995–99	2000–04	2005–09	2010–14	2015–20	Diff. 90–20
Georgia	67	67	67	67	67	67	0
Germany	67	67	67	67	67	67	0
Greece	67	67	67	67	67	67	0
Hungary	100	27	33	33	33	33	−67
Iceland	67	67	80	100	100	83	17
Ireland	33	33	33	33	33	67	33
Israel	33	33	33	33	33	33	0
Italy	27	33	67	67	67	100	73
Japan	67	67	67	67	67	67	0
Kosovo	-	-	50	50	50	50	0
Latvia	33	60	67	67	53	100	67
Liechtenstein	33	33	33	33	33	33	0
Lithuania	67	67	93	100	100	100	33
Luxembourg	67	67	67	67	67	72	6
Macedonia	0	0	30	50	50	50	50
Malta	67	67	67	73	100	100	33
Mexico	30	30	33	33	34	37	7
Moldova	0	0	0	0	33	78	78
Montenegro	33	33	40	87	100	100	67
Netherlands	67	67	67	67	67	67	0
Norway	33	33	60	67	67	67	33

Country	1990–94	1995–99	2000–04	2005–09	2010–14	2015–20	Diff. 90–20
Poland	80	100	100	100	100	72	–8
Portugal	50	60	100	100	100	100	50
Republic of Korea	33	67	67	67	67	67	33
Romania	0	0	27	33	33	33	33
Russian Federation	25	12	21	33	33	33	8
Serbia	0	0	23	53	58	61	61
Slovakia	33	40	87	100	100	100	67
Slovenia	40	67	67	67	40	67	27
South Africa	67	93	100	100	100	100	33
Spain	100	100	100	100	100	100	0
Sweden	67	67	67	67	67	67	0
Switzerland	99	99	99	99	99	99	0
Turkey	33	33	33	33	33	44	10
Ukraine	17	22	22	25	33	57	40
United Kingdom	67	67	67	67	67	67	0
United States of America	33	33	33	33	33	33	0
MEANS	47	49	57	60	61	65	18

Source: Authors' own.

scope at the local level: Albania and Romania have increased their scores by 56 and 34 points respectively (see Table 2.3). Others have seen a decrease in policy scope over the years, notably Hungary and Luxembourg with –37 and –31 points respectively. These two major downward spirals aside, we find only minor decreases in other countries (e.g. Bosnia and Herzegovina, Switzerland and the United Kingdom). Regarding this policy-scope dimension, no country reaches the maximum score, which is simply explained by the plethora of policy fields that would need to benefit from full autonomy in a country. Overall, given the major fluctuations among countries in positive and negative tendencies over time, policy scope has gained only five points over the 30-year period considered. The remaining countries show relatively stable scores over time, which can also be explained by the combination and aggregation of scores for all policy fields considered and coded. Here, the more detailed scores can provide more specific insights as to what areas policy reforms should be aimed at, if the general goal is to increase decentralized power in favour of the local level (see Chapter 7).

The political-discretion dimension shows dynamics similar to those of the policy-scope dimension: they are somewhat practically related since they express the functional responsibilities of local governments. However, whereas policy scope is a dimension built based on its namesake variable, political discretion is a compound weighted combination of institutional depth and effective political discretion, since both variables better reflect the decision-making autonomy of local governments in general and over public policies in particular. Since effective political discretion is made up of a wide range of sub-indicators related to the same array of services as for policy scope (see Appendix), some of this diversity is still reflected to some extent in the variance of scores among the 57 countries over time. The remainder of the changes can be attributed to changes in institutional depth. Among the noteworthy observations, Albania skyrocketed from having no political discretion to reaching 74 points, and other strong improvements include Montenegro and Romania (see Table 2.4). A few decreases appear mostly among Eastern European countries. Although we see a slight dip in cross-country political discretion between 2010–14 and 2015–20, the dimension has globally gained over the past three decades. Again, the compound character of this dimension and its construction leaves out some of the fluctuations and the ability to identify specific areas of strength and weakness (see Chapter 7).

The financial autonomy dimension draws a highly volatile picture, as both strong gains and losses are to be seen across various countries. Whereas some countries have faced big losses in financial autonomy (Colombia, Cyprus and Mexico among them), others clearly demonstrate the opposite trend, for example Belarus, Bulgaria and North Macedonia (see Table 2.5). Montenegro is singled out by its strong climb towards 90 points, only to tumble post-2009 by

Table 2.3 Policy scope, five-year means per country (N=57), standardized

Country	1990–94	1995–99	2000–04	2005–09	2010–14	2015–20	Diff. 90–20
Albania	0	0	40	54	54	56	56
Andorra	34	40	39	37	37	37	3
Argentina	34	34	35	43	45	46	12
Armenia	-	38	38	44	45	46	7
Australia	34	34	34	34	34	34	0
Austria	43	43	43	43	43	43	0
Belarus	74	74	74	74	74	74	0
Belgium	50	50	50	50	50	50	0
Bosnia and Herzegovina	-	46	46	46	46	46	0
Bulgaria	42	42	45	45	49	50	8
Canada	23	23	25	25	25	25	1
Chile	32	32	32	32	32	32	0
Colombia	60	63	63	63	66	66	6
Croatia	24	24	35	41	42	30	5
Cyprus	15	17	22	22	22	22	6
Czech Republic	20	37	37	37	37	37	17
Denmark	73	73	73	75	76	76	4
Estonia	57	57	57	57	57	57	0
Finland	76	76	76	76	76	76	0
France	79	79	79	79	79	79	0

Country	1990–94	1995–99	2000–04	2005–09	2010–14	2015–20	Diff. 90–20
Georgia	55	55	55	55	55	59	5
Germany	69	69	69	69	69	69	0
Greece	18	21	26	27	40	40	22
Hungary	83	83	83	83	78	46	–37
Iceland	39	49	53	53	55	55	16
Ireland	24	24	24	24	24	24	0
Israel	44	44	44	44	44	44	0
Italy	52	47	46	46	46	45	–7
Japan	58	58	58	60	60	60	2
Kosovo	-	-	41	42	50	50	9
Latvia	56	56	56	56	53	53	–4
Liechtenstein	66	66	66	66	66	66	0
Lithuania	46	49	58	58	59	59	13
Luxembourg	67	67	58	58	50	35	–31
Macedonia	38	38	50	58	58	41	3
Malta	3	3	3	5	10	10	7
Mexico	38	43	43	44	44	42	4
Moldova	23	30	37	31	31	31	8
Montenegro	12	21	21	18	26	30	19
Netherlands	53	57	60	63	63	65	12
Norway	59	59	59	59	59	59	0

Country	1990–94	1995–99	2000–04	2005–09	2010–14	2015–20	Diff. 90–20
Poland	49	60	60	60	60	60	11
Portugal	21	23	31	31	31	39	18
Republic of Korea	25	25	25	36	38	38	13
Romania	11	24	35	43	46	46	34
Russian Federation	10	5	20	41	41	40	30
Serbia	58	58	58	65	69	64	5
Slovakia	20	21	31	43	50	50	30
Slovenia	8	38	38	38	38	39	31
South Africa	47	34	31	31	31	31	–16
Spain	41	41	41	42	40	35	–6
Sweden	73	75	75	75	75	68	–6
Switzerland	61	63	63	60	58	58	–3
Turkey	38	38	38	38	38	38	0
Ukraine	60	55	52	52	52	56	–4
United Kingdom	65	65	65	65	59	59	–6
United States of America	67	67	67	67	67	67	0
MEANS	43	45	47	49	49	48	5

Source: Authors' own.

Table 2.4 *Political discretion, five-year means per country (N=57), standardized*

Country	1990–94	1995–99	2000–04	2005–09	2010–14	2015–20	Diff. 90–20
Albania	0	0	62	74	74	74	74
Andorra	37	39	38	37	37	34	–2
Argentina	48	48	48	50	51	51	4
Armenia	-	42	42	47	48	48	7
Australia	22	22	22	22	22	22	0
Austria	57	57	57	57	57	57	0
Belarus	50	41	44	44	46	49	–1
Belgium	56	56	56	56	56	56	0
Bosnia and Herzegovina	-	39	39	40	40	42	2
Bulgaria	36	42	55	60	62	54	19
Canada	24	25	29	31	31	32	8
Chile	31	31	36	36	37	38	7
Colombia	64	67	67	67	72	74	10
Croatia	41	41	43	46	46	46	5
Cyprus	16	18	24	24	24	24	8
Czech Republic	37	50	50	50	50	50	13
Denmark	69	69	69	71	72	80	11
Estonia	66	69	69	69	66	62	–5
Finland	74	82	87	87	87	87	13
France	76	76	76	76	76	76	0

Country	1990–94	1995–99	2000–04	2005–09	2010–14	2015–20	Diff. 90–20
Georgia	42	49	50	50	52	59	17
Germany	56	56	56	56	56	56	0
Greece	31	41	41	41	57	61	29
Hungary	69	66	66	66	64	55	–14
Iceland	53	60	63	63	64	64	12
Ireland	33	38	38	38	38	38	5
Israel	23	23	22	22	22	22	–1
Italy	61	44	58	63	63	53	–8
Japan	46	46	54	55	55	55	9
Kosovo	-	-	29	33	42	42	13
Latvia	65	63	61	61	61	60	–5
Liechtenstein	43	43	43	43	43	43	0
Lithuania	51	60	69	69	69	69	18
Luxembourg	60	60	55	55	51	51	–8
Macedonia	36	36	56	69	69	53	17
Malta	18	18	18	19	26	26	8
Mexico	43	43	44	44	44	44	1
Moldova	26	29	37	35	39	47	21
Montenegro	12	13	25	43	45	43	31
Netherlands	55	57	60	63	62	60	5
Norway	71	71	71	71	71	71	0

Country	1990–94	1995–99	2000–04	2005–09	2010–14	2015–20	Diff. 90–20
Poland	55	59	54	53	53	50	−5
Portugal	41	41	39	39	42	52	11
Republic of Korea	4	13	13	23	26	26	22
Romania	16	28	35	45	50	51	34
Russian Federation	7	4	11	23	19	6	−1
Serbia	52	49	54	57	61	55	3
Slovakia	34	34	44	58	63	63	28
Slovenia	39	48	48	48	48	45	5
South Africa	26	34	35	35	35	35	9
Spain	54	54	54	54	52	48	−6
Sweden	72	73	73	73	73	74	1
Switzerland	46	46	48	49	50	50	4
Turkey	28	28	28	28	27	27	−1
Ukraine	51	51	56	57	57	46	−5
United Kingdom	39	39	39	39	36	36	−4
United States of America	62	62	62	62	62	62	0
MEANS	43	45	48	50	51	50	7

Source: Authors' own.

Table 2.5 Financial autonomy, five-year means per country (N=57), standardized

Country	1990–94	1995–99	2000–04	2005–09	2010–14	2015–20	Diff. 90–20
Albania	0	0	34	47	47	19	19
Andorra	85	85	85	85	85	85	0
Argentina	46	54	46	44	44	54	8
Armenia	-	19	19	23	24	29	10
Australia	71	71	71	71	71	71	0
Austria	60	59	60	64	68	62	2
Belarus	0	0	0	6	15	30	30
Belgium	74	74	74	74	74	74	0
Bosnia and Herzegovina	-	24	24	24	28	28	4
Bulgaria	4	12	27	34	49	49	45
Canada	71	71	71	71	71	71	0
Chile	29	29	29	29	29	29	0
Colombia	87	89	70	70	70	70	–17
Croatia	44	51	54	50	48	44	0
Cyprus	56	58	64	64	64	30	–26
Czech Republic	45	54	40	39	39	39	–6
Denmark	76	76	68	65	65	80	4
Estonia	35	35	35	35	35	35	0
Finland	85	85	85	85	85	89	5
France	74	74	74	74	74	74	0

Country	1990–94	1995–99	2000–04	2005–09	2010–14	2015–20	Diff. 90–20
Georgia	25	36	50	40	25	23	–2
Germany	74	74	72	72	73	76	2
Greece	54	54	54	54	49	63	10
Hungary	37	39	39	39	34	30	–7
Iceland	89	89	89	89	86	85	–5
Ireland	69	69	69	69	69	69	0
Israel	58	58	58	58	58	58	0
Italy	41	55	56	60	62	69	28
Japan	41	45	52	57	58	62	21
Kosovo	-	-	25	27	30	30	5
Latvia	5	5	5	5	9	15	11
Liechtenstein	100	100	100	100	91	86	–14
Lithuania	35	35	35	35	35	35	0
Luxembourg	70	70	70	70	70	60	–11
Macedonia	0	0	0	44	44	44	44
Malta	19	22	33	33	33	33	14
Mexico	39	33	29	30	30	28	–11
Moldova	11	21	27	15	21	15	4
Montenegro	29	29	42	90	69	67	38
Netherlands	45	45	45	45	45	45	0
Norway	58	58	60	63	63	63	5

Country	1990–94	1995–99	2000–04	2005–09	2010–14	2015–20	Diff. 90–20
Poland	60	60	60	60	60	60	0
Portugal	49	49	53	60	60	74	25
Republic of Korea	58	58	58	58	58	58	0
Romania	21	40	48	40	40	37	15
Russian Federation	18	6	14	27	27	27	8
Serbia	30	30	30	52	60	57	27
Slovakia	54	54	54	60	60	40	−14
Slovenia	2	10	10	16	15	30	28
South Africa	60	83	89	89	89	89	30
Spain	74	74	74	74	68	74	0
Sweden	83	89	89	89	89	89	6
Switzerland	98	98	98	98	98	98	0
Turkey	44	44	44	44	44	44	0
Ukraine	17	17	15	14	14	23	6
United Kingdom	45	45	45	45	45	57	12
United States of America	75	75	75	75	75	75	0
MEANS	49	50	51	54	53	53	6

Source: Authors' own.

almost a third. A broad range of countries can be seen showing diminished financial autonomy between the periods of 2004–08 and 2009–14, of which many cases can be imputed to post-2008 financial crisis measures, when a number of state governments recentralized this dimension as a solution to crisis management. This precautionary trend is reflected in more recent years as well, since for many countries improvements in financial autonomy have been stable or marginal at best, which can also be observed in the decreasing mean value across all 57 countries. Indeed, the highest mean value can be observed during 2009–2014 and not the most recent 2015–20 period. Restrictions on financial autonomy show their impact over a longer period of time, and close observations over the coming years, including newly updated measurements, are warranted to assess the long-term impact of such a major crisis. That being said, this generally observed trend again does not apply to the entire list of countries under scrutiny, as some countries have only progressed in financial autonomy over the years, including during this specific era at the beginning of the twenty-first century. Issues related to financial autonomy are addressed in Chapter 6.

Organizational autonomy is the dimension that shows the greatest stability, displaying an overall lowest general progress among all dimensions, not even reaching 5 per cent (see Table 2.6). Dynamics-wise, we can report that the most significant increase is in Georgia (from 0 to 94), with a couple of strong decreases in Belarus and Italy. The numbers often appear to be well rounded: since they are based on a 100-point standardized scale at the weighted dimensional level, scores of 50, 75 and 100 appear quite regularly. This is because, at the lower variable level, many of the indicators are conditional. If a condition is fulfilled, a jump of 25 or 50 per cent happens casually. This explanation accounts for a multitude of drastic jumps in the scores observed across the table. The details of these scales and measurements on the political and administrative structural elements pertaining to organizational autonomy are found in the codebook (see Appendix), and more in-depth discussions on the limitations and implications of this way of measuring are found in Chapter 5. As for the stability among the remainder of countries, reforms related to organizational structure tend to be more tedious and scarcer than other policy or financial reforms, which could possibly explain the overall flatter progress line.

Noninterference, although it is the second-lowest-progressing dimension when considering overall means between 1990 and 2020 (5 points, see Table 2.7), seems to display more inter-country variation. Dynamics can be witnessed in both the upward and downward directions, as this is the dimension that sees the biggest amount of declines and fluctuations. More specific analyses of issues around access are discussed further in Chapter 8. The biggest backsliding trends (based on the observations of this dimension) are found

Table 2.6 Organizational autonomy, five-year means per country (N=57), standardized

Country	1990–94	1995–99	2000–04	2005–09	2010–14	2015–20	Diff. 90–20
Albania	63	63	63	63	63	63	0
Andorra	75	75	75	75	75	75	0
Argentina	80	80	80	81	81	81	1
Armenia	-	44	44	45	46	46	2
Australia	63	63	63	63	63	63	0
Austria	63	63	63	63	63	63	0
Belarus	88	40	25	25	25	25	−63
Belgium	25	75	75	75	75	75	50
Bosnia and Herzegovina	-	77	77	77	77	77	0
Bulgaria	45	70	75	75	75	75	30
Canada	87	87	87	87	87	87	0
Chile	40	50	50	50	50	50	10
Colombia	75	75	75	75	75	75	0
Croatia	63	63	63	63	63	63	0
Cyprus	63	63	63	63	63	63	0
Czech Republic	81	81	81	81	81	81	0
Denmark	100	100	100	100	100	100	0
Estonia	94	94	94	94	94	94	0
Finland	88	88	88	88	88	88	0
France	63	63	63	63	63	63	0

Country	1990–94	1995–99	2000–04	2005–09	2010–14	2015–20	Diff. 90–20
Georgia	0	0	0	0	5	94	94
Germany	63	63	63	63	63	63	0
Greece	44	44	44	44	44	48	4
Hungary	63	63	63	63	63	63	0
Iceland	100	100	100	100	100	100	0
Ireland	38	38	38	38	38	38	0
Israel	63	63	63	63	58	56	–6
Italy	70	75	75	75	75	50	–20
Japan	75	75	75	75	75	75	0
Kosovo	-	-	63	63	63	63	0
Latvia	75	75	75	75	63	63	–13
Liechtenstein	100	100	100	100	100	100	0
Lithuania	75	75	75	75	75	75	0
Luxembourg	25	25	25	25	25	63	38
Macedonia	56	56	56	56	56	56	0
Malta	25	25	25	25	25	38	13
Mexico	66	68	72	74	74	74	8
Moldova	25	30	50	50	50	50	25
Montenegro	75	75	75	75	75	69	–6
Netherlands	75	75	75	75	75	75	0
Norway	80	100	100	100	100	97	17

Country	1990–94	1995–99	2000–04	2005–09	2010–14	2015–20	Diff. 90–20
Poland	88	88	88	88	88	88	0
Portugal	75	75	75	75	75	75	0
Republic of Korea	19	44	44	44	44	44	25
Romania	63	63	65	73	63	71	8
Russian Federation	36	20	45	74	74	73	38
Serbia	75	75	75	75	75	73	–2
Slovakia	100	100	100	100	100	100	0
Slovenia	88	88	88	88	88	88	0
South Africa	50	70	75	75	75	75	25
Spain	75	75	75	75	55	73	–2
Sweden	100	100	100	100	100	100	0
Switzerland	100	100	100	100	100	100	0
Turkey	63	63	63	63	63	63	0
Ukraine	69	69	69	69	69	69	0
United Kingdom	50	50	50	50	50	50	0
United States of America	93	93	93	93	93	93	0
MEANS	66	68	69	69	69	71	5

Source: Authors' own.

Table 2.7 *Noninterference, five-year means per country (N=57), standardized*

Country	1990–94	1995–99	2000–04	2005–09	2010–14	2015–20	Diff. 90–20
Albania	17	17	27	33	33	50	33
Andorra	33	33	33	33	33	58	25
Argentina	87	87	87	88	88	88	0
Armenia	-	72	72	72	72	64	–8
Australia	50	50	50	50	50	50	0
Austria	67	67	67	67	67	67	0
Belarus	17	0	0	0	0	0	–17
Belgium	17	23	17	18	20	26	10
Bosnia and Herzegovina	-	73	64	64	64	64	–9
Bulgaria	33	60	53	33	33	17	–17
Canada	19	19	19	19	19	19	0
Chile	67	67	67	67	60	67	0
Colombia	30	33	33	33	33	33	3
Croatia	50	46	50	52	57	83	33
Cyprus	37	38	39	39	39	67	29
Czech Republic	63	67	53	63	60	67	3
Denmark	83	83	83	83	83	67	–17
Estonia	73	83	63	50	50	83	10
Finland	67	83	83	83	83	92	25
France	83	83	83	83	83	83	0

Country	1990–94	1995–99	2000–04	2005–09	2010–14	2015–20	Diff. 90–20
Georgia	0	0	0	10	20	67	67
Germany	63	64	65	66	66	67	3
Greece	83	83	83	83	83	89	6
Hungary	67	67	67	67	43	17	–50
Iceland	83	83	83	83	73	83	0
Ireland	23	33	33	33	30	17	–7
Israel	17	17	17	17	17	17	0
Italy	47	50	63	67	80	78	31
Japan	17	17	50	50	50	50	33
Kosovo	-	-	50	50	50	50	0
Latvia	50	67	67	67	67	50	0
Liechtenstein	67	67	67	67	67	67	0
Lithuania	23	27	50	50	50	50	27
Luxembourg	73	67	67	67	67	67	–7
Macedonia	67	67	67	67	67	67	0
Malta	83	83	83	83	83	83	0
Mexico	60	56	36	34	30	28	–32
Moldova	0	0	0	0	0	0	0
Montenegro	83	83	83	57	40	33	–50
Netherlands	0	7	17	20	40	50	50
Norway	70	83	83	83	83	79	9

Country	1990–94	1995–99	2000–04	2005–09	2010–14	2015–20	Diff. 90–20
Poland	67	67	67	67	67	57	–9
Portugal	83	83	83	83	83	83	0
Republic of Korea	33	40	37	50	50	50	17
Romania	28	40	40	30	33	39	11
Russian Federation	25	17	21	33	33	33	8
Serbia	50	50	60	77	83	75	25
Slovakia	50	50	50	50	50	50	0
Slovenia	67	67	67	67	67	83	17
South Africa	50	77	83	83	83	83	33
Spain	83	83	83	83	83	83	0
Sweden	83	83	83	83	83	67	–17
Switzerland	39	38	39	42	47	48	9
Turkey	83	83	83	83	83	83	0
Ukraine	33	33	39	45	43	58	25
United Kingdom	65	65	65	65	65	50	–15
United States of America	50	50	50	50	50	50	0
MEANS	51	54	55	55	55	57	5

Source: Authors' own.

in Hungary and Montenegro (–50 points each). Other countries that scored a lesser amount in recent years cannot be pinpointed to a specific region of the world. In the majority of cases where noninterference was reduced (conversely, political control from higher levels increased), the change mainly occurred over the final two recorded periods of 2010–14 and 2015–20. In countries where recentralization tendencies can be observed in the overall LAI score (e.g. Hungary, Poland, Belarus), we see a very definite plunge in scores for the access dimension, one of the first to be impacted whenever more centralized control is exerted.

THE VARIOUS DYNAMICS OF THE OVERALL INDEX BY COUNTRY AND AFFILIATION

To expand on the general observations per dimension addressed in the previous section, in a more comparative perspective, we can also observe different dynamics across all seven dimensions depending on affiliations to international organizations, but also when grouping federal states together. Compared to the overall averages for all 57 countries together, federalist countries display a lesser degree of policy scope and political discretion, as well as a lower level of noninterference (see Figure 2.2). This might be explained by the addition of an intermediate government, whose federalist status implies decision-making and executive competencies regarding public policies and control over local governments (see Chapter 9). On the other hand, organizational and financial autonomy is considerably higher in the federal group than in any other group presented in the diagram. Affiliation-wise, different dynamics across the dimensions emerge depending on what grouping is considered. Countries belonging to the EU collectively tend to have greater legal autonomy, access, political discretion and noninterference than those of other groups. CoE member states do not stand out in any dimension, whereas OECD member states tend to have the upper hand when it comes to financial and organizational autonomy, but not at the expense of policy scope and political discretion as is the case for federal states.

Here, it is very relevant to mention that many of the countries under scrutiny joined the various international organizations that are considered in this chapter at different times. Sometimes, their affiliation only starts at a later point in time, which should be taken into account when observing the general trends over five-year periods as they have been highlighted in this chapter. For example, Colombia joined the OECD only in 2020, but is therefore included in the OECD member state group in our database, which means that Colombia's values are accounted for in the means for all time periods, when we look at the evolution of the LAI 2.0 scores and its underlying dimensions.

Source: Authors' own.

Figure 2.2 *LAI 2.0 dimensions, 2015–20 means by affiliation or federalist structure, standardized*

Finally, a look at the overall LAI 2.0 per country and per affiliation shows an interesting variety of dynamics. First, for the individual countries, when aggregating weighted dimensions into the LAI 2.0, the biggest anomalies tend to flatten themselves out, to a certain extent. The most dramatic jumps in augmented local autonomy across time are to be found in Albania, Bulgaria and Georgia (see Table 2.8). The biggest downfall in local autonomy, based on our numbers, is awarded to Hungary with an overall loss of 20 per cent. Hungary is the only country which experienced centralization at both regional and local levels (see Chapter 9). A certain number of other states also show some very small decreases in local autonomy: Belarus, Cyprus, Estonia, Liechtenstein, Luxembourg, Mexico and Poland. In most countries, however, the trend leans towards significantly strengthening autonomy in a more decentralizing context, as the mean value for the LAI 2.0 moves from 50 to 57 over the span of 30 years (i.e. 7 per cent).

Returning to the question of the importance of international affiliations and/ or a federalist structure, the graph indicates a few intriguing clear separations of LAI 2.0 average scores (see Figure 2.3). More reasoning on why federalist countries behave differently is discussed more extensively in Chapter 4 on

Table 2.8 LAI 2.0, five-year means per country (N=57), standardized

Country	1990–94	1995–99	2000–04	2005–09	2010–14	2015–20	Diff. 1990–2020
Albania	13	15	50	59	59	54	40
Andorra	57	59	59	58	58	59	2
Argentina	54	57	55	56	57	60	5
Armenia	-	39	39	42	43	45	6
Australia	50	50	50	50	50	50	0
Austria	61	61	61	62	63	62	0
Belarus	45	33	30	32	34	38	−7
Belgium	53	61	61	61	61	61	8
Bosnia and Herzegovina	-	48	50	50	51	52	3
Bulgaria	32	44	57	58	63	60	28
Canada	43	43	45	45	45	45	2
Chile	39	42	43	43	43	46	7
Colombia	67	70	66	66	67	68	0
Croatia	46	47	50	51	51	50	5
Cyprus	42	43	47	47	46	41	−1
Czech Republic	47	56	53	54	54	57	10
Denmark	75	75	73	74	74	76	0
Estonia	65	68	65	62	61	63	−2
Finland	80	83	84	84	84	86	6
France	73	73	74	76	76	76	3

Country	1990–94	1995–99	2000–04	2005–09	2010–14	2015–20	Diff. 1990–2020
Georgia	29	34	39	40	39	57	28
Germany	65	66	65	65	65	66	1
Greece	47	50	50	51	55	61	13
Hungary	65	59	59	59	55	45	–20
Iceland	71	74	76	78	77	76	5
Ireland	37	40	42	42	42	43	6
Israel	40	40	40	40	39	39	–1
Italy	53	53	60	62	64	62	9
Japan	52	53	59	61	61	62	10
Kosovo	-	-	36	40	47	47	11
Latvia	46	51	51	51	48	52	6
Liechtenstein	74	74	74	74	72	71	–3
Lithuania	48	51	60	61	61	62	14
Luxembourg	60	59	57	57	55	59	–1
Macedonia	36	36	44	60	60	54	18
Malta	30	30	33	34	38	40	11
Mexico	46	46	45	45	45	44	–2
Moldova	17	21	31	27	31	36	19
Montenegro	37	38	45	63	60	59	22
Netherlands	53	55	57	58	59	60	7
Norway	59	63	66	67	67	69	10

Country	1990–94	1995–99	2000–04	2005–09	2010–14	2015–20	Diff. 1990–2020
Poland	64	68	67	67	67	62	–2
Portugal	53	55	59	61	62	68	15
Republic of Korea	34	43	43	48	49	49	15
Romania	30	40	47	50	50	51	21
Russian Federation	21	16	27	42	41	38	16
Serbia	50	49	53	63	67	64	14
Slovakia	53	54	61	68	70	66	13
Slovenia	36	51	51	50	47	53	17
South Africa	51	64	67	67	67	67	16
Spain	65	65	69	69	64	67	1
Sweden	77	79	79	79	79	76	0
Switzerland	76	76	77	77	77	77	1
Turkey	44	44	44	43	43	44	1
Ukraine	42	44	45	46	46	49	7
United Kingdom	50	50	50	50	48	50	0
United States of America	67	67	67	67	67	67	0
MEANS	50	52	54	56	57	57	7

Source: Authors' own.

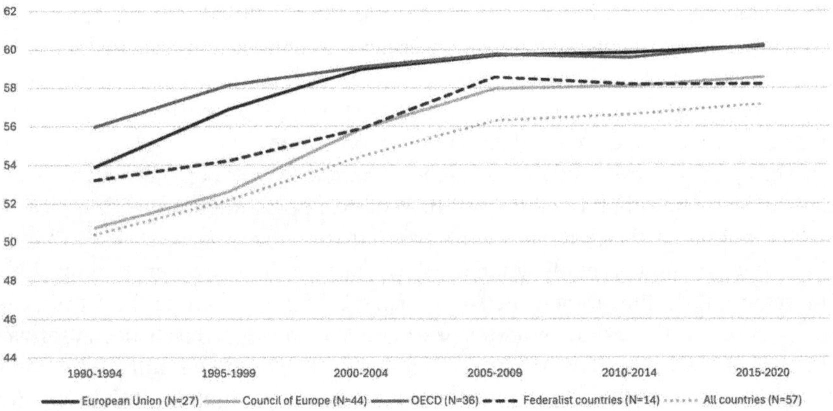

Source: Authors' own.

Figure 2.3 LAI 2.0, five-year means per affiliation, standardized

asymmetric decentralization. From a longitudinal perspective, we observe a certain convergence over the years, displaying fewer and fewer differences between our highlighted groupings. This coalescing phenomenon can be linked to the fact that more and more countries are adhering to certain international bodies, signing the European Charter of Local Self-Government and adhering to other standards of decentralization and good governance (see Chapters 12 and 14). In the first period (1990–94) OECD member states clearly disposed of more local autonomy than the general pool of 57 countries or any other group shown in the figure. In the most recent period under scrutiny (2015–20), the most blatant differences between groups seem to have faded away. Here, we find EU and OECD member states at the top, followed by CoE member states. The latter, as a group, display the biggest general increase in local autonomy over time (almost 8 per cent), which could be attributed to the majority of countries in the Eastern European group, where many countries have demonstrated immense progress since the early 1990s.

CONCLUSION

Over the course of the chapter, a whole variety of results have been outlined in a somewhat extensive display of tables and figures, accompanied by some general comments and interpretations. There are of course too many detailed discussions around the dynamics of the 11 variables, seven dimensions and the LAI as a whole, at least for a single chapter. This is the rationale behind the remainder of the book: to examine in a more detailed fashion how these dynamics can be explained, and what issues and outcomes are related to these observations. For example, Chapter 13 examines how rapid changes in autonomy are an important part of the institutional-reform approach, whether they reflect a process of decentralization or centralization.

The main general trends show an increase in local autonomy across all variables, dimensions and the index itself. What is interesting however, especially when looking at the dynamics across countries, which we were able to highlight here, is how general tendencies pan out differently when looking into more detail, i.e. the seven dimensions or the LAI 2.0 overall, at the individual country level. For example, countries that have shown a recent decentralization trend with overall decreasing scores for local autonomy (Hungary, Poland and Belarus), can also show stability or increases depending on which specific dimension is observed. Also, federalist countries show a different configuration of local autonomy when observing the dimensions, which opens the door to an interesting discussion on the link between local autonomy and regional authority in a multilevel governance context (see Chapter 9). Finally, degrees of local autonomy and their progressions vary depending on whether a country belongs to the EU, CoE or OECD. This raises questions about the impact of certain ratifications, one that is broadly developed in this volume being the European Charter of Local Self-Government (see Chapter 12). These insights and diverse results all indicate that local autonomy is truly a complex and multi-dimensional phenomenon that merits deeper thought and analysis.

3. Self-rule versus interactive rule: towards a cross-national empirical typology of local autonomy

INTRODUCTION

In the bulk of this book, aspects and dimensions of local autonomy are contrasted on a country-by-country basis. This focus on national political systems remains the standard in most comparative studies (Caramani 2023). Given that local autonomy takes shape in intergovernmental relations with the national centre, such an outlook also seems pertinent to our topic. However, beyond the default focus on the state, attempts should also be made at 're-placing the nation' (Sellers 2005, 2019). This raises the question of whether and how certain *types* of countries can be discerned as clusters with similar configurations of local autonomy underlying the multifaceted patterns of the separate nations (Ladner et al. 2019). Such clusters of course represent an attempt at analytical generalization. Typologies tend to synthesize more nuanced findings. They help us to gain a deeper and broader understanding of the specific blend of local autonomy found in each country. By giving structure to comparison, they also aid in juxtaposing and contextualizing the designated cases. However, clustering equally implies the risk of 'pigeon-holing' by placing nuanced practices in time and space into clearcut and fixed categories. In that sense, typologies are more ideal than real (Collier et al. 2008; Hendriks et al. 2012: 729–731).

Against that backdrop, the aim of this chapter is to develop an *empirical* typology of local autonomy with a broad *cross-national* appeal (inside and outside Europe). The terms in italics matter to understand the approach taken. First, the typology is not a top-down deductive theoretical endeavour. It rather arises from our findings. It thus provides a bottom-up and inductive description of typical classes of local autonomy (Collier et al. 2008). Second, our exercise seeks to go beyond mere geographical areas (between and within the various continents included) and/or the traditional typologies of intergovernmental relations often used in comparative local government studies.

The chapter therefore proceeds as follows. First, it provides a synthetic overview of existing typologies of intergovernmental relations with a focus on local autonomy (to provide a base for our endeavour).[1] Second, it discusses the design, methods and data used to discern the dimensions and categories of our typology. Based on two components stemming from a factor analysis on our data (interpreted as *self-rule* versus *interactive* rule) we define four 'ideal types' (*champions of local autonomy*, *local policy autonomy*, *local polity autonomy* and *opponents of local autonomy*). Third, the chapter expands upon the results of our analyses. Cases are placed in classes whose features are further discussed. We thus empirically check how close to one of the ideal types a specific country is (with a keen eye on the heterogeneity within and between the categories). The fourth concluding section reflects on our findings.

EXISTING TYPOLOGIES CONSIDERING LOCAL AUTONOMY

Given the overall aim of the chapter, this section situates the current exercise against the extant typologies found in the literature. It discusses key developments in the building of these anterior classifications with a particular concern for the position and role of characteristics of local autonomy therein. Our review only summarizes the main trends and tendencies. Table 3.1a and Table 3.1b highlight the key contributions (exemplary rather than exhaustive), central variables (with those most pertinent to local autonomy in bold) and types discerned in existing typologies pertinent to our topic. The discussions below will not address each of these typologies in much detail. A more extensive elaboration on the features of specific classifications and subsequent categories can be found elsewhere (see e.g. Ladner et al. 2019: 258–263; Steyvers 2019). We do not set our endeavour here against the typology developed for the first edition of the Local Autonomy Index ('the LAI 1.0'). This is the main basis to which we try to add further scope and depth (i.e. more countries, up to date aspects and dimensions).The typologies relevant to our theme emerged during the so-called second phase of comparative local-government research focusing on path-dependent systemic similarities and differences tied to state traditions (Stoker 2006; Steyvers 2019). Earlier versions adopted a qualitative and categorical approach wherein experts estimated the position of specific countries on theoretically relevant dimensions (mainly captured in broadly defined nominal classes). Categories with geographical labels were often distinguished. As Table 3.1a indicates, with time these labels gained in nuance. This pertained in particular to the need for (sub-)division(s) in the Northern part of Europe

[1] This implies we do not consider other kinds of typologies (e.g. focusing on intragovernmental relations, democracy modes or state–society interactions) used to comparatively classify local government systems (for an overview, see Heinelt et al. 2018a, 2018b; Steyvers 2019).

Table 3.1a Existing typologies of intergovernmental relations with a focus on local autonomy: qualitative and categorical

Key contributions	Central variables	Types discerned
Page & Goldsmith (1987a, 1987b)[a]	Functions **Discretion** Access	North & South European
Hesse & Sharpe (1991)	Constitutional status **Discretion** Rationale	North and Middle European, Anglo & Franco[b]
Bennett (1993)	**Competencies**	Dual, fused & mixed
Loughlin et al. (2012)	Legal basis for the state State–society relations Basis of policy style **Form of political organization** **Form of decentralization**	Nordic states, Rhinelandic states, British Isles, Southern European & new democracies

Notes: Central variables most pertinent to estimate local autonomy in bold. [a] Alternatively summarized as legal (functions and discretion) and political (access) localism versus centralism (Page 1991). [b] Based on a common history and the decentralization wave of the 1990s, Heinelt and Hlepas (2006) add the Central East European type to the original typology.

(none, two or more). Aspects of local autonomy featured prominently in all these attempts. At times, autonomy comprised a central variable on its own. At others, it formed part of a wider component (such as competencies or decentralization). This vein mainly conceived of autonomy as general freedom from central interference with either statutory or administrative modes of regulation respectively implying substantial and limited discretion for place-bound authorities. Most contributions also emphasized the interplay between different dimensions of intergovernmental relations marking out the type discerned (the interaction between functions, discretion and access being a seminal case in point).

Later variants differed in two respects. First, qualitative and categorical approaches gave way to quantitative and discrete counterparts. These aimed to objectify and refine the initial assertions empirically by espousing numerical indicators over nominal classes. Driven by current accounts of reforms of and changes in the erstwhile traditions, scores on scales captured an increasing number of aspects and dimensions of intergovernmental relations (such as territorial organization or functional decentralization). These typologies subsequently considered local autonomy as a multifaceted characteristic. Rather

Table 3.1b Existing typologies of intergovernmental relations with a focus on local autonomy: quantitative and discrete

Key contributions	Central variables	Types discerned
Sellers & Lidström (2007)	**Capacities** (political-administrative, fiscal) **Supervision** (political-administrative, fiscal)	State monopoly, state-dependent, society-dependent & autonomous
Swianiewicz (2014)	Territorial organization Functional decentralization **Financial discretion** Horizontal power relations	Champions of decentralization, relative decentralization, Balkan, high level of territorial consolidation & strong centralization and territorial fragmentation
Heinelt & Hlepas (2018)	Municipal spending as a percentage of GDP **Institutional depth** **Institutional autonomy** **Administrative supervision** **Financial self-reliance** **Financial transfers** **Local tax autonomy**	Type I–IX
Ladner et al. (2019)	Political discretion Financial autonomy	Partnership, chained democracy, guided democracy, *tutelle* & transitional

Note: Central variables most pertinent to estimate local autonomy in bold.

than a general degree of freedom or mode of regulation, discretion can have various specific faces (potentially looking in different directions). Next to the traditional noninterference (freedom from), the ability to make place-bound choices (freedom to) entered the conceptual fray. Thus, the 'triangle of local autonomy' has legal, political and financial points, with additional traits (such as organization or functions) along the lines (Ladner et al. 2019: 224). This also entails ideal types distinct from mere regional circumscriptions.

Second, an overt concern with the rest of Europe replaced a covert bias towards the West. This particularly came into play regarding the Central and Eastern parts of Europe. Previously, they had been either denoted as terra incognita or conveniently compressed as new democracies (often based on the communist past and a common trajectory of transition or transformation); now, scholars increasingly acknowledged internal variation and external differentiation of local government systems in the region (Swianiewicz 2014). These efforts often paid particular attention to developments in financial and fiscal autonomy, given their centrality in the countries concerned. This resulted in additional clusters within the region, overlapping only partly with existing categorizations. Also, beyond the European continent, autonomy gained relevance in the study of intergovernmental relations (e.g. Do Vale 2015)

Closest to our own endeavour, Ladner et al. (2019: 257–278) developed a quantitative empirical typology of local autonomy for 39 European countries between 1990 and 2014. The authors focused on two dimensions deemed most important in the LAI 1.0: on the one hand political discretion (covering institutional depth and effective policy discretion), on the other financial autonomy (comprising fiscal autonomy, financial self-reliance and borrowing autonomy). Both referred to more leeway for local choice (in terms of policy or means). The associated scale scores were recategorized in three classes (low, medium and high). The combination rendered nine potential types, of which four were denoted as pure (low-low or *tutelle*, low-high or *guided democracy*, high-low or *chained democracy* and high-high or *partnership*) and five as transitional. Ladner and colleagues thereby considered three points in time (1990, 2004 and 2014).

Their results demonstrated the existence of all potential types (at least at some point in time, sometimes including only one country). This typology thus offered a more diversified classification of countries according to their level of local autonomy than hitherto available. The types appeared sufficiently homogeneous even if some groups remained internally diversified. Geography or state tradition mattered but only to a certain extent. *Partnership* could be found in the Nordic countries and some of the Rhineland. *Tutelle* could be found in countries of the Franco (Mediterranean) group, some states in Central and Eastern Europe, and the United Kingdom (foundational to the Anglo-Saxon model). Other types showed a more mixed composition beyond north versus south or west versus east.

Over time, change relatively trumped stability (54 per cent versus 46 per cent of all countries moving or staying in classes in the period under study). Such dynamics came about to different extents and with specific patterns. They were most pronounced in Central and Eastern Europe taking the early 1990s as a reference. This was due to the progress in decentralization reforms in the region moving cases upwards in terms of local autonomy. Nevertheless, a more recent tendency of recentralization seemed to emerge in some cases. Even if the overall evolution implied a certain convergence in local autonomy, the authors emphasized that their typology primarily offered a series of snapshots. Developing a universal or encompassing classification valid for the long term therefore proved elusive: 'we have no doubt that the typology might be different again in five to ten years from now … even if the methodology to construct types might have a more stable character' (Ladner et al. 2019: 276).

DESIGN, METHODS AND DATA

The data for the LAI 2.0 allow us to pick up the thread concluding the preceding section. Relying on the extant literature (with a keen eye on the LAI 1.0), we have built our typology based on the following preliminary assumptions. First, we have sought to include as many aspects and dimensions of local autonomy as possible, rather than work with a selection of (key) variables. We thus wanted to go beyond confining ourselves to the (features comprising) effective political discretion and financial autonomy of Ladner and colleagues. Second, we have taken into consideration the (pre-existing) theoretical and empirical cohesion of the various aspects of local autonomy – in preference to focusing on all single variables separately or looking at mere sums of scales (as in the raw scores of self-rule or interactive rule). We therefore started from the seven (standardized) dimensions of local autonomy discerned in the current version of the index (Ladner and Keuffer 2021; Ladner et al. 2021).[2]

Third, our typology attempts to transcend a single point in time, which would make it too sensitive to particular alterations in certain cases. Nevertheless, it must remain sufficiently timely and encompassing in terms of the number of countries covered. Thus, we have not limited our attempt to the most recent point in time (2020) but have rather looked at the 2015–20 means (which are available for all the 57 states covered in the index). Adopting the means likely provides additional robustness to the findings, but this inevitably remains relative. Typologies only persist as time-bound snapshots (Swianiewicz 2014). Particular changes in specific countries can affect their positioning in or out of a given category.[3] Also, this update and extension of the LAI precludes the more longitudinal perspective of Ladner and his colleagues (comparing three points in time over almost a quarter of a century). The issue of stability or change can therefore only be contemplated indirectly (also given the broader basis of our endeavour).

2 This also trumps considering the values in the eventual LAI as a basis, even if a categorization of countries in five types (of LAI-score ranges) already existed (very high, medium-high, medium, medium-low and very low, see Ladner et al. 2021: 70–71). Such an approach remains a little more one-dimensional (although the aggregations add weight to the previously discerned dimensions).

3 A PCA (principal component analysis) was explored for 2015 and 2020 separately. This led to the same two components identified in the means with highly similar factor loadings for both dimensions.

Table 3.2 *Principal component analysis of dimensions of local autonomy (2015–2020 means)*

Dimension	Component 1	Component 2
Policy scope	.865	-
Effective political discretion	.825	-
Financial autonomy	.466	-
Organizational autonomy	.698	-
Noninterference	-	.716
Legal autonomy	-	.629
Access	-	.658

Note: Rotation method: varimax with Kaiser normalization; factor loadings < .400 not displayed.
Source: Authors' own.

Following these assumptions, the (standardized) scores on the seven dimensions of local autonomy (2015–20 means) were included in a principal component analysis (PCA).[4] This determined two components that together explain about 54 per cent of the variance found (or respectively 32 per cent and 22 per cent). The factor loadings for each dimension (as items in the analysis) are displayed in Table 3.2 and further interpreted below.The first component includes the dimensions policy scope, effective political discretion, financial autonomy and organizational autonomy. This could be termed the self-rule component. It includes all the original items from the codebook under that heading except one (cf. infra). The second component is formed of the dimensions noninterference, legal autonomy and access – in other words, the interactive rule component. However, it also includes the financial-transfer system as part of noninterference (Ladner and Keuffer 2021). That item was initially denoted as part of self-rule in the codebook. Of course, the labels of the components must be interpreted with caution. As the table demonstrates, the correlations between certain initial items and their respective components are statistically significant and predominantly (very) strong. However, they invariably deviate from a perfect association (see e.g. financial autonomy). The factor score on the components cannot entirely capture the variation in the single items (and the other way around). This methodological fact can have empirical consequences. Even if the typology created appears generally valid, it may invoke results that

[4] We also explored K-means cluster analysis as a substitute. However, this did not produce very meaningful results and largely depends on the number of predefined clusters.

are more difficult to interpret for specific cases given the labels chosen for the principal components. These might appear at odds with a description of the countries via single items. The findings of the analyses in this chapter should thus always be seen in the light of these components (and their composition and configuration).

Together, these two components thus cover all the dimensions and aspects of local autonomy considered. This aligns with our first intention, to develop a typology as information-rich as possible. They also reflect the assumed conceptual and empirical structure of local autonomy as sought in the second aim. Whereas the classification of Ladner et al. (2019) remained confined to (aspects of) self-rule, the current attempt complements this with (all items of) interactive rule. This provides a more comprehensive and integrated basis for further categorization. In addition, the associated factor scores were adopted for a further distinction into low, medium or high ranges of values on both components.[5] As in the first version of the index, this produces nine categories. Again, four can be considered ideal-typical. In the first, the scores on both self-rule as well as interactive rule are high. This type (high-high) can be denoted as *champions of local autonomy*. It is the most decentralized type. In the second, self-rule is high, but interactive rule low. This type (high-low) represents *local policy autonomy*. Here, local authorities have scope and discretion in many domains and can finance and organize themselves accordingly. In the third, the opposite applies (low on self-rule, high on interactive rule). This type (low-high) can be termed as *local polity autonomy*. Here, scope and discretion are notably smaller, but local authorities are nevertheless acknowledged as self-standing political entities in their own right. In the fourth and final ideal type, scores on both dimensions are low. This type (low-low) stands as *opponents of local autonomy*. It is the most centralized type. Of course, these labels should be interpreted with caution. Classes are defined by their relative standing towards one another as captured by the two underlying components. The five remaining categories are transitional (with medium values on one or both dimensions). They somehow deviate from the pure types.

RESULTS

Subsequently, the countries included were placed into these categories. We thus aimed to determine how closely they resemble one of the ideal types. The

[5] Calculating Cronbach's alpha did not produce very consistent and reliable sum scales (respectively .680 and .458). The categorization for each dimension is based on the marginal frequency distribution of the factor scores (each range comprises about one third of the cases). This yields the breaking points for the division of the dimensions into particular classes.

Table 3.3 *Typology of local autonomy (relative factor score of countries on self-rule versus interactive rule – 2015–2020 mean)*

		Self-rule component (factor based on *policy scope, effective political discretion, financial autonomy & organizational autonomy*)		
		Low	Medium	High
Interactive rule component (factor based on *noninterference, legal autonomy & access*)	Low	**Type 9** *Opponents of autonomy* Armenia, Canada, Ireland, Israel, Kosovo, Mexico, Moldova, Russian Federation (N = 8)	**Type 7** Albania, Belarus, Hungary, Romania, Ukraine, United Kingdom (N = 6)	**Type 2** *Policy autonomy* Belgium, Colombia, Denmark, United States of America (N = 4)
	Medium	**Type 8** Australia, Bosnia and Herzegovina, Croatia, Cyprus, Turkey (N = 5)	**Type 5** Argentina, Bulgaria, Latvia, Lithuania, Macedonia (N = 5)	**Type 3** Estonia, Georgia, Germany, Japan, Liechtenstein, Norway, Poland, Serbia, Sweden (N = 9)
	High	**Type 6** *Polity autonomy* Chile, Luxembourg, Malta, Montenegro, Republic of Korea, South Africa (N = 6)	**Type 4** Andorra, Austria, Czech Republic, Greece, Italy, Portugal, Slovenia, Spain (N = 8)	**Type 1** *Champions of autonomy* Finland, France, Iceland, Netherlands, Slovakia, Switzerland (N = 6)

Source: Authors' own.

result of that exercise can be found in Table 3.3. It sets the four (shaded) ideal types against their transitory counterparts. All types are labelled by numbers that represent a descending value (2015–20 means) on the overall index of local autonomy (1 = highest; 9 = lowest). The exact values of the latter by type can be found in Table 3A.1 in the Appendix to this chapter.

Overall, our typology appears to meet the quality criteria set forth in the methodological literature. It comprises mutually exclusive and collectively exhaustive types that represent categorized ranges of quantitative (factor) scores on self-rule and interactive rule (two central dimensions of the overarching concept of local autonomy empirically enclosing all scrutinized aspects). These types are classificatory and foster a more structured descriptive comparison of the country cases included in the study (Collier et al. 2008, 2012).

Each of the subsequent types includes a substantial number of cases (from four to nine countries). Together, the ideal types cover a minority of cases (24, or 42 per cent of all countries).

Type 1 includes six countries with the highest level of both self-rule and interactive rule (and the subsequent highest value on the LAI). It comprises two Nordic (Finland and Iceland) and two Rhinelandic countries (the Netherlands and Switzerland) along with France and Slovakia. These are the *champions of autonomy*. The counterpart can be found in Type 9, with low self-rule and interactive rule (thus lowest on the LAI). This type comprises eight countries, of which four are (Central and) Eastern European (Armenia, Moldova, Kosovo and the Russian Federation) and two stemming from the Anglo-Saxon state tradition (Canada and Ireland) in addition to Israel and Mexico. These thus comprise the *opponents of autonomy*.

Types 2–5 score above the overall mean on the LAI. For 2 and 3, this comes with a high score on self-rule. The four Type 2 countries (Belgium, Colombia, Denmark and the United States) are spread across different continents and state traditions. Moreover, they combine their high score on self-rule with a low one on interactive rule. Here, *autonomy* is thus more a matter of *policy* than polity. The nine in Type 3 come from the (Central and) Eastern European (Estonia, Georgia, Poland and Serbia), Nordic (Norway and Sweden) or Rhinelandic (Germany and Liechtenstein) group supplemented with Japan. Type 4 scores medium on self-rule but remains high in interactive rule. Five of the eight countries in this group are from Southern Europe (Andorra, Greece, Italy, Portugal and Spain). Two are from (Central and) Eastern Europe (Czech Republic and Slovenia), with Austria making up the eight. Apart from Argentina, the cases from Type 5 (medium on both dimensions) are situated in (Central and) Eastern Europe (Bulgaria, Latvia, Lithuania and Macedonia).

The remaining types (Types 6–8) score below the overall mean on the LAI. They are each low on one of the dimensions (6 and 8 on self-rule versus 7 on interactive rule). The six cases of Type 6 combine their high score on interactive rule with a low one on self-rule. Here, *autonomy* tends to *polity* rather than policy. The cases are dispersed geographically. This holds for those in Europe (Luxembourg, Malta and Montenegro) as well as those beyond (Chile, the Republic of Korea and South Africa). Except the United Kingdom, all Type 7 countries can be found in (Central and) Eastern Europe (Albania, Belarus, Hungary, Romania and Ukraine). Type 8 includes cases from (Central and) Eastern Europe (Bosnia and Herzegovina, and Croatia), Southern Europe (Cyprus and Turkey) and Australia.

In sum, there is some but definitely not overall regional clustering and/or reference to the traditional typologies often used in cross-national studies of intergovernmental relations. Trends and tendencies in that regard often come with exceptions. It can be noted that all Nordic European cases are high on self-rule (but vary on interactive rule). For most Anglo-Saxon ones, a different pattern holds (low on interactive rule, variable on self-rule). The bulk of Southern European countries score high on interactive rule. Those beyond Europe tend to position low on self-rule (with the exception of Argentina and the United States of America). However, cases from (Central and) Eastern Europe have a differentiated profile (present in all types except Type 2). Such a result may be expected. Our focus is on constitutive (rather than effective) local autonomy (the potential for more rather than the actual use of discretion). Moreover, the analysis includes cases well beyond the traditional empirical core.

The above summarizes the types by their constitutive components and overall degree of local autonomy. However, these may differ on more specific features, and shared characteristics can blur internal diversification. This could occur for each of the dimensions of local autonomy included. Figure 3.1 takes

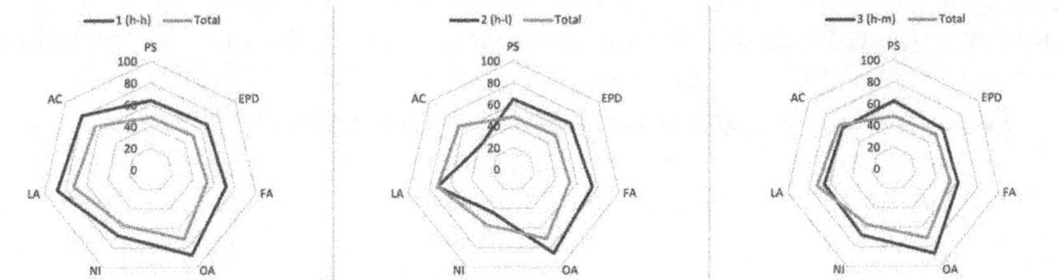

Source: Authors' own.

Figure 3.1 *Dimensions of local autonomy by type (means 2015–20)*

this into account. It represents the (mean) scores on these dimensions for the different types (set off against those for the total). The radar graphs help us to visualize the configuration of local autonomy characterizing each type. The values behind the figure (including standard deviations to estimate the heterogeneity within the types) can be found in Table 3A.1 in the Appendix to this chapter.

Appendix Table 3A.1 and the graphs demonstrate the pronounced features of the ideal types. In Type 1 (*champions of autonomy*), the means for all dimensions are higher than those for the total. In turn, these prove consistently lower for Type 9 (*opponents to autonomy*). For Type 2 (*policy autonomy*), the scores on policy scope, effective political discretion, financial autonomy and organizational autonomy turn out higher (as well as on legal autonomy). For Type 6 (*polity autonomy*), this is the case for noninterference, legal autonomy and access (but also financial autonomy). As can be expected, the transitional types take an intermediate position. When a type is characterized by high scores on self-rule, all the associated dimensions tend to reflect this. A similar tendency holds for interactive rule (and *mutatis mutandis* when a type tallies low on either of these components).

The different types appear fairly homogeneous internally. For most dimensions, the standard deviations for the separate types are (substantially) lower than those for the total (suggesting higher variation between than within the groups). However, there are some exceptions. These pertain less to dimensions of self-rule than to those of interactive rule. Regarding the former, only for Type 1 is the variation in terms of financial autonomy higher than that of the total. For the latter and noninterference, the same holds for Type 5. Legal autonomy differs a bit more in Types 2 and 9 than on average. Access to the regional or central level varies above average in Types 4, 5 and 8.

CONCLUSION

In this chapter, we developed an empirical typology of local autonomy. The aim was to cluster countries with similar configurations beyond geographical areas and traditional classifications of intergovernmental relations. Building on the attempt made for the LAI 1.0, our current exercise considered all aspects of local autonomy while acknowledging their underlying cohesion in dimensions. It provided a robust update of the last five years and an extension to the 57 countries included in the LAI 2.0.

A PCA of the (mean) country scores on the seven dimensions of local autonomy during that period revealed the existence of two underlying constituents. Given the item loadings, these could be interpreted as pertaining respectively to self-rule and interactive rule. This rendered a comprehensive and integrated basis for subsequent categorization. Factor scores distinguished low, medium and high ranges on both components, producing a typology with nine categories. We termed four of these as ideal types: *champions of autonomy* (high on self-rule – high on interactive rule), *policy autonomy* (high-low), *polity autonomy* (low-high) and *opponents of autonomy* (low-low). The remaining five are transitional (medium on at least one of the two dimensions).

The results show some but no regional patterns and/or alignment with the existing typologies. For each rule in the findings exceptions must also be noted. All Nordic countries scored high on self-rule (but differed in interactive rule). They could in a sense be contrasted with their Anglo-Saxon counterparts (low on interactive rule; variable on self-rule). Most Southern European states proved high on interactive rule. Cases outside Europe tended to turn out low on self-rule (with exceptions). Those from (Central and) Eastern Europe displayed much variation (present in nearly all types).

Beyond the constitutive components of local autonomy, types equally differed on more specific characteristics. Further analyses of the dimensions demonstrated that the pure types showed the most pronounced and consistent (low or high) features. Their transitional counterparts positioned as more intermediate. Overall, high (or low) scores on self-rule (and vice versa interactive rule) tended to reappear in the associated dimensions. Common features may cover internal variety. However, the different types seemed relatively homogeneous. Variation was larger between than within the designated cluster of countries (with some exceptions mainly for interactive rule).

In sum, the current venture adds empirical scope (time, space) and depth (aspects, dimensions) to the existing typologies. It allows us to better comprehend contextualization of the selected cases in shared configurations of local autonomy. However, as with previous endeavours, it is neither universal nor static. Future research should update and extend the current snapshot of five particular years and discuss whether and how this should be done on a similar or different basis. Moreover, scholars could also probe into the question of matter. Focusing on the dimensions of local autonomy, our typology does not cover all pertinent aspects of local government systems. To what extent and how does the position of a country in a given type also associate with wider features such as territorial organization, functional decentralization or even horizontal power relations?[6] Does type also affect outcomes at a more systemic level and why (e.g. satisfaction with provisions and services or democracy or

[6] A first exploration suggests no clear relationship with territorial organization, i.e. conceived as the mean or median number of municipalities or their inhabitants. Such indicators do not align with the levels of local autonomy the types stand for. Moreover, standard deviations often transcend the aforementioned means (suggesting a large variation in territorial organization within a designated type).

trust in political actors)? In the vocabulary of the chapter, these are the *types* of questions further efforts will likely *cluster* around.

APPENDIX

Table 3A.1 *Features of types (dimensions of local autonomy – means 2015–20)*

	LAI		PS		EPD		FA		OA		NI		LA		AC	
Type (SRC-IRC)	**X**	**S**	**X**	**S**	**X**	**S**	**X**	**S**	**X**	**S**	**X**	**S**	**X**	**S**	**X**	**S**
1 (h-h)	73	9	64	12	67	13	72	24	88	16	68	20	88	17	80	16
2 (h-l)	68	6	65	11	68	11	75	4	86	13	44	18	73	33	38	8
3 (h-m)	66	6	63	4	58	10	61	22	87	14	68	10	66	25	60	13
4 (m-h)	61	5	39	3	50	8	62	19	69	14	76	11	87	15	79	25
5 (m-m)	58	4	50	7	58	7	39	15	70	10	54	26	85	15	77	31
6 (l-h)	53	10	30	10	37	10	56	22	56	15	64	20	94	14	83	19
7 (m-l)	48	5	56	10	52	13	33	14	57	17	36	23	60	25	48	17
8 (l-m)	48	5	34	9	32	11	43	17	65	7	69	14	57	22	67	28
9 (l-l)	42	4	38	10	35	15	41	22	61	17	28	20	48	32	46	17
Total	**57**	**12**	**48**	**15**	**50**	**16**	**54**	**23**	**71**	**18**	**57**	**24**	**72**	**27**	**65**	**24**

Note: Type number according to LAI value (2015–20). Abbreviations, see dimensions as in Table 3.2.
Source: Authors' own.

PART II

ISSUES OF LOCAL AUTONOMY

4. Asymmetric decentralization at the subnational level: varied arrangements of local autonomy

INTRODUCTION

In the study of intergovernmental relations, autonomy is often interpreted as a uniform characteristic of a given tier of governance. At the local level, this implies that all municipalities enjoy the same freedom *from* central control *to* exercise their place-bound authority. Hence, in principle immunity and initiation are created equal amongst all (Ladner et al. 2019), and this approach remains the default in contemporary practice. However, in some states the allocation of autonomy continues to differ systematically across local entities (Ladner et al. 2023). In such institutional settings, certain municipalities are more autonomous than others. This form of asymmetric decentralization has been well studied in regional and federal studies as an alternative to the trade-offs between the advantages and disadvantages of centralized versus decentralized provisions. It allows the specificities of some jurisdictions to be accommodated in the management of multilevel governance (Hooghe et al. 2016; Fiorillo et al. 2021).

Much less research exists that pertains to municipalities. This chapter therefore scrutinizes asymmetric decentralization at the subnational level by probing into varied arrangements of local autonomy within states. It proceeds as follows. First, the phenomenon is situated in the extant literature. Second, the empirical patterns in asymmetry are assessed at the local and the regional level. For each level, we outline the implied countries and units. We subsequently discuss local autonomy as the interplay between self- and interactive rule and how these (or aspects thereof) differ (or not) in the respective subunits. The conclusions present a summary of the main findings and discusses their implications against existing insights.

LOCAL AUTONOMY: UNIFORM BY DEFAULT, VARIED AS DEVIATION

Local government in the contemporary nation-state is often (and almost by default) conceived of in terms of symmetry. The historical pattern of uniformity was mainly induced by the diffusion of the Napoleonic model in Europe (Loughlin et al. 2012). This adds up to the more current discourse of territorial justice. Regardless of place, citizens (under similar circumstances) should be able to make an equal appeal to (a nationally determined minimum standard of) local public services and provisions. This reasoning based on equity gained traction with the development of the (local) welfare state in the twentieth century (Sellers et al. 2020).[1] Local self-government is thus not only a matter of the ability to make specific place-bound choices: it also pertains to a territorially homogenous level of municipal capabilities reflected in a similar institutional setting.

Despite these dynamics, instances of asymmetric arrangements still occur. These have been compared most systematically by Lidström (2019) with a specific focus on the unequal division of functions at the local level. The author argues that such arrangements emerge to handle differences in municipal capacity or stem from regional asymmetries. The question of capacity concerns the general urban–rural divide or specific local authorities with particularly weak or strong capacities. It also includes the need for flexibility. The question of asymmetries pertains to areas with a particular ethnic-cultural identity and city or metropolitan regions. With distinct rationales come various institutional solutions. Some asymmetries are general and comprehensive (e.g. in developing a ladder of responsibility or standardizing diversification along with urbanization). Others tend to be more specific and limited (e.g. by giving some authorities fewer tasks and others more, letting negotiations determine their division or outsourcing these to neighbouring entities, metropolitan governance structures or higher tiers of government).

Functional asymmetries exist all over Europe (regardless of geographical area or (local) government system). They may occur for political, administrative or fiscal reasons. Sometimes they persist in path dependencies. In other cases, asymmetries are subject to institutional change (either by being abolished or newly introduced). Recent accounts by the OECD (Organisation for Economic Co-operation and Development) even suggest an increase in

[1] Earlier on and/or elsewhere, asymmetry was dominant (based on the rationale of different functions for different needs). The development of local government thereby tended to follow separate trajectories for towns (or cities) and the countryside (Lidström, 2019).

asymmetric decentralization, moving from the regional level (historically the most common form) to major urban areas (from capital cities to metropolitan regions) or applied at the municipal level (based on number of inhabitants and/or urbanization). Once introduced, these differentiated forms of governance tend to persist on a long-term basis (OECD 2019; Allain-Dupré et al. 2020).[2]

Lidström's analysis is one of the rare systematic assertions of asymmetric arrangements at the local level. However, it takes a mere functional perspective. It considers only the (delegated) tasks, responsibilities and competencies of local government. The issue of diverging authority can evidently be approached more broadly, covering all aspects and dimensions of local autonomy. Hence the central question in this chapter: *to what extent are asymmetries visible in the wider configuration of local autonomy*? We also widen the range of countries covered. Lidström draws on illustrative examples derived from the scholarly literature in Europe. Our geographical scope and empirical rigour are more extensive.

The exercise in this chapter builds on the distinction between the unit of analysis and aggregation made in the collection and processing of the project data (see Chapter 1 in this volume). The first refers to the lowest and most important unit of effective self-government,[3] the second to the final level of measurement (for cross-national comparison). Here, unitary states were distinguished from their federal counterparts. Furthermore, systems where all municipalities have the same degree of autonomy were set apart from those where there are asymmetric arrangements with different units at the subnational level. The latter include local and regional variations (Ladner et al. 2023). The assignment of cases to the designated categories was at the discretion of the country experts and to the extent that it implied differences in the aspects of local autonomy studied.

---

[2] These broader subnational assessments see political, administrative and fiscal rationales for introducing asymmetries. The latter can be found at the regional, metropolitan or local level. The first is the historical locus with a continued rising trend. The second is thus also waning (from traditional arrangements for capital cities to timely city-regional configurations). The third stems from divergences in the capacities or classifications of municipalities, often along the urban–rural divide.

[3] This is the first tier of local government (often denoted as the municipality or equivalent). We thus exclude the second tier (with intermediate authorities such as districts, counties, provinces or metropolitan governance).

ASYMMETRIES AT THE LOCAL LEVEL

In our sample, there are 13 (mainly European) countries (or about 23 per cent of the total) where asymmetries can be found at the local level (see Table 4.1). These pertain to varied arrangements of autonomy between specific (categories of) municipalities. This is higher than the number of countries where such divergencies exist at the regional level (10 or about 18 per cent, cf. infra) but lower than that where these are absent (34 countries or about 60 per cent of the total). In our sample of countries, asymmetry in local autonomy thus appears to be more the exception than the rule, although with an overall figure of about 40 per cent, it is not uncommon either.

The number of units marked by local-level asymmetries varies from two (seven countries) or three (four countries) to four (two countries). Thus, the more units, the fewer countries. These asymmetries seem to revolve around the degree of urbanization of a given entity (with some functional equivalents). The prevalence of the distinction between (ordinary) municipalities and cities in most of the countries included is a case in point (alternative bases are number of inhabitants or metropolitan status). Sometimes, the dichotomy is further refined (i.e. when distinguishing settlements, villages and/or towns). At others, it pertains to specific (types of) cities only. These can be the national capital or other designated authorities (by name or nature). As expected (but with some exceptions), there are more municipalities (or settlements, villages and towns) with the standard arrangements than (particular) cities (or types thereof) with exceptions.

To what extent do these asymmetries matter for local autonomy? Given the prime importance of urbanization as a basis for the arrangements, can we assume that local autonomy is higher for cities (in general, by type or particular) than for the default municipalities (or their functional equivalents)? If so, is this driven by (aspects of) self-rule, interactive rule or both as introduced in Chapter 1 (see Table 1.1).

The table shows that asymmetries indeed come with different degrees of autonomy (even if this is not the case for all countries and/or units). The assumption made above holds in most instances. The degree of local autonomy indeed tends to be higher for (specific) cities than for municipalities (the baseline). Exceptions are found only in France (cf. lower scores for Paris) and the Russian Federation (cf. lower scores for the federal cities). The latter also displays the biggest difference in terms of local autonomy between two types of units (8.5 points of variation between lowest and highest).[4]

---

[4] As outlined in the country profile, the municipal units in the three federal cities of Russia (Moscow, St Petersburg and Sebastopol) are deprived of almost

Table 4.1 *Asymmetric decentralization at the local level – overview of cases*

Country	Units	Number of authorities (2020)
Armenia	Communities (*Hamaynk*)	481
	Yerevan (Capital)	1
Belarus	Municipalities (*Raion*)	1309
	Cities (*Oblast*)	1328
Croatia	Municipalities (*Općina*)	531
	Cities (*Grad*)	24
	Zagreb (Capital)	1
Cyprus	Communities (*Koinotites*)	39
	Municipalities (*Dimoi*)	39
France	Municipalities (Communes)	35 087
	Lyon	1
	Marseille	1
	Paris (Capital)	1
Japan	Villages and towns (*Mura/Chō*)	926
	Cities (*Shi*)	791
Poland	Municipalities (*Gminy*)	2411
	Cities (*Miasta na prawach powiatu*)	66
Russian Federation	Settlements	16 821
	Urban (*Okrugs*)	635
	Federal cities	267[a]
Serbia	Municipalities (*Opštine*)	122
	Cities (*Gradovi*)	22
	Belgrade (Capital)	1
Slovenia	Municipalities (Občin)	201
	Cities (Mestna občina)	11
Spain	< 20 000 inhabitants	7715
	> 20 000 inhabitants	416
Turkey	Municipalities (*Belediye*)	1398
	Municipalities within metropolitan municipalities	519
	Metropolitan municipalities	30
Ukraine	Villages and settlements (*Sela*)	8310
	Amalgamated (*Hromadas*)	872
	Towns (*Selyshcha*)	198
	Cities (*Mista*)	145

Note: [a] The number refers to municipal entities as territories within the three federal cities.
Source: Chapter 1 of this volume (Table 1.1).

Differences in local autonomy are mainly due to variation in self-rule. This can be found in 11 of the 13 countries (not in Slovenia and Turkey). Only in four (Armenia, Serbia, Turkey and Ukraine) are there differences in terms of interactive rule. These generally add up to those in self-rule (in Turkey alone, solely interactive rule leads to the ultimate difference in local autonomy for one type of unit).

The sum scores in Table 4.2 provide a general picture of similarities and differences in (the main rule areas of) local autonomy. An additional analysis focuses on the more particular aspects of each form of rule (self- or interactive). Variation may be concentrated in one or more of these aspects or hidden by diverging configurations under the same overall heading. Table 4A.1 (appended to this chapter) displays the scores for each unit on the eight aspects of self-rule. It shows that, apart from institutional depth, at least some variation can be found for each aspect. However, there are aspects for which this is clearly more pronounced than for others.

Differences are most frequent with regard to the intertwined pair of policy scope (responsibility for the delivery of services or provisions in certain fields) and effective political discretion (authoritative decision-making power).[5] Here, variation can be found in a large majority of cases (nine and ten respectively). Again (but also with exceptions), (certain (types of)) cities tend to have more scope and/or discretion than (non-urban) municipalities (or their equivalents). Thus, local level asymmetries first and foremost imply differences in functional autonomy. Some entities (mainly cities) have a larger range of tasks, responsibilities and/or competences than others (even if the general scope remains similar). In this regard, duty likely equals jurisdiction. Further explorations show this involves a wide range of fields and services predominantly related to the welfare state.[6] These probably require a certain scale and governing capacity reserved for cities (or supralocal bodies).

all functions. They only retain limited review and control over services and provisions assumed by their city governments. The latter can effectively be considered as state bodies. This functional void extends to its financial counterpart. These entities have no tax authority and limited own sources and cannot borrow.

[5] Also in terms of local level asymmetries, policy scope and effective politial discretion tend to covary. However, there are instances where differences in policy scope remain unmatched by those in effective politial discretion or vice versa. There are also examples where the pattern inverts.

[6] Greater scope and/or discretion applies to a majority of cases in welfare-state fields such as social assistance (N = 6), education (N = 5) and health (N = 5). It is also fairly common in the related field of caregiving or in the territorial counterpart of land use (both N = 4). It is less frequent in policing (N = 2) and housing (N = 1). Sometimes the patterns stem from (specific) cities equally having county

Table 4.2 *Asymmetric decentralization at the local level – autonomy as self- vs. interactive rule*

Country	Units	Self-rule (0–28)	Interactive rule (0–9)	Local autonomy (0–37)
Armenia	Municipalities	11.75	5	16.75
	Yerevan	**16**	**6**	**22**
Belarus	Municipalities	9	2	11
	Cities	12	2	14
Croatia	Municipalities	14.5	5.5	20
	Cities	**16.5**	5.5	**22**
	Zagreb	**17.5**	5.5	**23**
Cyprus	Communities	9.5	5	14.5
	Municipalities	**11.5**	5	**16.5**
France	Municipalities	22.5	7	29.5
	Lyon	22.5	7	29.5
	Marseille	22.5	7	29.5
	Paris	*20.5*	7	*27.5*
Japan	Villages and towns	17	6	23
	Cities	**19**	6	**25**
Poland	Municipalities	16.5	5.5	22
	Cities	**20.5**	5.5	**26**
Russian Federation	Settlements	8	6	14
	Urban *Okrugs*	**11**	6	**17**
	Federal cities	*2.5*	6	*8.5*
Serbia	Municipalities	18.5	5.75	24.25
	Cities	**19.5**	5.75	**25.25**
	Belgrade	**19.25**	**6.75**	**26**
Slovenia	Municipalities	15	7	22
	Cities	15	7	22
Spain	< 20 000	17	9	26
	> 20 000	**19**	9	**28**
Turkey	Municipalities	14.5	4	18.5
	Municipalities within metropolitan municipalities	14.5	**5**	**19.5**
	Metropolitan municipalities	14.5	4	18.5

status (thus also assuming second-tier tasks, responsibilities or competences). This can be found in Croatia and Poland, for example. Together with Ukraine, these are also the countries where scope and/or discretion differ for the largest number of

Country	Units	Self-rule (0–28)	Interactive rule (0–9)	Local autonomy (0–37)
Ukraine	Villages and settlements	8.75	5.5	14.25
	Amalgamated *Hromadas*	**13.75**	**6.5**	**20.25**
	Towns	**9.75**	**6.5**	**16.25**
	Cities	**13.75**	**6.5**	**20.25**

Note: Units where self-rule, interactive rule and/or local autonomy are higher than for baseline authorities (i.e. the most numerous, smallest or rural) in bold; where lower in italics.

For all other aspects of self-rule, only a minority of cases exhibit differences between units. This holds for each indicator pertaining to the financial autonomy of local authorities (in descending order of the frequency of differences: financial self-reliance, financial transfer system, borrowing autonomy and fiscal autonomy). If such variation does exist, cities tend to be more financially autonomous than other entities. This is most apparent in the larger proportion of their income derived from own sources and the share of transfers received that are unconditional.[7] Only two cases (slightly) differ in terms of organizational autonomy. There are two cases (Armenia and the Russian Federation) where differences can be found in (aspects of) functional, financial and organizational autonomy (but the pattern goes in opposite directions). In four others, this pertains to functional and financial autonomy only (Belarus, Poland, Japan and Ukraine).

Table 4A.2 (appended to this chapter) subsequently presents the scores for each unit on the three aspects of interactive rule. In view of the previous discussion, there are far fewer instances where differences by unit appear. These are, for example, entirely absent regarding legal protection. There is only one case (Armenia) where they exist in terms of administrative supervision, i.e. the difference between including budgetary matters or being limited to legality (the capital). In three countries, central or regional access is higher for some units than for others. Further analysis shows this to be a matter of formal representation and/or informal channels. This combination is the case for the capital city of Belgrade in Serbia, municipalities within metropolitan municipalities

fields (N = 4). In France, the lower score for Paris is due to (administrative) policing. In the capital, responsibilities in this field are shared with the prefecture.

7 The meaning of 'more' and 'larger' differs, however, with the initial level of financial autonomy for the baseline as a benchmark. In this regard, one can compare Armenia with Ukraine.

in Turkey or those beyond the level of villages and settlements in Ukraine. No differences appear in terms of formal consultation.

ASYMMETRIES AT THE REGIONAL LEVEL

As already mentioned, there are ten countries (or about 18 per cent of the total) where asymmetries can be found at the regional level (see Table 4.3). These refer to varied arrangements of local autonomy between substate entities of the same national political system. We found that, in sum, this pertains to 162 regions in countries inside or outside Europe. Such arrangements comprise all municipalities of the designated region. Evidently, the number of substate entities determines the number of units affected (and subsequently that of local authorities). This varies between two (Bosnia and Herzegovina) and 51 (United States). However, we will demonstrate that in some states actual differences in local autonomy pertain to all and in others to only some regions. As the table clarifies, almost all countries implied are federal states. Innate in their constitutional set-up, the constitutive discretion regarding local government tends to be situated at the substate level. This also affects local autonomy.[8] The United Kingdom forms the notable exception. Here, local autonomy differs between the devolved entities of the (formally) still unitary state.

Resuming the approach taken above, we subsequently discuss local autonomy as the combination of self-rule and interactive rule. To what extent and how are regional variations visible? Tables 4.4a to 4.4j provide the overview. Other than in the previous analysis, a baseline category involving the bulk of all cases cannot be discerned. Therefore, we took the overall country mean as a reference for regional (standard) deviations (explanation of the highlighting at the bottom of Table 4.4a).

Tables 4.4a–j show that in a little over a quarter of the regions included (42 out of 162), local autonomy is one standard deviation lower (italic) or higher (bold) than the overall national mean. In these cases, varied arrangements thus imply more or less significant regional differences in the overall summative index. This is relatively evenly distributed between regions above and below the country mean, although the former (22 cases) is more prevalent than the latter (20 instances). Regions with such deviations can be found in seven out of the ten states concerned. The one with the most is Switzerland (found in 11 out of 26 *cantons*). That with the least is Mexico (two out of 32 *estados*). The

8 In this respect, Germany appears to be the exception. Although the *Länder* do have such constitutive discretion, no differences could be found in the coding of any aspect of local autonomy.

largest regional difference in local autonomy can be found in Argentina (eight points between the lowest and the highest scoring *provincias*).

Again, differences in the overall index are largely driven by those in self-rule rather than interactive rule. The overall index and self-rule demonstrate a largely similar pattern of variation (in frequency and direction). Differences in interactive rule remain less prevalent. Standard deviations from the mean

Table 4.3 Asymmetric decentralization at the regional level – overview of cases

Country	Units (Number of local authorities – 2020)[a]
Argentina	Buenos Aires (135), Catamarca (36), Chaco (69), Chubut (47), Córdoba (427), Corrientes (75), Entre Ríos (136), Formosa (55), Jujuy (60), La Pampa (79), La Rioja (18), Mendoza (18), Misiones (77), Neuquén (57), Río Negro (75), Salta (60), San Juan (19), San Luis (65), Santa Cruz (20), Santa Fe (365), Santiago del Estero (165), Tierra del Fuego (3) and Tucumán (112)
Australia	New South Wales (128), Queensland (77), South Australia (68), Tasmania (29), Victoria (79) and Western Australia (137)
Austria	Burgenland (171), Kärnten (132), Niederösterreich (573), Oberösterreich (438), Salzburg (119), Steiermark (286), Tirol (279) and Vorarlberg (96)
Belgium	Brussels Capital (19), Flanders (300) and Wallonia (262)
Bosnia and Herzegovina	Federation of BiH (8) and Republika Srpska (64)
Canada	Alberta (333), British Columbia (162), Manitoba (137), New Brunswick (104), Newfoundland and Labrador (276), Nova Scotia (50), Ontario (444), Prince Edward Island (63), Québec (1134) and Saskatchewan (773)
Mexico	Aguascalientes (11), Baja California (6), Baja California Sur (5), Campeche (12), Chiapas (124), Chihuahua (67), Coahuila (38), Colima (10), Durango (39), Guanajuato (46), Guerrero (81), Hidalgo (84), Jalisco (125), México (125), Mexico City (16), Michoacán (113), Morelos (36), Nayarit (20), Nuevo León (51), Oaxaca (570), Puebla (217), Querétaro (18), Quintana Roo (11), San Luis Potosí (58), Sinaloa (18), Sonora (72), Tabasco (17), Tamaulipas (43), Tlaxcala (70), Veracruz (212), Yucatán (106) and Zacatecas (58)
Switzerland	Aargau (210), Appenzell Ausserrhoden (20), Appenzell Innerrhoden (6), Basel Landschaft (86), Basel Stadt (3), Bern (342), Fribourg (133), Genève (45), Glarus (3), Graubünden (105), Jura (53), Luzern (82), Neuchâtel (31), Nidwalden (11), Obwalden (7), Schaffhausen (26), Schwyz (30), Solothurn (109), St Gallen (77), Thurgau (80), Ticino (115), Uri (20), Valais (126), Vaud (309), Zug (11) and Zürich (162)

Country	Units (Number of local authorities – 2020)[a]
United States	Alabama (1195), Alaska (179), Arizona (658), Arkansas (1541), California (4444), Colorado (3141), Connecticut (625), DC (2), Delaware (334), Florida (1712), Georgia (1380), Hawaii (21), Idaho (1170), Illinois (6918), Indiana (2638), Iowa (1941), Kansas (3792), Kentucky (1322), Louisiana (516), Maine (834), Maryland (344), Massachusetts (858), Michigan (2863), Minnesota (3643), Mississippi (969), Missouri (3768), Montana (1226), Nebraska (2538), Nevada (189), New Hampshire (541), New Jersey (1338), New Mexico (1013), New York (3450), North Carolina (970), North Dakota (2664), Ohio (3897), Oklahoma (1830), Oregon (1510), Pennsylvania (4830), Rhode Island (129), South Carolina (671), South Dakota (1916), Tennessee (906), Texas (5343), Utah (619), Vermont (729), Virginia (517), Washington (1900), West Virginia (651), Wisconsin (3096) and Wyoming (794)
United Kingdom	England (339), Northern Ireland (11), Scotland (32) and Wales (22)

Note: [a] In the United States, the number of local authorities pertains to 2017 (the latest nationwide census of local governments).
Source: Chapter 1 in this volume.

can be found in a lower number of regions or states (respectively 27 and five). In addition, deviations below the mean are more frequent than those above. In that sense, they tend to lower overall autonomy, at times compensated for by higher self-rule. The reverse might also be true. Both rule areas of local autonomy can but do not always coincide. However, there are no countries where standard deviations on interactive rule occur without those in self-rule also materializing.

To what extent and how do these regional differences occur in the particular aspects underlying the general picture of the components or the composite of local autonomy? Tables 4A.3a–j (appended to this chapter) present the within-country variation for the eight aspects of self-rule. Notably, regional (standard) deviations from the overall country mean appear in all. They also tend to go in different directions indicating both higher or lower scores in a distinct facet of autonomy. However, for some this is clearly more prevalent than others. Moreover, variation tends to be concentrated in one or more specific paths and/or countries. Deviations can most often be found with regard to organizational autonomy (42 out of 162 regions). These are mainly situated in Argentina (where some *provincias* fare better than others) and the United States (in which the pattern goes in different directions). This is followed by policy scope (37 regions) and financial autonomy (29 instances). The former is again concentrated in Argentina (where some regions have a more restricted portfolio)

Table 4.4a *Asymmetric decentralization at the regional level – autonomy as self- vs interactive rule: Argentina*

Region	Self-rule (0–28)	Interactive rule (0–9)	Local autonomy (0–37)
Buenos Aires	*17*	*5*	*22*
Catamarca	19	6	25
Chaco	21	6	27
Chubut	**22**	6	28
Córdoba	20	**8**	28
Corrientes	**23**	**7**	**30**
Entre Ríos	19	6	25
Formosa	**22**	6	28
Jujuy	20	**7**	27
La Pampa	18	6	24
La Rioja	*17*	6	*23*
Mendoza	*17*	*5*	*22*
Misiones	18	6	24
Neuquén	**22**	6	28
Río Negro	18	**7**	25
Salta	**22**	6	28
San Juan	18	6	24
San Luis	18	6	24
Santa Cruz	21	6	27
Santa Fe	*16*	6	*22*
Santiago del Estero	18	6	24
Tierra del Fuego	**23**	**7**	**30**
Tucumán	*16*	**7**	*23*
Mean	19.35	6.22	25.57
Standard deviation	2.25	0.67	2.52

Notes: For tables 4.4a–j-: 1 sd or > country mean: Self-rule (0–28): 23 (14.2%); Interactive rule (0–9): 8 (4.9%); Local autonomy (0–37): 22 (13.6%). 1 sd or < country mean: Self-rule (0–28): 21 (13%); Interactive rule (0–9): 19 (11.7%); Local autonomy (0–37): 20 (12.3%). < or >. N = 162 regions.

Table 4.4b *Asymmetric decentralization at the regional level – autonomy as self- vs interactive rule: Australia*

Region	Self-rule (0–28)	Interactive rule (0–9)	Local autonomy (0–37)
New South Wales	15.5	4	19.5
Queensland	15.5	4	19.5
South Australia	16.5	4	20.5
Tasmania	15.5	4	19.5
Victoria	16.5	4	20.5
Western Australia	16.5	4	20.5
Mean	16	4	20
Standard deviation	0.55	0	0.55

and the United States (with much internal variation), the latter remarkably in Argentina (where the ability to independently tax the population swings from total absence to full discretion). Much less deflection occurs for financial self-reliance, the financial-transfer system (but note the higher levels in some Swiss *cantons*) or effective policy discretion (respectively in three, seven and nine regions). Borrowing autonomy and institutional depth (note the lower levels in some Argentinian *provincias*) are in between.

Table 4.4c *Asymmetric decentralization at the regional level – autonomy as self- vs interactive rule: Austria*

Region	Self-rule (0–28)	Interactive rule (0–9)	Local autonomy (0–37)
Burgenland	*15.5*	7	*22.5*
Kärnten	*15.5*	7	*22.5*
Niederösterreich	16.5	7	23.5
Oberösterreich	16.5	7	23.5
Salzburg	16.5	7	23.5
Steiermark	16.5	7	23.5
Tirol	16.5	7	23.5
Vorarlberg	**17**	7	**24**
Mean	16.31	7	23.31
Standard deviation	0.53	0	0.53

Table 4.4d Asymmetric decentralization at the regional level – autonomy as self- vs interactive rule: Belgium

Region	Self-rule (0–28)	Interactive rule (0–9)	Local autonomy (0–37)
Brussels Capital	18	4	22
Flanders	**19**	4	**23**
Wallonia	18	4	22
Mean	18.33	4	22.33
Standard deviation	0.58	0	0.58

Table 4.4e Asymmetric decentralization at the regional level – autonomy as self- vs interactive rule: Bosnia and Herzegovina

Region	Self-rule (0–28)	Interactive rule (0–9)	Local autonomy (0–37)
Federation of BiH	11	8	19
Republika Srpska	15.25	4.5	19.75
Mean	13.13	6.25	19.38
Standard deviation	3.01	2.47	0.53

Also for the three aspects of interactive rule, significant regional differences come to the fore, albeit to a lesser extent (see Table 4A.4a–j appended to this chapter). They are most prevalent for legal protection (23 cases), all indicating a lower level of constitutional or legal means to assert local autonomy in some regions (with a majority of these cases found in the United States). Regional variation occurs the least in terms of central or regional access (five instances). In all but one case, the extent to which local authorities have channels to influence higher-level decision-making is higher in some regions than others. Administrative supervision remains in between and displays mixed orientations.

CONCLUSION

Symmetry is the historical and normative principle underpinning most local government systems. Uniform practices prevail, but do not necessarily preclude uneven arrangements. In previous studies these have been scrutinized mainly from a functional perspective. Extant research demonstrates the unequal

Table 4.4f Asymmetric decentralization at the regional level – autonomy as self- vs interactive rule: Canada

Region	Self-rule (0–28)	Interactive rule (0–9)	Local autonomy (0–37)
Alberta	14.5	2	16.5
British Columbia	13.5	**3.5**	**17**
Manitoba	13.5	2	15.5
New Brunswick	13.5	2	15.5
Newfoundland and Labrador	*12*	2	*14*
Nova Scotia	*12.5*	2	*14.5*
Ontario	**15.5**	2	**17.5**
Prince Edward Island	14.5	2	16.5
Québec	13.5	2	15.5
Saskatchewan	13.5	2	15.5
Mean	13.65	2.15	15.8
Standard deviation	1	0.47	1.09

Table 4.4g Asymmetric decentralization at the regional level – autonomy as self- vs interactive rule: Mexico

Region	Self-rule (0–28)	Interactive rule (0–9)	Local autonomy (0–37)
Aguascalientes	*9*	4	*13*
Baja California	10	4	14
Baja California Sur	10	4	14
Campeche	10	4	14
Chiapas	10	4	14
Chihuahua	10	4	14
Coahuila	10	4	14
Colima	10	4	14
Durango	10	4	14
Guanajuato	10	4	14
Guerrero	10	4	14
Hidalgo	10	4	14
Jalisco	10	4	14

Region	Self-rule (0–28)	Interactive rule (0–9)	Local autonomy (0–37)
México	10	4	14
Mexico City	*5.5*	**5**	*10.5*
Michoacán	10	4	14
Morelos	10	4	14
Nayarit	10	4	14
Nuevo León	10	4	14
Oaxaca	10	4	14
Puebla	10	4	14
Querétaro	10	4	14
Quintana Roo	10	4	14
San Luis Potosí	10	4	14
Sinaloa	10	4	14
Sonora	10	4	14
Tabasco	10	4	14
Tamaulipas	10	4	14
Tlaxcala	10	4	14
Veracruz	10	4	14
Yucatán	10	4	14
Zacatecas	10	4	14
Mean	9.83	4.03	13.86
Standard deviation	0.81	0.18	0.64

division of tasks, functions and competences stems from different rationales and comes with various institutional solutions. These often address disparities in capacity originating from intermunicipal variation (in terms of size or urbanization). They can be general or specific and comprehensive or limited. This chapter builds on that research, extending the scope to all aspects of local autonomy. In our wider selection of countries, we include varied arrangements of local autonomy both at the local and at the regional level. Can we determine wider asymmetries at the first tier of local government in our selected countries? What similarities and differences exist in various types of rule and their constitutive aspects? Our findings are summarized below.

Asymmetric decentralization remains the exception. However, it is not uncommon. It characterizes about 40 per cent of all countries included in the analysis. Those at the local level are mostly situated in (the Eastern part of)

Table 4.4h *Asymmetric decentralization at the regional level – autonomy as self- vs interactive rule: Switzerland*

Region	Self-rule (0–28)	Interactive rule (0–9)	Local autonomy (0–37)
Aargau	**24**	8	**32**
Appenzell_Arh	23	9	**32**
Appenzell Irh	23	9	**32**
Basel Landschaft	23	9	**32**
Basel Stadt	22	8	30
Bern	22	8	30
Fribourg	22	*5*	*27*
Genève	*18*	9	*27*
Glarus	23	8	31
Graubünden	22	7	29
Jura	21	7	*28*
Luzern	23	*6*	29
Neuchâtel	21	9	30
Nidwalden	**24**	9	**33**
Obwalden	23	9	**32**
Schaffhausen	22	8	30
Schwyz	**24**	*6*	30
Solothurn	22	9	31
St Gallen	**24**	7	31
Thurgau	22	8	30
Ticino	**24**	8	**32**
Uri	22	9	31
Valais	**24**	8	**32**
Vaud	*20*	9	29
Zug	22	9	31
Zürich	21	8	29
Mean	22.35	8.04	30.39
Standard deviation	1.41	1.11	1.6

Table 4.4i *Asymmetric decentralization at the regional level – autonomy as self- vs interactive rule: United States*

Region	Self-rule (0–28)	Interactive rule (0–9)	Local autonomy (0–37)
Alabama	*16*	5.5	*21.5*
Alaska	17	6	23
Arizona	19	*5*	24
Arkansas	*16.5*	*5*	*21.5*
California	**20**	6	**26**
Colorado	**20**	6	**26**
Connecticut	17.5	5.5	23
DC	17.5	*5*	22.5
Delaware	*15.5*	*5*	*20.5*
Florida	19	6	25
Georgia	**20.5**	6	**26.5**
Hawaii	17	6	23
Idaho	18	*5*	23
Illinois	18	6	24
Indiana	17	*5*	22
Iowa	18.5	6	24.5
Kansas	18.5	5.5	24
Kentucky	18.5	*5*	23.5
Louisiana	19	6	25
Maine	*16.5*	5.5	22
Maryland	17.5	6	23.5
Massachusetts	17.5	5.5	23
Michigan	18	6	24
Minnesota	**21**	6	**27**
Mississippi	17.5	*5*	22.5
Missouri	18	6	24
Montana	19	6	25
Nebraska	*16*	*5*	*21*
Nevada	17	5.5	22.5
New Hampshire	17.5	*5*	22.5
New Jersey	18	*5*	23
New Mexico	18	6	24

Region	Self-rule (0–28)	Interactive rule (0–9)	Local autonomy (0–37)
New York	**20**	6	**26**
North Carolina	17	*5*	22
North Dakota	19	5.5	24.5
Ohio	**20**	6	**26**
Oklahoma	*16.5*	5.5	22
Oregon	17.5	6	23.5
Pennsylvania	18.5	6	24.5
Rhode Island	*16*	5.5	*21.5*
South Carolina	**20**	6	**26**
South Dakota	19	6	25
Tennessee	**21**	6	**27**
Texas	17.5	5.5	23
Utah	18.5	5.5	24
Vermont	*14*	*5*	*19*
Virginia	18	*5*	23
Washington	19	6	25
West Virginia	17.5	5.5	23
Wisconsin	19	5.5	24.5
Wyoming	17.5	5.5	23
Mean	18.04	5.59	23.63
Standard deviation	1.43	0.42	1.7

Table 4.4j *Asymmetric decentralization at the regional level – autonomy as self- vs interactive rule: United Kingdom*

Region	Self-rule (0–28)	Interactive rule (0–9)	Local autonomy (0–37)
England	14	5	19
Northern Ireland	10	5	15
Scotland	13	5	18
Wales	13	5	18
Mean	12.5	5	17.5
Standard deviation	1.73	0	1.73

Europe (but can equally be found elsewhere). It tends to involve two types of units (although more is possible) and galvanizes around urbanization (a striking parallel with its earlier prevalence). This sets (certain (types) of) cities apart from ordinary municipalities (or their equivalents). At times, there exists a specific arrangement for the capital of the nation. The pattern for asymmetries at the regional levels appears more dispersed. Examples are not limited to Europe. They can be found in all continents. As expected, these tend to coincide with a federal political system.

Asymmetry matters for autonomy, but for some authorities and aspects more than others. Regarding local level asymmetries, urban units tend to enjoy more autonomy than the default entities in their country (with notable exceptions). Asymmetry can be found more often in the area of self-rule than in that of interactive rule. For self-rule, it is more functional than financial or organizational. It is primarily visible in the extended scope and discretion of these units and mainly appears in welfare-related fields such as social assistance, education and health. Providing a more systematic and comprehensive picture, this largely confirms the earlier account by Lidström (2019). It also appears in the predominance of own or unconditional sources of income. For interactive rule, it is more additional than exclusive and mainly occurs through enhanced access to central or regional government via formal representation or informal channels.

Asymmetries at the regional level are both similar to and different from those found for their local counterparts. Actual variation may impact all or only some regions. It can go in different directions (with greater or lesser autonomy for the local authorities involved). In some states the differences are also more significant (for some regions) than others (conceived as a standard deviation from the country mean). Here also, significant variation in self-rule prevails over that in interactive rule. However, for both, it pertains to all aspects under study. Variation in self-rule is more organizational than functional or financial. Variation in autonomy between regions is thus most often a matter of greater or lesser discretion in terms of the local electoral system or administrative structures. Moreover, differences in policy scope do not necessarily entail differences in effective political discretion. The latter sometimes adds to but sometimes detracts from local autonomy. It also tends to involve (fewer) legal means to ensure local autonomy rather than (more) channels of access into higher levels of government.

The findings of this chapter add to the existing literature. First, in some countries, asymmetry clearly goes beyond tasks, responsibilities and competences, even if this is often the basis for diverging arrangements. It also has organizational or financial dimensions. Second, varieties in local autonomy within countries also come in different shades: at times more superficial and narrow, at times more profound and broad. Third, variation at the local and regional levels cannot be equalized: their prevalence and characteristics differ. Since this chapter mainly provides a more systematic and integrated description of the phenomenon, future research should probe further into the causes, forms and consequences of these exceptions to the general rule of uniformity. Why and how do these lasting asymmetries occur and matter?

APPENDIX

Table 4A.1 Asymmetric decentralization at the local level – aspects of self-rule

Country	Units	ID	PS	EPD	FA	FTS	FSR	BA	OA
Armenia	Municipalities	2	2	2	0	2	1	1	1.75
	Yerevan	2	**3**	**3**	0	**3**	**2**	1	**2**
Belarus	Municipalities	1	3	2	1	0	0	1	1
	Cities	1	3	**3**	1	0	**2**	1	1
Croatia	Municipalities	3	1	1	1	3	2	1	2.5
	Cities	3	**2**	**2**	1	3	2	1	2.5
	Zagreb	3	**3**	**2**	1	3	2	1	2.5
Cyprus	Communities	1	1	1	1	1	1	1	2.5
	Municipalities	1	**2**	**2**	1	1	1	1	2.5
France	Municipalities	2	4	4	2	3	3	2	2.5
	Lyon	2	4	4	2	3	3	2	2.5
	Marseille	2	4	4	2	3	3	2	2.5
	Paris	2	*3*	*3*	2	3	3	2	2.5
Japan	Villages and towns	3	2	2	2	1	1	3	3
	Cities	3	**3**	2	2	1	**2**	3	3
Poland	Municipalities	2	2	2	2	1	2	2	3.5
	Cities	2	**4**	**3**	2	**2**	2	2	3.5
Russian Federation	Settlements	0	1	1	1	0	0	2	3
	Urban *Okrugs*	0	**3**	1	1	0	**1**	2	3
	Federal cities	0	0	*0*	*0*	0	0	*0*	*2.5*
Serbia	Municipalities	2	3	2	2	3	2	1.5	3
	Cities	2	3	**3**	2	3	2	1.5	3
	Belgrade	2	3	**3**	2	3	2	1.5	2.75
Slovenia	Municipalities	2.5	2	2	1	2	1	1	3.5
	Cities	2.5	2	2	1	2	1	1	3.5
Spain	< 20 000	3	1	1	2	2	3	2	3
	> 20 000	3	**2**	**2**	2	2	3	2	3
Turkey	Municipalities	2	2	1	1	3	2	1	2.5
	Municipalities within metropolitan municipalities	2	2	1	1	3	2	1	2.5
	Metropolitan municipalities	2	2	1	1	3	2	1	2.5

Country	Units	ID	PS	EPD	FA	FTS	FSR	BA	OA
Ukraine	Villages and settlements	2	2	1	1	0	0	0	2.75
	Amalgamated *Hromadas*	2	**3**	**2**	1	**1**	**1**	**1**	2.75
	Towns	2	2	1	1	0	0	**1**	2.75
	Cities	2	**3**	**2**	1	**1**	**1**	**1**	2.75

Notes: ID = institutional depth (0–3), PS = policy scope (0–4), EPD = effective political discretion (0–4), FA = financial autonomy (0–4), FTS = financial-transfer system (0–3), FSR = financial self-reliance (0–3), BA = borrowing autonomy (0–3) and OA = organizational autonomy (0–4). Units where self-rule, interactive rule and/or local autonomy are higher than for baseline authorities (i.e. the most numerous, smallest or rural) in bold; where lower in italics.

Table 4A.2 Asymmetric decentralization at the local level – aspects of interactive rule

Country	Units	LP	AS	CRA
Armenia	Municipalities	3	1	1
	Yerevan	3	**2**	1
Belarus	Municipalities	1	0	1
	Cities	1	0	1
Croatia	Municipalities	2.5	2	1
	Cities	2.5	2	1
	Zagreb	2.5	2	1
Cyprus	Communities	2	1	2
	Municipalities	2	1	2
France	Municipalities	3	2	2
	Lyon	3	2	2
	Marseille	3	2	2
	Paris	3	2	2
Japan	Villages and towns	2	2	2
	Cities	2	2	2
Poland	Municipalities	1.5	2	2
	Cities	1.5	2	2
Russian Federation	Settlements	3	2	1
	Urban *Okrugs*	3	2	1
	Federal cities	3	2	1
Serbia	Municipalities	2.5	1.5	1.75
	Cities	2.5	1.5	1.75
	Belgrade	2.5	1.5	**2.75**
Slovenia	Municipalities	2	3	2
	Cities	2	3	2
Spain	< 20 000	3	3	3
	> 20 000	3	3	3
Turkey	Municipalities	1	2	1
	Municipalities within metropolitan municipalities	1	2	**2**
	Metropolitan municipalities	1	2	1
Ukraine	Villages and settlements	1.5	3	1
	Amalgamated *Hromadas*	1.5	3	**2**
	Towns	1.5	3	**2**
	Cities	1.5	3	**2**

Notes: LP = legal protection (0–3), AS = administrative supervision (0–3) and CRA = central or regional access (0–3). Units where self-rule, interactive rule and/or local autonomy are higher than for baseline authorities (i.e. the most numerous, smallest or rural) in bold; where lower in italics.

Table 4A.3a Asymmetric decentralization at the regional level – aspects of self-rule: Argentina

Region	ID	PS	EPD	FA	FTS	FSR	BA	OA
Buenos Aires	*1.00*	2.00	3.00	*0.00*	3.00	3.00	2.00	3.00
Catamarca	2.00	2.00	3.00	*0.00*	3.00	3.00	2.00	4.00
Chaco	2.00	2.00	2.00	4.00	3.00	3.00	2.00	3.00
Chubut	2.00	2.00	2.00	4.00	3.00	3.00	2.00	4.00
Córdoba	2.00	3.00	3.00	*0.00*	3.00	3.00	2.00	4.00
Corrientes	2.00	3.00	2.00	4.00	3.00	3.00	2.00	4.00
Entre Ríos	2.00	3.00	3.00	*0.00*	3.00	3.00	2.00	3.00
Formosa	2.00	3.00	2.00	4.00	3.00	3.00	2.00	3.00
Jujuy	2.00	2.00	2.00	3.00	3.00	3.00	2.00	3.00
La Pampa	2.00	3.00	2.00	*0.00*	3.00	3.00	2.00	3.00
La Rioja	2.00	2.00	2.00	*0.00*	3.00	3.00	2.00	3.00
Mendoza	*1.00*	2.00	2.00	*0.00*	3.00	3.00	2.00	4.00
Misiones	2.00	3.00	2.00	*0.00*	3.00	3.00	2.00	3.00
Neuquén	2.00	3.00	2.00	3.00	3.00	3.00	2.00	4.00
Río Negro	2.00	2.00	2.00	*0.00*	3.00	3.00	2.00	4.00
Salta	2.00	3.00	2.00	4.00	3.00	3.00	2.00	3.00
San Juan	2.00	3.00	2.00	*0.00*	3.00	3.00	2.00	3.00
San Luis	2.00	2.00	2.00	*0.00*	3.00	3.00	2.00	4.00
Santa Cruz	2.00	2.00	2.00	4.00	3.00	3.00	2.00	3.00
Santa Fe	*1.00*	2.00	2.00	*0.00*	3.00	3.00	2.00	3.00
Santiago del Estero	2.00	3.00	2.00	*0.00*	3.00	3.00	2.00	3.00
Tierra del Fuego	2.00	3.00	2.00	4.00	3.00	3.00	2.00	4.00
Tucumán	2.00	2.00	2.00	*0.00*	3.00	3.00	2.00	3.00
Mean	1.87	2.48	2.17	1.24	3.00	3.00	2.00	3.39
Standard deviation	0.34	0.51	0.39	1.81	0.00	0.00	0.00	0.50

Table 4A.3b *Asymmetric decentralization at the regional level – aspects of self-rule: Argentina*

Region	ID	PS	EPD	FA	FTS	FSR	BA	OA
New South Wales	1.00	2.00	1.00	2.00	3.00	3.00	1.00	2.50
Queensland	1.00	2.00	1.00	2.00	3.00	3.00	1.00	2.50
South Australia	1.00	2.00	1.00	2.00	3.00	3.00	2.00	2.50
Tasmania	1.00	2.00	1.00	2.00	3.00	3.00	1.00	2.50
Victoria	1.00	2.00	1.00	2.00	3.00	3.00	2.00	2.50
Western Australia	1.00	2.00	1.00	2.00	3.00	3.00	2.00	2.50
Mean	1.00	2.00	1.00	2.00	3.00	3.00	1.50	2.50
Standard deviation	0.00	0.00	0.00	0.00	0.00	0.00	0.55	0.00

Table 4A.3c *Asymmetric decentralization at the regional level – aspects of self-rule: Austria*

Region	ID	PS	EPD	FA	FTS	FSR	BA	OA
Burgenland	3.00	2.00	2.00	3.00	2.00	0.00	*1.00*	2.50
Kärnten	3.00	2.00	2.00	3.00	2.00	0.00	*1.00*	2.50
Niederösterreich	3.00	2.00	2.00	3.00	2.00	0.00	2.00	2.50
Oberösterreich	3.00	2.00	2.00	3.00	2.00	0.00	2.00	2.50
Salzburg	3.00	2.00	2.00	3.00	2.00	0.00	2.00	2.50
Steiermark	3.00	2.00	2.00	3.00	2.00	0.00	2.00	2.50
Tirol	3.00	2.00	2.00	3.00	2.00	0.00	2.00	2.50
Vorarlberg	3.00	2.00	2.00	3.00	2.00	0.00	2.00	3.00
Mean	3.00	2.00	2.00	3.00	2.00	0.00	1.75	2.56
Standard deviation	0.00	0.00	0.00	0.00	0.00	0.00	0.46	0.18

Table 4A.3d *Asymmetric decentralization at the regional level – aspects of self-rule: Belgium*

Region	ID	PS	EPD	FA	FTS	FSR	BA	OA
Brussels Capital	3.00	2.00	2.00	2.00	1.00	3.00	2.00	3.00
Flanders	3.00	2.00	2.00	2.00	2.00	3.00	2.00	3.00
Wallonia	3.00	2.00	2.00	2.00	1.00	3.00	2.00	3.00
Mean	3.00	2.00	2.00	2.00	1.33	3.00	2.00	3.00
Standard deviation	0.00	0.00	0.00	0.00	0.58	0.00	0.00	0.00

Table 4A.3e *Asymmetric decentralization at the regional level – aspects of self-rule: Bosnia and Herzegovina*

Region	ID	PS	EPD	FA	FTS	FSR	BA	OA
Federation of BiH	0.00	2.00	3.00	0.00	1.00	1.00	1.00	3.00
Republika Srpska	1.00	2.00	2.00	1.00	3.00	2.00	1.00	3.25
Mean	0.50	2.00	2.50	0.50	2.00	1.50	1.00	3.13
Standard deviation	0.71	0.00	0.71	0.71	1.41	0.71	0.00	0.18

Table 4A.3f *Asymmetric decentralization at the regional level – aspects of self-rule: Canada*

Region	ID	PS	EPD	FA	FTS	FSR	BA	OA
Alberta	2.00	1.00	1.00	2.00	0.00	3.00	2.00	3.50
British Columbia	2.00	1.00	1.00	2.00	0.00	3.00	1.00	3.50
Manitoba	2.00	1.00	1.00	2.00	0.00	3.00	1.00	3.50
New Brunswick	2.00	1.00	1.00	2.00	0.00	3.00	1.00	3.50
Newfoundland and Labrador	*1.00*	1.00	1.00	2.00	0.00	3.00	1.00	3.50
Nova Scotia	*1.00*	1.00	1.00	2.00	0.00	3.00	1.00	3.50
Ontario	2.00	2.00	1.00	2.00	0.00	3.00	2.00	3.50
Prince Edward Island	2.00	1.00	1.00	2.00	0.00	3.00	2.00	3.50
Québec	2.00	1.00	1.00	2.00	0.00	3.00	1.00	3.50
Saskatchewan	2.00	1.00	1.00	2.00	0.00	3.00	1.00	3.50
Mean	1.80	1.10	1.00	2.00	0.00	3.00	1.30	3.50
Standard deviation	0.42	0.32	0.00	0.00	0.00	0.00	0.48	0.00

Table 4A.3g *Asymmetric decentralization at the regional level – aspects of self-rule: Mexico*

Region	ID	PS	EPD	FA	FTS	FSR	BA	OA
Aguascalientes	1.00	2.00	2.00	1.00	0.00	0.00	*0.00*	3.00
Baja California	1.00	2.00	2.00	1.00	0.00	0.00	1.00	3.00
Baja California Sur	1.00	2.00	2.00	1.00	0.00	0.00	1.00	3.00
Campeche	1.00	2.00	2.00	1.00	0.00	0.00	1.00	3.00
Chiapas	1.00	2.00	2.00	1.00	0.00	0.00	1.00	3.00
Chihuahua	1.00	2.00	2.00	1.00	0.00	0.00	1.00	3.00
Coahuila	1.00	2.00	2.00	1.00	0.00	0.00	1.00	3.00
Colima	1.00	2.00	2.00	1.00	0.00	0.00	1.00	3.00
Durango	1.00	2.00	2.00	1.00	0.00	0.00	1.00	3.00
Guanajuato	1.00	2.00	2.00	1.00	0.00	0.00	1.00	3.00
Guerrero	1.00	2.00	2.00	1.00	0.00	0.00	1.00	3.00
Hidalgo	1.00	2.00	2.00	1.00	0.00	0.00	1.00	3.00
Jalisco	1.00	2.00	2.00	1.00	0.00	0.00	1.00	3.00
México	1.00	2.00	2.00	1.00	0.00	0.00	*0.00*	3.00
Mexico City	*0.00*	*1.00*	2.00	*0.00*	0.00	0.00	1.00	*2.50*
Michoacán	1.00	2.00	2.00	1.00	0.00	0.00	1.00	3.00
Morelos	1.00	2.00	2.00	1.00	0.00	0.00	1.00	3.00
Nayarit	1.00	2.00	2.00	1.00	0.00	0.00	1.00	3.00
Nuevo León	1.00	2.00	2.00	1.00	0.00	0.00	1.00	3.00
Oaxaca	1.00	2.00	2.00	1.00	0.00	0.00	1.00	3.00

Region	ID	PS	EPD	FA	FTS	FSR	BA	OA
Puebla	1.00	2.00	2.00	1.00	0.00	0.00	1.00	3.00
Querétaro	1.00	2.00	2.00	1.00	0.00	0.00	1.00	3.00
Quintana Roo	1.00	2.00	2.00	1.00	0.00	0.00	1.00	3.00
San Luis Potosí	1.00	2.00	2.00	1.00	0.00	0.00	1.00	3.00
Sinaloa	1.00	2.00	2.00	1.00	0.00	0.00	1.00	3.00
Sonora	1.00	2.00	2.00	1.00	0.00	0.00	1.00	3.00
Tabasco	1.00	2.00	2.00	1.00	0.00	0.00	1.00	3.00
Tamaulipas	1.00	2.00	2.00	1.00	0.00	0.00	1.00	3.00
Tlaxcala	1.00	2.00	2.00	1.00	0.00	0.00	1.00	3.00
Veracruz	1.00	2.00	2.00	1.00	0.00	0.00	1.00	3.00
Yucatán	1.00	2.00	2.00	1.00	0.00	0.00	1.00	3.00
Zacatecas	1.00	2.00	2.00	1.00	0.00	0.00	1.00	3.00
Mean	0.97	1.97	2.00	0.97	0.00	0.00	0.94	2.98
Standard deviation	0.18	0.18	0.00	0.18	0.00	0.00	0.25	0.09

Table 4A.3h *Asymmetric decentralization at the regional level – aspects of self-rule: Switzerland*

Region	ID	PS	EPD	FA	FTS	FSR	BA	OA
Aargau	3.00	3.00	2.00	4.00	2.00	3.00	3.00	4.00
Appenzell_Arh	3.00	3.00	2.00	4.00	1.00	3.00	3.00	4.00
Appenzell Irh	3.00	3.00	2.00	4.00	1.00	3.00	3.00	4.00
Basel Landschaft	3.00	3.00	2.00	4.00	1.00	3.00	3.00	4.00
Basel Stadt	3.00	3.00	2.00	4.00	0.00	3.00	3.00	4.00
Bern	3.00	3.00	2.00	4.00	0.00	3.00	3.00	4.00
Fribourg	3.00	*2.00*	2.00	4.00	1.00	3.00	3.00	4.00
Genève	3.00	*2.00*	*1.00*	4.00	0.00	3.00	*1.00*	4.00
Glarus	3.00	3.00	2.00	4.00	1.00	3.00	3.00	4.00
Graubünden	3.00	3.00	2.00	4.00	0.00	3.00	3.00	4.00
Jura	3.00	*2.00*	2.00	4.00	0.00	3.00	3.00	4.00
Luzern	3.00	3.00	2.00	4.00	1.00	3.00	3.00	4.00
Neuchâtel	3.00	*2.00*	2.00	4.00	0.00	3.00	3.00	4.00
Nidwalden	3.00	3.00	2.00	4.00	2.00	3.00	3.00	4.00
Obwalden	3.00	3.00	2.00	4.00	1.00	3.00	3.00	4.00
Schaffhausen	3.00	3.00	2.00	4.00	0.00	3.00	3.00	4.00
Schwyz	3.00	3.00	2.00	4.00	2.00	3.00	3.00	4.00
Solothurn	3.00	3.00	2.00	4.00	0.00	3.00	3.00	4.00
St Gallen	3.00	3.00	2.00	4.00	2.00	3.00	3.00	4.00
Thurgau	3.00	3.00	2.00	4.00	0.00	3.00	3.00	4.00

Region	ID	PS	EPD	FA	FTS	FSR	BA	OA
Ticino	3.00	3.00	2.00	4.00	2.00	3.00	3.00	4.00
Uri	3.00	3.00	2.00	4.00	0.00	3.00	3.00	4.00
Valais	3.00	3.00	2.00	4.00	2.00	3.00	3.00	4.00
Vaud	3.00	*2.00*	2.00	4.00	1.00	3.00	*1.00*	4.00
Zug	3.00	3.00	2.00	4.00	0.00	3.00	3.00	4.00
Zürich	3.00	3.00	2.00	4.00	0.00	3.00	*2.00*	4.00
Mean	3.00	2.81	1.96	4.00	0.77	3.00	2.81	4.00
Standard deviation	0.00	0.40	0.20	0.00	0.82	0.00	0.57	0.00

Table 4A.3i *Asymmetric decentralization at the regional level – aspects of self-rule: United States*

Region	ID	PS	EPD	FA	FTS	FSR	BA	OA
Alabama	*0.00*	3.00	3.00	2.00	0.00	3.00	2.00	*3.00*
Alaska	1.00	3.00	3.00	2.00	0.00	3.00	2.00	*3.00*
Arizona	2.00	3.00	3.00	2.00	0.00	3.00	2.00	4.00
Arkansas	1.00	3.00	3.00	2.00	0.00	*2.00*	2.00	3.50
California	2.00	4.00	3.00	2.00	0.00	3.00	2.00	4.00
Colorado	2.00	4.00	3.00	2.00	0.00	3.00	2.00	4.00
Connecticut	1.00	*2.00*	3.00	3.00	0.00	3.00	2.00	3.50
DC	*0.00*	4.00	3.00	2.00	0.00	3.00	2.00	3.40
Delaware	1.00	*2.00*	*2.00*	2.00	0.00	3.00	2.00	3.50
Florida	2.00	3.00	3.00	2.00	0.00	3.00	2.00	4.00
Georgia	2.00	3.00	3.00	4.00	0.00	3.00	2.00	3.50
Hawaii	1.00	*2.00*	*2.00*	3.00	0.00	3.00	2.00	4.00
Idaho	2.00	3.00	3.00	2.00	0.00	3.00	2.00	*3.00*
Illinois	1.00	3.00	3.00	2.00	0.00	3.00	2.00	4.00
Indiana	1.00	3.00	3.00	2.00	0.00	3.00	2.00	*3.00*
Iowa	2.00	3.00	3.00	2.00	0.00	3.00	2.00	3.50
Kansas	2.00	3.00	3.00	2.00	0.00	3.00	2.00	3.50
Kentucky	2.00	3.00	3.00	2.00	0.00	3.00	2.00	3.50
Louisiana	2.00	3.00	3.00	2.00	0.00	3.00	2.00	4.00
Maine	1.00	*2.00*	3.00	2.00	0.00	3.00	2.00	3.50

Region	ID	PS	EPD	FA	FTS	FSR	BA	OA
Maryland	2.00	*2.00*	3.00	2.00	0.00	3.00	2.00	3.50
Massachusetts	1.00	3.00	3.00	2.00	0.00	3.00	2.00	3.50
Michigan	1.00	3.00	3.00	2.00	0.00	3.00	2.00	4.00
Minnesota	2.00	4.00	3.00	3.00	0.00	3.00	2.00	4.00
Mississippi	1.00	3.00	3.00	2.00	0.00	3.00	2.00	3.50
Missouri	1.00	3.00	3.00	2.00	0.00	3.00	2.00	4.00
Montana	2.00	3.00	3.00	2.00	0.00	3.00	2.00	4.00
Nebraska	*0.00*	3.00	3.00	2.00	0.00	3.00	2.00	*3.00*
Nevada	1.00	3.00	3.00	2.00	0.00	3.00	2.00	*3.00*
New Hampshire	1.00	*2.00*	3.00	3.00	0.00	3.00	2.00	3.50
New Jersey	2.00	*2.00*	3.00	2.00	0.00	3.00	2.00	4.00
New Mexico	2.00	3.00	3.00	2.00	0.00	2.00	2.00	4.00
New York	2.00	4.00	3.00	2.00	0.00	3.00	2.00	4.00
North Carolina	*0.00*	4.00	3.00	2.00	0.00	3.00	2.00	*3.00*
North Dakota	2.00	3.00	3.00	2.00	0.00	3.00	2.00	4.00
Ohio	2.00	4.00	3.00	2.00	0.00	3.00	2.00	4.00
Oklahoma	*0.00*	3.00	3.00	2.00	0.00	3.00	2.00	3.50
Oregon	1.00	3.00	3.00	2.00	0.00	3.00	2.00	3.50
Pennsylvania	1.00	4.00	3.00	2.00	0.00	3.00	2.00	3.50
Rhode Island	1.00	*2.00*	*2.00*	2.00	0.00	3.00	2.00	4.00
South Carolina	2.00	3.00	3.00	3.00	0.00	3.00	2.00	4.00

Region	ID	PS	EPD	FA	FTS	FSR	BA	OA
South Dakota	2.00	3.00	3.00	2.00	0.00	3.00	2.00	4.00
Tennessee	2.00	3.00	3.00	4.00	0.00	3.00	2.00	4.00
Texas	1.00	3.00	3.00	2.00	0.00	3.00	2.00	3.50
Utah	2.00	3.00	3.00	2.00	0.00	3.00	2.00	3.50
Vermont	*0.00*	*2.00*	3.00	2.00	0.00	*2.00*	2.00	*3.00*
Virginia	1.00	4.00	3.00	2.00	0.00	3.00	2.00	*3.00*
Washington	2.00	3.00	3.00	2.00	0.00	3.00	2.00	4.00
West Virginia	1.00	3.00	3.00	2.00	0.00	3.00	2.00	3.50
Wisconsin	2.00	3.00	3.00	2.00	0.00	3.00	2.00	4.00
Wyoming	1.00	3.00	3.00	2.00	0.00	3.00	2.00	3.50
Mean	1.53	3.00	2.94	2.18	0.00	2.94	2.00	3.63
Standard deviation	0.69	0.60	0.24	0.48	0.00	0.24	0.00	0.37

Table 4A.3j *Asymmetric decentralization at the regional level – aspects of self-rule: United States*

Region	ID	PS	EPD	FA	FTS	FSR	BA	OA
England	0.00	3.00	2.00	2.00	1.00	2.00	2.00	2.00
Northern Ireland	0.00	*1.00*	*1.00*	2.00	1.00	1.00	2.00	2.00
Scotland	0.00	3.00	2.00	2.00	1.00	1.00	2.00	2.00
Wales	0.00	3.00	2.00	2.00	1.00	1.00	2.00	2.00
Mean	0.00	2.50	1.75	2.00	1.00	1.25	2.00	2.00
Standard deviation	0.00	1.00	0.50	0.00	0.00	0.50	0.00	0.00

Table 4A.4a *Asymmetric decentralization at the regional level – aspects of interactive rule: Argentina*

Region	LP	AS	CRA
Buenos Aires	*2.00*	2.00	1.00
Catamarca	3.00	2.00	1.00
Chaco	3.00	2.00	1.00
Chubut	3.00	2.00	1.00
Córdoba	3.00	3.00	2.00
Corrientes	3.00	3.00	1.00
Entre Ríos	3.00	2.00	1.00
Formosa	3.00	2.00	1.00
Jujuy	3.00	2.00	2.00
La Pampa	3.00	2.00	1.00
La Rioja	3.00	2.00	1.00
Mendoza	3.00	2.00	1.00
Misiones	3.00	2.00	1.00
Neuquén	3.00	2.00	1.00
Río Negro	3.00	3.00	1.00
Salta	3.00	2.00	1.00
San Juan	3.00	2.00	1.00
San Luis	3.00	2.00	1.00
Santa Cruz	3.00	2.00	1.00
Santa Fe	*2.00*	3.00	1.00
Santiago del Estero	3.00	2.00	1.00
Tierra del Fuego	3.00	3.00	1.00
Tucumán	3.00	3.00	1.00
Mean	2.91	2.26	1.09
Standard deviation	0.29	0.45	0.29

Table 4A.4b *Asymmetric decentralization at the regional level – aspects of interactive rule: Australia*

Region	LP	AS	CRA
New South Wales	1.00	0.00	3.00
Queensland	1.00	0.00	3.00
South Australia	1.00	0.00	3.00
Tasmania	1.00	0.00	3.00
Victoria	1.00	0.00	3.00
Western Australia	1.00	0.00	3.00
Mean	1.00	0.00	3.00
Standard deviation	0.00	0.00	0.00

Table 4A.4c *Asymmetric decentralization at the regional level – aspects of interactive rule: Austria*

Region	LP	AS	CRA
Burgenland	2.00	2.00	3.00
Kärnten	2.00	2.00	3.00
Niederösterreich	2.00	2.00	3.00
Oberösterreich	2.00	2.00	3.00
Salzburg	2.00	2.00	3.00
Steiermark	2.00	2.00	3.00
Tirol	2.00	2.00	3.00
Vorarlberg	2.00	2.00	3.00
Mean	2.00	2.00	3.00
Standard deviation	0.00	0.00	0.00

Table 4A.4d *Asymmetric decentralization at the regional level – aspects of interactive rule: Belgium*

Region	LP	AS	CRA
Brussels Capital	3.00	0.00	1.00
Flanders	3.00	0.00	1.00
Wallonia	3.00	0.00	1.00
Mean	3.00	0.00	1.00
Standard deviation	0.00	0.00	0.00

Table 4A.4e *Asymmetric decentralization at the regional level – aspects of interactive rule: Bosnia and Herzegovina*

Region	LP	AS	CRA
Federation of BiH	2.00	3.00	3.00
Republika Srpska	2.00	0.50	2.00
Mean	2.00	1.75	2.50
Standard deviation	0.00	1.77	0.71

Table 4A.4f *Asymmetric decentralization at the regional level – aspects of interactive rule: Canada*

Region	LP	AS	CRA
Alberta	0.00	1.00	1.00
British Columbia	0.00	2.00	1.50
Manitoba	0.00	1.00	1.00
New Brunswick	0.00	1.00	1.00
Newfoundland and Labrador	0.00	1.00	1.00
Nova Scotia	0.00	1.00	1.00
Ontario	0.00	1.00	1.00
Prince Edward Island	0.00	1.00	1.00
Québec	0.00	1.00	1.00
Saskatchewan	0.00	1.00	1.00
Mean	0.00	1.10	1.05
Standard deviation	0.00	0.32	0.16

Table 4A.4g *Asymmetric decentralization at the regional level – aspects of interactive rule: Mexico*

Region	LP	AS	CRA
Aguascalientes	2.00	1.00	1.00
Baja California	2.00	1.00	1.00
Baja California Sur	2.00	1.00	1.00
Campeche	2.00	1.00	1.00
Chiapas	2.00	1.00	1.00
Chihuahua	2.00	1.00	1.00
Coahuila	2.00	1.00	1.00
Colima	2.00	1.00	1.00
Durango	2.00	1.00	1.00
Guanajuato	2.00	1.00	1.00
Guerrero	2.00	1.00	1.00
Hidalgo	2.00	1.00	1.00
Jalisco	2.00	1.00	1.00
México	2.00	1.00	1.00
Mexico City	2.00	*0.00*	3.00
Michoacán	2.00	1.00	1.00
Morelos	2.00	1.00	1.00
Nayarit	2.00	1.00	1.00
Nuevo León	2.00	1.00	1.00
Oaxaca	2.00	1.00	1.00
Puebla	2.00	1.00	1.00
Querétaro	2.00	1.00	1.00
Quintana Roo	2.00	1.00	1.00
San Luis Potosí	2.00	1.00	1.00
Sinaloa	2.00	1.00	1.00
Sonora	2.00	1.00	1.00
Tabasco	2.00	1.00	1.00
Tamaulipas	2.00	1.00	1.00
Tlaxcala	2.00	1.00	1.00
Veracruz	2.00	1.00	1.00
Yucatán	2.00	1.00	1.00
Zacatecas	2.00	1.00	1.00

Region	LP	AS	CRA
Mean	2.00	0.97	1.06
Standard deviation	0.00	0.18	0.35

Table 4A.4h *Asymmetric decentralization at the regional level – aspects of interactive rule: Switzerland*

Region	LP	AS	CRA
Aargau	3.00	2.00	3.00
Appenzell_Arh	3.00	3.00	3.00
Appenzell Irh	3.00	3.00	3.00
Basel Landschaft	3.00	3.00	3.00
Basel Stadt	3.00	3.00	*2.00*
Bern	3.00	2.00	3.00
Fribourg	*2.00*	*0.00*	3.00
Genève	3.00	3.00	3.00
Glarus	*2.00*	3.00	3.00
Graubünden	*2.00*	2.00	3.00
Jura	*2.00*	2.00	3.00
Luzern	3.00	*0.00*	3.00
Neuchâtel	3.00	3.00	3.00
Nidwalden	3.00	3.00	3.00
Obwalden	3.00	3.00	3.00
Schaffhausen	3.00	2.00	3.00
Schwyz	3.00	*0.00*	3.00
Solothurn	3.00	3.00	3.00
St Gallen	3.00	*1.00*	3.00
Thurgau	*2.00*	3.00	3.00
Ticino	*2.00*	3.00	3.00
Uri	3.00	3.00	3.00
Valais	*2.00*	3.00	3.00
Vaud	3.00	3.00	3.00
Zug	3.00	3.00	3.00
Zürich	3.00	2.00	3.00
Mean	2.73	2.35	2.96
Standard deviation	0.45	1.02	0.20

Table 4A.4i Asymmetric decentralization at the regional level – aspects of interactive rule: United States

Region	LP	AS	CRA
Alabama	1.50	3.00	1.00
Alaska	2.00	3.00	1.00
Arizona	*1.00*	3.00	1.00
Arkansas	*1.00*	3.00	1.00
California	2.00	3.00	1.00
Colorado	2.00	3.00	1.00
Connecticut	1.50	3.00	1.00
DC	*1.00*	3.00	1.00
Delaware	*1.00*	3.00	1.00
Florida	2.00	3.00	1.00
Georgia	2.00	3.00	1.00
Hawaii	2.00	3.00	1.00
Idaho	*1.00*	3.00	1.00
Illinois	2.00	3.00	1.00
Indiana	*1.00*	3.00	1.00
Iowa	2.00	3.00	1.00
Kansas	1.50	3.00	1.00
Kentucky	*1.00*	3.00	1.00
Louisiana	2.00	3.00	1.00
Maine	1.50	3.00	1.00
Maryland	2.00	3.00	1.00
Massachusetts	1.50	3.00	1.00
Michigan	2.00	3.00	1.00
Minnesota	2.00	3.00	1.00
Mississippi	*1.00*	3.00	1.00
Missouri	2.00	3.00	1.00
Montana	2.00	3.00	1.00
Nebraska	*1.00*	3.00	1.00
Nevada	1.50	3.00	1.00
New Hampshire	*1.00*	3.00	1.00
New Jersey	*1.00*	3.00	1.00
New Mexico	2.00	3.00	1.00

Region	LP	AS	CRA
New York	2.00	3.00	1.00
North Carolina	*1.00*	3.00	1.00
North Dakota	1.50	3.00	1.00
Ohio	2.00	3.00	1.00
Oklahoma	1.50	3.00	1.00
Oregon	2.00	3.00	1.00
Pennsylvania	2.00	3.00	1.00
Rhode Island	1.50	3.00	1.00
South Carolina	2.00	3.00	1.00
South Dakota	2.00	3.00	1.00
Tennessee	2.00	3.00	1.00
Texas	1.50	3.00	1.00
Utah	1.50	3.00	1.00
Vermont	*1.00*	3.00	1.00
Virginia	*1.00*	3.00	1.00
Washington	2.00	3.00	1.00
West Virginia	1.50	3.00	1.00
Wisconsin	1.50	3.00	1.00
Wyoming	1.50	3.00	1.00
Mean	1.59	3.00	1.00
Standard deviation	0.42	0.00	0.00

Table 4A.4j *Asymmetric decentralization at the regional level – aspects of interactive rule: United Kingdom*

Region	LP	AS	CRA
England	1.00	2.00	2.00
Northern Ireland	1.00	2.00	2.00
Scotland	1.00	2.00	2.00
Wales	1.00	2.00	2.00
Mean	1.00	2.00	2.00
Standard deviation	0.00	0.00	0.00

5. Organizational autonomy

INTRODUCTION

Local autonomy is reflected in organizational aspects. Organizational autonomy – the degree of discretion that municipalities have in organizing themselves and carrying out their functions – is at the core of local self-government. Embedded in it is Dahl and Tufte's concept of system capacity in its aspects of institutional structures, administrative efficiency and responsiveness of government to societal demands (Dahl and Tufte 1973). Other approaches also emphasize its key role in being able to act effectively and efficiently (Reddy et al. 2015). Indeed, organizational autonomy can have an impact on the ability of municipalities to manage public affairs and respond to the interests of the local population, which is the essence of local autonomy. In deciding on their internal structure, local governments will try to adapt to local needs and ensure effective management. By having the authority to define core elements of the political system such as electoral rules, they can improve the input aspects of democratic legitimacy. Are such decisions made at other levels of government, or can local authorities adapt their political institutions and administration to their needs and preferences?

Organizational autonomy covers the two dimensions into which the concept can be disaggregated: political organization and administrative organization. Both are equally relevant. Political aspects involve choices made in designing the elements of the electoral system, while administrative aspects refer to decisions on the organizational structure of local authorities and staff-related issues. International organizations such as the Council of Europe (CoE) have included both elements when setting thresholds for what constitutes a sufficient level of organizational freedom. On the political axis, the European Charter of Local Self-Government (ECLSG) states that autonomy should be exercised by councils or assemblies composed of democratically elected members and that the executive branch of local government should be accountable to the legislature. The CoE does not favour a particular electoral system as long as representatives are freely elected on the basis of direct, equal, universal suffrage (ECLSG art. 3). The CoE also links administration issues to organizational autonomy, such as the right of local authorities to determine their own internal administrative structures, the conditions that allow the recruitment of staff on the basis of merit and competence and the adequate training opportunities, remuneration and career prospects (ECLSG art. 7).

This chapter looks at the actual level of organizational autonomy in countries around the world, taking a cross-country and over-time perspective. After exploring the notion of organizational autonomy and the different aspects embedded in it, the chapter presents empirical evidence from previous measurements of local autonomy. A following section, drawing on a database with information from the 57 countries under analysis, examines the countries' achievement in this dimension of autonomy and discusses patterns of similarities and differences. The chapter ends with a reflection on the limited usefulness of organizational autonomy for assessing specific characteristics of politico-administrative configurations in municipalities, thus making it an insufficient measurement for conducting a detailed analysis on precise governance outcomes.

POLITICAL AND ADMINISTRATIVE ORGANIZATIONAL AUTONOMY

In terms of political organization, there are two key choices that shape the conditions under which local representatives obtain and exercise their mandates. One involves the model of horizontal power relations among the main pillars of local democracy (assembly and executive), while the other involves the electoral rules put in place.

In horizontal power relations, the main choice is on how the separation of power between the legislative and executive branches is structured. From a theoretical perspective, there are two typologies that allow the alternatives at stake to be identified. First, there is the classical distinction between parliamentary and presidential systems or, as applied to local government, between the local assembly (council) and the local executive. This depends on how the local executive is designed. Where the mayor/executive is elected or appointed by the local assembly, the system resembles a parliamentary model. Where the executive/mayor is elected directly by the local population, it resembles a presidential model. Second, a typology specifically conceived for local government systems looks at how power is distributed between, in this case, the three main elements of local governance (mayor – council – top administrator) and distinguishes between the so-called strong-mayor, collective, committee-leader and council-manager forms of local government (Mouritzen and Svara 2002). Each of these forms places emphasis on one of the various (all desirable) principles of political action: political leadership (strong-mayor form), democratic representation (collective and committee-leader forms) and professionalism (council-manager form).

Local authorities' autonomy to choose among forms of horizontal power relations is limited, since these issues are more likely to be regulated by national or state laws. In any case, from a normative point of view, no one form is better than another. Countries have tended to opt for one or another type based on elements of political culture, historical tradition or response to a particular challenge. In Europe, for instance, there has been a recent shift to stronger executives – to presidential or strong-mayor systems – with the aim of increasing their legitimacy and effectiveness in intergovernmental relations (Heinelt et al. 2018a, 2018b).

When it comes to electoral rules, legislations opt between majority and proportional systems to elect members of the local assembly and between direct and indirect election of the head of the executive. Among European countries, the proportional system is by far the most popular, with 38 cases opting for the electoral proportional system and only ten for the plurality/majority system (Gendźwiłł et al. 2022). In the election of mayors, however, the figures are more evenly balanced between the direct and indirect election models. In 19 countries heads of the executive are elected by the members of the council, while in 23 others mayors are elected directly (Gendźwiłł et al. 2022). Academic debate in this area has failed to identify any of these models as superior. Again, the choices made are related to historical legacies or to the trade-offs made between different values, such as input and output legitimacy, effectiveness or efficiency. For example, the recent popularity of the direct election of mayors mentioned above, motivated by a desire to increase legitimacy and to favour political leadership, raises the question of the potential risk of a monopoly of power (Sweeting 2017).

In general, national rules tend to establish the organizing principles of horizontal distribution of power and electoral systems. However, in some countries, local authorities have some discretion to decide on some elements of their political system. For the purposes of this book, a high degree of political organizational autonomy implies that local executives are elected by the municipal council or directly by the citizens and that local governments can decide core elements of the political system such as the electoral districts, the number of seats in the council or aspects of the electoral system.

As for administrative organization, the aspects that define this notion involve the internal organization of the local administrative structure and choices about its staff. Self-government is reflected in the different constellations of departments and units that municipalities choose for the purpose of implementing their policies, in the diversity of organizational structures, and in the recruitment of personnel and incentive systems to increase effectiveness and efficiency. A local authority that wants to emphasize the priority that it attaches to, for example, climate change mitigation, social services for vulnerable groups, or corruption issues will organize a departmental structure that reflects these policy options. Local authorities could also organize themselves in rigid silo structures or, conversely, in cross-cutting ways that allow complex problems to be tackled comprehensively.

Systems can also vary from giving the lead role in administration to the traditional secretary, responsible for legal compliance of administrative processes, to one supported by a more active CEO or manager with a more strategic role, applying new public management (NPM) measures or strategies such as performance measurement and accountability, customer focus, or flexibility and innovation. NPM can also be seen in human resource policies, which include strategies such as performance-related pay, merit-based promotion and the introduction of more flexible employment practices to attract and retain talent.

In general, municipalities have autonomy to decide on the size and structure of their administrations and the rules governing their human resources policies. But sometimes higher levels of government impose top-down policies for municipal organization. The status of staff may be largely determined by national norms. These norms can also mandate the set-up of specific structures at the local level, such as transparency units, or put limits on the employee salaries. For the purposes of this book, a high degree of administrative organizational autonomy implies that local authorities can hire their own staff, set the salary of their employees, choose their organizational structure and the status of the staff and establish legal entities and municipal enterprises.

PREVIOUS MEASUREMENT OF ORGANIZATIONAL AUTONOMY

Organizational autonomy has been already explored with regard to the countries belonging to the CoE that have signed the ECLSG. The earlier research project of which this is a continuation considered the organizational dimension of local self-government in terms similar to those employed in the present analysis and measured it in 39 countries over the period of 1990–2014 (Ladner et al. 2019). The analysis showed that the average score for organizational autonomy was rather high in comparison with other dimensions of local autonomy and that it has remained relatively stable over two and a half decades (Ladner et al. 2019). It also identified considerable diversity among the different countries. In general, there are more chances for countries to reach maximum scores in the administrative dimension of organizational autonomy than in the political one. In a significant number of countries all electoral elements are decided by the central government, although there are cases in which local authorities are also involved in these decisions. A few countries allow local authorities to decide on elements such as the number and size of their electoral districts, whether they prefer majority or proportional representation, or the form and size of their local executive. In contrast, municipalities rank relatively well in the administrative dimension of local autonomy. They are generally free to employ their staff, set their salaries (sometimes within limits set by the central government), choose their organizational structure and set up legal entities and municipal enterprises, although many countries encounter various types of restrictions.

Only eight out of the 39 countries attained the highest score (4) in the last year of the analysis of the LAI 1.0 (Local Autonomy Index), 2014, while five countries were at the lowest score (1). The Czech Republic, Denmark, Estonia, Iceland, Norway and Switzerland were in the first group, while France, Ireland, Malta, Luxembourg and Georgia were consistently at the bottom. Political autonomy tends to be more difficult to achieve, as there is a strong pattern of all electoral elements of local autonomy being decided by the central government. In a study of local electoral systems in Europe, Gendźwiłł et al. (2022) report that most countries (28 out of 40 under analysis) have uniform electoral rules that are applied throughout.

Organizational autonomy shows one of the most stable trajectories of all the autonomy dimensions over the two-and-a-half decades covered by the analysis. Changes over time have been minimal, and these mainly reflect the remarkable growth of organizational autonomy experienced in Central and Eastern European countries in the early 1990s as they underwent democratic transitions alongside decentralization processes. There have been a few cases of slight drops in organizational autonomy linked to the impact of the global financial crisis and measures taken by central authorities in Latvia and Spain. In these cases, the decrease is related to restrictions on salary decisions due to stricter fiscal discipline.

DYNAMICS OF ORGANIZATIONAL AUTONOMY – EMPIRICAL RESULTS

The picture displayed by the previous measurement has not greatly changed after the inclusion of 18 additional countries for the period 1990–2014 and an examination of the 2015–20 period for all 57 countries. Once again, stability has been the outstanding characteristic of this variable: in the 2015–20 period, minor changes emerged only in Spain, Greece, Romania and Norway. The latter is an outlier since it was the only country where organizational autonomy decreased, even though only by 0.25 points. Norway had reached the maximum score of 4.00 points back in 1994, but in recent years national staffing norms (e.g. in preschools or primary education) have increasingly been imposed on local authorities, limiting organizational autonomy (–0.25 points since 2017).

In Spain, restrictions imposed on hiring staff and setting salaries caused a drop from 3.00 (in 2010) to 2.00 points in 2013. Following economic recovery, these losses were restored, on the condition that the criteria of a balanced budget were met, and Spain again reached a score of 3.00 in 2017. In the same year, Greek municipalities were allowed to hire personnel in some categories, which caused a 0.25 point increase. Romanian municipalities have also experienced restrictions. Ceilings on staffing levels on personnel spending were introduced, while a system of bonuses and allowances was scrapped. The latter was slowly rebuilt until local governments were allowed (in 2017) to set the base wage of their employees while staffing level restrictions were maintained. As a result, the Romanian score increased by 0.50.

The stability of organizational autonomy seems also to prevail among the 18 countries that were added to this research project, including the 1990–2014 period. In Argentina, there was an increase only in political autonomy in one region (Corrientes). In Armenia, there was no change after the establishment of democratic local self-government in 1996. The same applies to Bosnia and Herzegovina, since 1992 also to Chile (where democratic transition took place in 1990), and since 2000 to Kosovo. Stability has prevailed since 1990 in Colombia, Japan, Australia and Canada. In the Republic of Korea, election of the executive was first introduced in 1995 but since then all sub-variables of organizational autonomy have remained unchanged. In South Africa, all four 'administrative' sub-variables of organizational autonomy changed and reached maximum scores in 1996, soon after the first fully nonracial democratic elections in 1994, and there has been no change since then. In Mexico, all sub-variables of organizational autonomy have been stable for 30 years, except for the discretion to establish legal entities that was gradually given (until 2014) to municipalities in all states, but not to Mexico City. In the Russian Federation, while organizational autonomy has been stable in settlements for 30 years, it considerably increased in federal cities in 2001 and urban okrugs in 2003 with the election of councils and the powers to hire staff and set salaries as well as to define organizational structures and establish legal entities.

Sometimes change has moved in the opposite direction. For instance, starting from 2011, municipal corporations in Israel have been subject to quite strict regulatory constraints, including a selective policy of approving the establishment of new corporations. This reduced the relevant score by 0.25 points. In Montenegro, there was pressure from the central government to reduce the number of employees in local authorities (–0.25). In Belarus, executives in municipalities have not been elected since 1995; local authorities have no discretion on core elements of the political system, nor can they set the salary of their employees or choose the status of their staff and their organizational structure.

The question of why organizational autonomy has been so stable in the great majority of our 57 country cases is not easy to answer. Features like the architecture of the local political system and local discretion on the organizational structure are usually the result of long-lasting processes, institutional legacies and path dependencies, which are difficult to change. On the other hand, hiring and spending on staff salaries can have far-reaching consequences on public finance, debt and labour relations, especially in times of economic crisis and fiscal stress. Central governments then tend to restrict local discretion, as has also been the case in countries heavily affected by the 2007–08 financial crisis.

Regarding the different sub-variables of organizational autonomy (see Table 5.1), the election of local executives is a self-evident fact in nearly all 57 countries, the exceptions being Armenia, Belarus, Ireland and the United Kingdom. The power to decide on core elements of the political system ('political autonomy') is given to municipalities in Denmark, Iceland, Liechtenstein, Lithuania, Norway, Slovakia, Slovenia, Sweden, Switzerland and the United States (in the majority of states). In Argentina, 14 out of 23 regions and the autonomous city of Buenos Aires have given this power to local authorities. In most countries, municipalities are allowed to establish legal entities and municipal enterprises, choose their organizational structure and status of staff (e.g. public or private) and hire their staff, but discretion to set their salary is less common, probably for reasons of macroeconomic and fiscal stability since state grants constitute a considerable part of municipal revenue in most countries.

After conducting an analytical examination of various aspects of organizational autonomy across different countries and tracing its evolution from 2015 to 2020, attention is once again drawn to its two fundamental components: political autonomy and administrative autonomy (Table 5.2). Figure 5.1 illustrates that countries achieving higher levels of political autonomy are clearly fewer than those attaining high scores in administrative autonomy. Municipal elections can significantly impact national political balance and are typically conducted nationwide simultaneously, with few exceptions primarily observed in federal states. Legislators at higher levels of governance appear hesitant to delegate regulatory authority concerning the electoral system to municipalities. This reluctance, in some instances, reflects a lack of confidence, or at least a fear that electoral regulations could be manipulated by unscrupulous local majorities. In contrast, concerns regarding administrative autonomy seem less pronounced, since the discretion of local decision-makers is constrained by the need for practical efficiency and by fundamental principles governing the organization and operation of modern public administration. Consequently, as depicted in Figure 5.1, most countries are clustered at higher levels of administrative autonomy.

Table 5.1 Scores in different aspects of organizational autonomy, means 2015–2020 and changes 2015–2020

Country	Electoral system	Elements of polit. system	Hire staff	Set salary	Org. structure Staff status	Establish entities	OA 2020 change after 2015	Mean (2015–2020)
Albania	1.00	0.00	0.50	0.00	0.50	0.50	2.50 No	2.50
Andorra	1.00	0.00	0.50	0.50	0.50	0.50	3.00 No	3.00
Argentina	1.00	0.60	0.50	0.50	0.50	0.50	3.23 No	3.23
Armenia	0.00	0.00	0.50	0.25	0.50	0.50	1.84 No	1.84
Australia	1.00	0.00	0.50	0.50	0.50	0.00	2.50 No	2.50
Austria	1.00	0.00	0.50	0.00	0.50	0.50	2.53 No	2.53
Belarus	0.00	0.00	0.50	0.00	0.00	0.50	1.00 No	1.00
Belgium	1.00	0.00	0.50	0.50	0.50	0.50	3.00 No	3.00
Bosnia/Herzeg.	1.00	0.00	0.50	0.50	0.50	0.50	3.09 No	3.09
Bulgaria	1.00	0.00	0.50	0.50	0.50	0.50	3.00 No	3.00
Canada	1.00	0.50	0.50	0.50	0.50	0.50	3.49 No	3.49
Chile	1.00	0.00	0.25	0.25	0.25	0.25	2.00 No	2.00
Colombia	1.00	0.00	0.50	0.50	0.50	0.50	3.00 No	3.00
Croatia	1.00	0.00	0.50	0.25	0.25	0.50	2.50 No	2.50
Cyprus	1.00	0.00	0.50	0.00	0.50	0.50	2.50 No	2.50
Czech Republic	1.00	0.50	0.25	0.50	0.50	0.50	3.25 No	3.25
Denmark	1.00	1.00	0.50	0.50	0.50	0.50	4.00 No	4.00
Estonia	1.00	0.75	0.50	0.50	0.50	0.50	3.75 No	3.75

Country	Electoral system	Elements of polit. system	Hire staff	Set salary	Org. structure Staff status	Establish entities	OA 2020 change after 2015	Mean (2015–2020)
Finland	1.00	0.50	0.50	0.50	0.50	0.50	3.50 No	3.50
France	1.00	0.00	0.50	0.00	0.50	0.50	2.50 No	2.50
Georgia	1.00	0.75	0.50	0.50	0.50	0.50	3.75 No	3.75
Germany	1.00	0.00	0.50	0.00	0.50	0.50	2.50 No	2.50
Greece	1.00	0.00	0.25	0.00	0.25	0.50	2.00 Yes +0.25 Hire staff since 2017	1.92
Hungary	1.00	0.00	0.50	0.00	0.50	0.50	2.50 No	2.50
Iceland	1.00	1.00	0.50	0.50	0.50	0.50	4.00 No	4.00
Ireland	0.00	0.00	0.50	0.00	0.50	0.50	1.50 No	1.50
Israel	1.00	0.00	0.50	0.25	0.25	0.25	2.25 No	2.25
Italy	1.00	0.00	0.25	0.00	0.25	0.50	2.00 No	2.00
Japan	1.00	0.50	0.25	0.50	0.50	0.25	3.00 No	3.00
Kosovo	1.00	0.00	0.50	0.00	0.50	0.50	2.50 No	2.50
Latvia	1.00	0.00	0.50	0.00	0.50	0.50	2.50 No	2.50
Liechtenstein	1.00	1.00	0.50	0.50	0.50	0.50	4.00 No	4.00
Lithuania	1.00	0.00	0.50	0.50	0.50	0.50	3.00 No	3.00
Luxembourg	1.00	0.00	0.50	0.00	0.50	0.50	2.50 No	2.50
Malta	1.00	0.00	0.50	0.00	0.00	0.00	1.50 No	2.25

Country	Electoral system	Elements of polit. system	Hire staff	Set salary	Org. structure Staff status	Establish entities	OA 2020 change after 2015	Mean (2015–2020)
Mexico	1.00	0.00	0.50	0.50	0.50	0.50	2.96 No	1.50
Moldova	1.00	0.00	0.50	0.00	0.00	0.50	2.00 No	2.96
Montenegro	1.00	0.00	0.25	0.50	0.50	0.50	2.75 No	2.00
Netherlands	1.00	0.00	0.50	0.50	0.50	0.50	3.00 No	2.75
North Macedonia	1.00	0.00	0.25	0.00	0.50	0.50	2.25 No	3.00
Norway	1.00	1.00	0.50	0.50	0.25	0.50	3.88 Yes −0.25 Org. Structure	3.88
Poland	1.00	0.50	0.50	0.50	0.50	0.50	3.50 No	3.50
Portugal	1.00	0.00	0.50	0.50	0.50	0.50	3.00 No	3.00
Republic of Korea	1.00	0.00	0.25	0.00	0.25	0.25	1.75 No	1.75
Romania	1.00	0.00	0.50	0.50	0.50	0.50	2.83 Yes +0.50 Set salaries	2.83
Russian Federation	1.00	0.00	0.50	0.50	0.50	0.50	2.94 No	2.94
Serbia	1.00	0.25	0.50	0.25	0.50	0.50	2.94 No	2.94
Slovakia	1.00	1.00	0.50	0.50	0.50	0.50	4.00 No	4.00
Slovenia	1.00	1.00	0.50	0.00	0.50	0.50	3.50 No	3.50
South Africa	1.00	0.00	0.50	0.50	0.50	0.50	3.00 No	3.00

Country	Electoral system	Elements of polit. system	Hire staff	Set salary	Org. structure Staff status	Establish entities	OA 2020 change after 2015	Mean (2015–2020)
Spain	1.00	0.00	0.50	0.50	0.50	0.50	2.92 Yes +0.50 Hire staff since 2017	2.92
Sweden	1.00	1.00	0.50	0.50	0.50	0.50	4.00 No	4.00
Switzerland	1.00	1.00	0.50	0.50	0.50	0.50	4.00 No	4.00
Turkey	1.00	0.00	0.25	0.25	0.50	0.50	2.50 No	2.50
Ukraine	1.00	0.00	0.50	0.25	0.50	0.50	2.75 No	2.75
United Kingdom	0.00	0.00	0.50	0.50	0.50	0.50	2.00 No	2.00
United States of America	1.00	1.00	0.50	0.50	0.50	0.50	3.72 Yes +0.01	3.72

Source: Authors' own.

Table 5.2 *Mean and median scores in political autonomy and administrative autonomy (57 countries – 2020)*

	OA_pol_index	OA_adm_index
N – Valid	57	57
N – Missing	0	0
Mean	0.5805	0.4203
Median	0.5	0.4375
Mode	0.5	0.5

COULD ORGANIZATIONAL AUTONOMY BE USED TO ASSESS DEMOCRATIC VALUES?

Modern developments of local governmental and bureaucratic structures have been shaped by decentralization and organizational autonomy among other phenomena (Kuhlmann and Wollmann 2019). However, efforts to measure the specific impact on good governance or legitimacy using only organizational autonomy as a measurement have been thwarted, and a more general approach using the entire LAI was used instead (see Chapter 14).

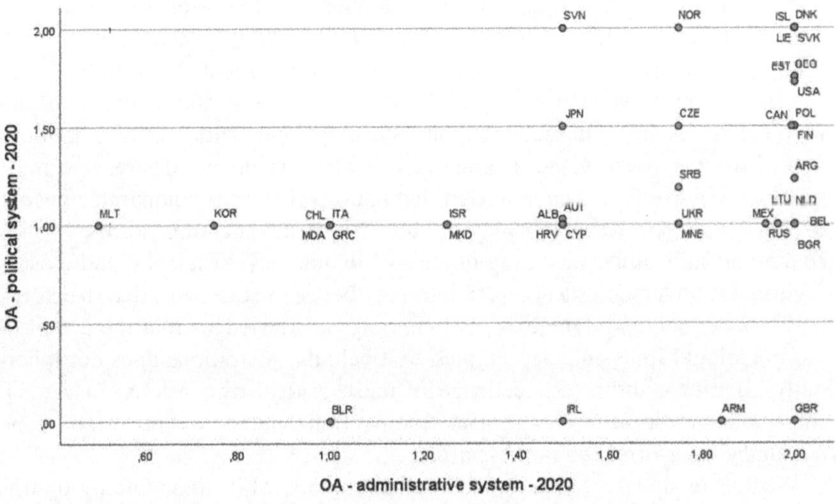

Source: Authors' own.

Figure 5.1 *Political autonomy and administrative autonomy in 2020*

As a reminder, the composite concept of local autonomy and organizational autonomy as a component dimension is derived from the LAI 2.0 (for more on the construction of the updated and extended LAI 2.0, see Ladner et al. 2023). The codebook (see Appendix) highlights the exact coding instructions for the organizational autonomy variable.

While the dimension of organizational autonomy effectively gauges the breadth of possibilities in structuring the politico-administrative landscape of local governments, it remains a framework of possibilities rather than a definitive tool for measurement outlining specific configurations. To achieve a comprehensive understanding of the choices underlying these configurations, it is imperative to undertake more refined, context-specific studies.

As can be noted from the broad and conditional wording of the codebook, the criteria for defining organizational autonomy do not allow for precise evaluation of politico-administrative organizational configurations. For example, the elements of administrative organizational autonomy that were chosen as determinant criteria are marked down in a conditional fashion, i.e. answerable either positively or negatively. This makes it possible to arrive at a general picture of how much organizational freedom is held by local public administrations, but it does not provide any quantitative detail beyond the qualitative country profiles provided by the LAI 2.0 project (Ladner et al. 2021). The same applies to both conditional 0–1 scales pertaining to political organizational autonomy. There is no doubt that core elements of organizing the local political system have an impact on governance outcomes, but the extent of this impact, what precise elements are crucial and how exactly they are implemented, remains to be discovered through more precise case-oriented research.

Consequently, when thinking of how organizational autonomy, as measured here presently, can matter beyond the simple calculation of free politico-administrative space to be arranged as local governments desire, one must proceed with caution. The assertion that nations sharing a comparable degree of organizational autonomy may exhibit divergent outcomes across various functional indicators, including quality of democracy, efficiency and overall legitimacy, underscores a complex interplay between administrative structures and broader societal dynamics. This finding acknowledges that the extent of organizational independence granted to local administrations does not inherently guarantee uniform excellence in these critical dimensions. Instead, it implies that multiple factors beyond organizational autonomy intricately shape a country's performance in these areas.

We thus recognize that organizational autonomy, while undoubtedly significant, does not exist in isolation. Rather, it exists within a multifaceted ecosystem influenced by historical legacies, cultural nuances, institutional capacities and prevailing political climates (Ladner et al. 2019). Hence, attributing variations in functional indicators solely to the degree of organizational autonomy oversimplifies the intricate causal web that underlies local-governance outcomes. For instance, a country may grant substantial organizational autonomy to its local administrations, yet still grapple with inefficiencies due to factors such as inadequate resource allocation, bureaucratic inertia or corruption. Similarly, while a high degree of autonomy might bolster the perceived legitimacy of local-governance structures in one context, in another, it could engender power imbalances or undermine accountability.

Organizational autonomy can play a role in enhancing local-governance outcomes, but it interacts with other determinants and is not a self-sufficient constitutive dimension. Other dimensions must be considered jointly with organizational autonomy. A country with extensive autonomy might excel in the quality of local governance if it had robust participatory mechanisms, whereas another with similar autonomy might falter if political freedoms were curtailed for other reasons.

CONCLUSIONS

The degree of discretion granted to municipalities in structuring themselves and carrying out their functions lies at the heart of local autonomy. If local authorities have the flexibility to tailor their political institutions and administration and adapt them to their specific needs and preferences, we can expect them to be in a better position to manage public affairs effectively.

This chapter has assessed the two dimensions in which organizational autonomy is encompassed (political and administrative) in 57 countries for the period 2015–20. The assessment is a follow-up to the one carried out for 1990–2014 in European countries only. The way in which this composite aspect of autonomy is measured has remained unchanged in this second project, but its two dimensions and the elements within them can now be distinguished individually, allowing a more nuanced and precise analysis.

Extending the measurement to new countries and a new period does not change the dynamics previously identified. Levels of local autonomy are relatively high and stable over time. With regard to political organization, the election of local executives is a self-evident fact in nearly all 57 countries and, in general, national legislation defines the parameters of local elections. Only in a few countries do municipalities possess the authority to determine aspects of their electoral system, such as the configuration of electoral districts, the choice between majority elections or proportional representation, and the form of their local executive. Concerning local administration, the freedom to recruit personnel, set employee salaries, determine organizational structures and establish legal entities and municipal enterprises is a prerogative enjoyed by most countries. Free setting of salaries is the only administrative element that is more restricted in some countries. Stability also marks the pattern identified. Only minor changes emerged in a minority of countries. Some of these changes relate to the lifting of constraints imposed after the global financial crisis.

Although the organizational dimension of autonomy and its operationalization in this project serves to assess the range of options available for structuring the political-administrative landscape of local governments effectively, it has its limitations. It serves more as a map to show the possibilities for local authorities to decide on relevant issues than to assess the impact of this freedom. Countries with similar levels of organizational autonomy can have different outcomes in terms of values such as efficiency, legitimacy and the quality of democracy. This highlights the complex interaction between administrative structures and broader societal dynamics. Organizational autonomy, as relevant as it is, does not exist in isolation. Only in interaction with other societal and political dynamics does it produce a specific outcome, which remains to be discovered through more detailed case-oriented research.

6. Financial autonomy as local democratic space

INTRODUCTION

The purpose of this chapter is to explore the space for local democratic decision-making as it emerges through the regulatory frameworks of local finances across the countries covered by this study. The chapter's point of departure is the normative assumption of the European Charter of Local Self-Government that a degree of local financial autonomy is a prerequisite for local democracy. If locally elected decision-makers do not have some control over local spending priorities and/or levels and sources of income, there is little point in having locally contested elections. *How much* autonomy is needed for local democracy to be a reality is, of course, to some extent a matter of normative judgement.

In the theories of fiscal federalism, local democracy is assigned a prominent role as a mechanism of allocative efficiency, as stated by the well-known 'decentralization theorem' (Oates 1972). The analytical challenge of fiscal federalism is to reconcile allocative efficiency with national regulation and support of local finances, which necessarily involves some restrictions on local autonomy. The OECD (Organisation for Economic Co-operation and Development) fiscal-federalism programme outlines several partly competing objectives for national regulatory frameworks beyond supporting allocative efficiency, such as restraining the size of the public sector overall, ensuring debt sustainability and coping with financial shocks.[1] Allocative efficiency may also necessitate central-government interventions in local finances through fiscal equalization across jurisdictions. These goals may require difficult trade-offs, as stated in another OECD document:

> It is challenging to design fiscal rules that can achieve all three of their main objectives: (i) promoting fiscal sustainability, (ii) fostering economic stability and (iii) improving the allocation of resources. There are trade-offs involved in the choice of

---

[1] Subcentral governments (scg) fiscal rules indicator. OECD Fiscal Decentralisation Database. https://www.oecd.org/tax/federalism/fiscal-decentralisation-database/sub-central-governments-fiscal-rules-indicator.pdf.

fiscal rules and, ultimately, the design of fiscal rules is a policy choice that favours one or more objectives.[2]

However, ensuring the vitality of local democracy does not figure prominently among the goals discussed in the OECD study quoted above. And, of course, local democracy has functions beyond that of allocative efficiency, e.g. as expressions of local identities or fostering civic virtue (Hooghe and Marks 2016).

In this chapter, first, trends in local-government financial autonomy are briefly outlined, including the additional countries covered since the LAI 1.0 (Local Autonomy Index). Second, the space for local democracy is analysed and, finally, drivers of financial autonomy are explored.

WHAT IS LOCAL FINANCIAL AUTONOMY, AND HOW HAS IT DEVELOPED?

Definitions: In the LAI, financial autonomy is measured through four sets of indicators: fiscal autonomy (or local taxation powers), financial-transfer systems (or degree of earmarking of expenditures), financial self-reliance (or local control over revenue sources) and borrowing autonomy. Theoretically, the indicators are based on core notions of fiscal federalism as well as normative ideas of local democracy expressed in the European Charter of Local Self-Government mentioned in the Introduction to the chapter. How a country scores on the financial autonomy index reflects the country's trade-off between national control and decentralized financial decision-making.

The details of the scoring system for financial autonomy are specified in the Appendix at the end of this book.

Trends: Figure 6.1 shows how the components of fiscal autonomy have developed since 1995 by groups of countries. The grouping of countries follows a logic of normative migration as formulated, for example, in theories of institutional isomorphism (DiMaggio and Powell 1983). New ideas of good governance emanate from a normative centre of prestige and power and travel gradually towards distant regions. The ideas of good governance, transparency and accountability adopted from fiscal federalism are espoused by such normative centres as OECD, the EU and CoE (Council of Europe). The greater the exposure (or pressure), the more likely countries are to have adopted the ideas.

---

2 Pietrangelo de Biase and Sean Dougherty, The past and future of subnational fiscal rules: An analysis of fiscal rules over time. OECD Working Papers on Fiscal Federalism October 2022, No. 41. https://www.oecd.org/content/dam/oecd/en/publications/reports/2022/10/the-past-and-future-of-subnational-fiscal-rules_77285223/d2798c9e-en.pdf.

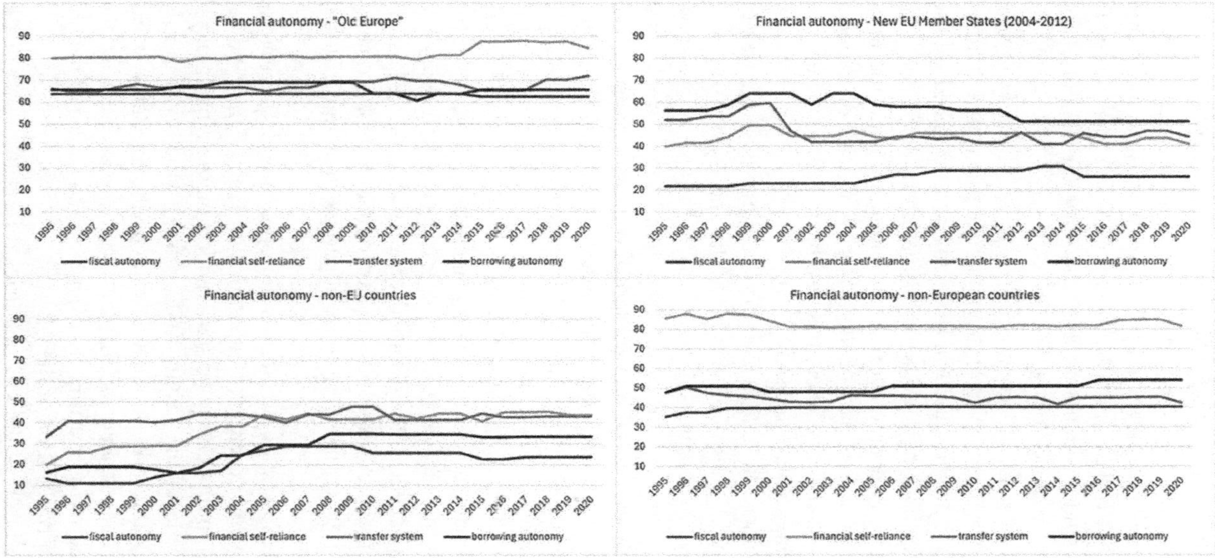

Notes: 'Old Europe' (EU15 and EFTA countries (Iceland, Liechtenstein, Norway and Switzerland)), 'New EU member states (post-2004 accession), 'Non-EU countries' (Balkans, former Soviet Union, Turkey).

Figure 6.1 *Index of financial autonomy by country group, standardized*

The 15 EU member states of before 2004 plus the associated EFTA countries constitute 'the Old Europe', presumably most heavily exposed to the normative centres. The new EU member states from 2004 onwards are 'the New Europe', strongly influenced through the long accession process. A third group is that of European countries that are not members of the EU (the West Balkans, former Soviet Union territories plus Turkey). Finally, there are the ten non-European countries covered by this study, which are members of the OECD but, naturally, not the European organizations of the EU and CoE.

The 'old Europe' countries (EU 15 countries plus those of the European Economic Area) obtain the highest scores of the municipal financial autonomy indices. Moreover, all four variables used in the study are 'balanced' in the sense that they all have similar, high levels. The situation in the 1995–2020 period was relatively stable. A drop of borrowing autonomy occurred after 2008, which may be interpreted as part of the austerity policies of national governments after the financial crisis. There has also been a slight increase of financial self-reliance during the last decade.

In the countries that joined the EU in 2004 or later (the 11 countries of post-communist Central and Eastern Europe plus Malta and Cyprus), all four variables have significantly lower scores compared to Old Europe. As we know from earlier analyses, the financial dimension has often been a 'weak spot' of decentralization reforms in Central and Eastern European countries. The level of fiscal autonomy is especially low – in most countries in this group, governments are reluctant to allocate significant discretion over tax policies to local governments. Municipalities are to a large extent financed by tax-sharing and transfers, so the level of financial self-reliance is relatively low as well. The trend regarding borrowing autonomy is very interesting: in some of the countries (the Czech Republic, Slovakia and to a lesser extent Hungary are good examples), in the last decade of the twentieth century there was a laissez-faire approach to local borrowing. However, the experience of debt problems in some of the cities made governments in those countries tighten the formal rules of borrowing.

The autonomy scores are lowest in the group of European non-EU countries (Western Balkans and several countries that originated from former Soviet Republics). However, even in this group we see a modest increase of financial autonomy in the first decade of the twenty-first century, which was mostly due to reforms in several Western Balkan countries applying for status as EU accession countries. As demonstrated in Chapter 12 on the adoption of the European Charter of Local Self-Government, a similar trend occurred in connection with the process of ratification of the Charter.

The pattern in the non-European OECD countries differs from that of the other groups. It is characterized by very high levels of financial self-reliance and rather low values on the other three variables. In most of the countries in this group the scope of functions provided by local governments is relatively narrow. Also, the level of horizontal equalization is low, so there is no need to spend significant amounts on transfers to local government. This explains the high proportion of revenues from own sources: the overall funding of local government is relatively low, the level of inequalities is high and local authorities are mostly financed by their own resources. The scores on the remaining three variables are rather low, reflecting low levels of financial decentralization. This is, however, a rather disparate group of countries in terms not only of geographic location but also of levels of financial autonomy. The four countries of Australia, Canada, South Africa and the United States all score above 70 points on overall financial autonomy, while the score of Chile is 29 and that of Mexico only 14. Obviously, further variables need to be taken into account to explain the variation within the non-European group.

SPACE FOR LOCAL DEMOCRACY

Fiscal federalism, with roots in the club model of Buchanan (1965) and the theory of fiscal equivalence of Mancur Olson (1969), and further developed through the decentralization theorem of Oates (1972, 2005), assigns a decisive role to the rational voter as a mechanism of allocative efficiency through local democracy. Space for local democracy means that there is room for elected local councils to make meaningful choices between fiscal alternatives as well as setting spending priorities. This again is a basis for local electoral democracy with competing electoral platforms and meaningful choices for voters. Voter choice is also, potentially, a source of political discipline and managerial rectitude through electoral accountability (Seabright 1996).

However, a concern with allocative efficiency at higher levels of government may also become a driver of financial restraints on local government, for example the introduction of equalization measures that redistribute revenues between local authorities through various mechanisms. The common-pool problem inherent in central grants and redistributive programmes is addressed in later versions of fiscal federalism (Prud'homme 1995; Goodspeed 2002).

The various restraints on local financial autonomy may be seen as a series of solutions to the common-pool problem. The varying levels of local financial autonomy may be interpreted as reflections of how pressing the problem is in various countries or of how tolerant the national systems are faced with such problems. The indicators of financial autonomy are, in fact, also indicators of national restrictions on autonomy: restrictions are just the other side of the coin of autonomy. In many cases, the indicators measure the absence of specific restriction, e.g. the absence of demands for prior approbations of borrowing. Consequently, the index also measures national preferences for regulating the local financial space.

In order to obtain a measure of local democratic space, the four indicators of financial autonomy are collated into two items: financial self-determination and spending independence. *Financial self-determination* is the combination of fiscal autonomy (or local taxation power) and borrowing autonomy. *Spending independence* combines the financial-transfer system (i.e. scores indicating the absence of earmarking) and financial self-reliance (or the proportion of revenues from own, local sources).

The first set of indicators measures the local freedom of financial decision-making (the extent to which local authorities can set base and rate of taxes, and whether they can finance operations through borrowing).[3]

The second set measures spending independence (the extent to which local authorities are unconstrained by earmarking of transfers, and the extent to which they have control over local sources of income to use at their own discretion).

In combination, the two consolidated measures indicate the extent of local democratic space – the extent to which local decision-makers have choices regarding how they can raise income and spend revenues. Presumably, a wide democratic space may leave much more room for local choices regarding financial policies and hence more room for debates than does a narrow space with few financial options. The combination of the measures yields a fourfold table that specifies a simplified world with four types of spaces, as demonstrated in Table 6.1.

Cell 2 may be termed 'rational-choice democracy' since decision-makers and voters theoretically have many options of tax and expenditure combinations to choose between. The opposite situation is in cell 3, denoted 'constrained democracy' since voters and decision-makers are left with a narrow band of options on both dimensions. In cell 4 there are few choices regarding revenue options but nevertheless local control over sources of income – which may be termed 'guided democracy' since expenditure priorities are guided by national earmarking. Situation 1 is 'incongruent' in the sense that decision-makers have choices regarding taxation and borrowing but little control over the revenue pool (for example, high level of earmarking of transfers and also few own resources).

Figure 6.2 shows how the local governments of the 57 countries in this study are distributed in local democratic space. First of all, the figure shows that the countries are spread out widely across the space, or in other words that

---

[3] These two variables have the same value for all municipalities in a given country. Exceptions to this rule may be found in federal countries with different local financial systems in different subjects of the federation, or in countries with asymmetric decentralization, typically allocating more functions and consequently different financial arrangements for larger cities.

Table 6.1 Local democratic spaces: four constellations of decision-making powers and financial independence

		Spending independence (level of earmarking + self-reliance)	
Financial freedom of choice (taxation + borrowing powers)		Low	High
	High	1 Incongruent democracy	2 Rational-choice democracy
	Low	3 Constrained democracy	4 Guided democracy

Source: Authors' own.

countries vary substantially as to how much space there is for democracy to unfold locally. National governments may grant much freedom on one dimension but retain tight control over another. Chile is an example of this, with a low score on financial freedom but a high score on revenue independence. It is definitely a case of guided democracy in terms of financial autonomy. Slovakia is an example in the opposite direction. Nevertheless, there is an overall linear relationship between the two sides of space, as demonstrated by the overall pattern in Figure 6.2. Although the relationship is not very tight, the pattern signifies a distribution of financial regimes spread out between the pure types of rational choice and constrained regimes. Finland and Sweden, in the upper right-hand part of the figure, come close to the rational choice type, whereas Moldova and Mexico are close to the constrained type with little space for local rational democracy.

Table 6.2 presents details of the scoring of some of the cases at the extremes of Figure 6.2 and also of some cases with a mixed scoring. The scoring profiles of the two cases at the extremes of Figure 6.2, Sweden and Mexico, may not be so surprising – they receive top and (almost) bottom scores respectively. The four cases exemplify different solutions to the overarching dilemmas of local autonomy versus macroeconomic control. The Mexican solution is quite straightforward: to prioritize national control over local autonomy. The Swedish case is instructive in the sense that the Swedes have managed to strike a balance that implies a reasonable degree of national control while largely respecting the norms of the European Charter of Local Self-Government.

The two cases with mixed profiles – Norway and Poland – illustrate the situation of the majority of cases in this study: a series of compromises that yield distinctive national solutions to the dilemmas of local financial autonomy. The

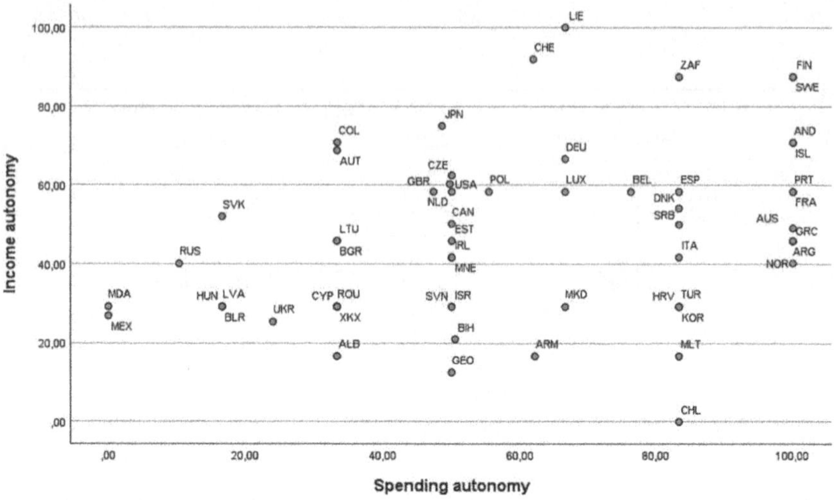

Source: Authors' own.

Figure 6.2 *Distribution of countries in local democratic space (2020)*

cases of Norway and Poland are documented in more detail in Box 6.1 and Box 6.2.

Table 6.2 *Components of financial autonomy 2020 by types of local democratic space*

Financial indicators (scale in brackets):	Sweden – rational	Mexico – constrained	Norway – mixed	Poland – mixed
Fiscal autonomy (0–4)	3	1	1	2
Financial transfer system (0–3)	3	2	3	2
Financial self-reliance (0–3)	3	1	3	2
Borrowing autonomy (0–3)	3	1	2	2
Financial autonomy total	12	5	9	8

BOX 6.1 THE CASE OF NORWAY

Norway is an interesting case of cell 4, guided democracy. How did Norway end up there, while the other Nordic countries are all in cell 2, rational-choice democracies?

The explanation of the Norwegian position on local financial autonomy is largely the low score on fiscal autonomy and the consequent absence of variation across municipalities regarding local tax rates on personal incomes. This is by far the most important local tax. The tax rate is in practice set by Parliament at a standard rate for all municipalities. Another consequence is that the local income tax is not an issue in public debate locally or at the national level, nor is it an issue in local elections. There is no tax competition between municipalities. Local political debate is almost exclusively focused on spending priorities, while revenue levels are more or less taken for granted or follow automatically from the workings of the overall financial systems. Consequently, the institutional setting of Norwegian local finances does not make for a rational-choice type of local democracy.

The issues mostly hotly debated are features of the transfer and equalization system. As pointed out above, the level of formal earmarking is low: national support is mostly given as a lump sum, or 'free revenues' in the terminology of the financial system. The sum transferred to a municipality is the result, first, of a set of complex criteria that seek to account for variations in spending needs across municipalities, and second, calculations to equalize tax-base variations.

A recurring debate is concerned with the criteria applied to calculate spending needs. Large cities, for example, can be heard to argue that their special needs are not properly reflected in the criteria, while small, peripheral municipalities may claim that problems related to small-scale operations are not sufficiently acknowledged.

The financial system is mostly a consumer democracy concerned with spending priorities, ripe with fiscal illusions and often optimistic over-budgeting. The disciplinary connection to the taxpayer is absent. Budgetary discipline is maintained through bureaucratic means – through the administrative supervision of state agents. If a municipality engenders a deficit it is obliged to recover the deficit within the next three years. If not, an overseer regime takes over, suspending borrowing autonomy, and enforces recovery as the top priority.

BOX 6.2 THE CASE OF POLAND

Polish debates on financing local governments focus, first of all, on the sufficiency of local revenues (including transfers received) relative to compulsory standards of locally provided services. The funding of salaries of schoolteachers – salaries are set at the central level of government but paid from local budgets – is the most salient example of such debates.

In recent years another important topic of debates has been the change in the composition (and size) of local revenues. After 2015, the importance of own revenues, and especially of PIT (personal income tax) tax-sharing, has been reduced at the expense of earmarked grant programmes.

More technical debates on local finance are relatively less visible, being limited to the narrow group of experts and interested local politicians. The topics of those niche debates include:

- Possible reform of the property tax, which is by far the most important local tax in Poland.
- Financial equalization system. There are two issues in this debate. The first concerns horizontal equalization, through the so-called 'Robin Hood tax', which in the case of municipalities provides only a marginal share of transfers but is often questioned by more affluent local authorities. The second debate originates from the fact that financial equalization in Poland is based on revenue potential only, while factors influencing variation of spending needs are almost totally ignored.

As regards the borrowing regulation, the current system is not questioned (except in terms of some technical details). But the main concern is that inadequate financing of current expenditures reduces the size of the operating surplus of the budget, which effectively limits the borrowing capacity of local authorities.

DRIVERS OF DEMOCRATIC SPACE

Why do countries vary so much in the nature of their local-government financial regimes? Although financial autonomy is regarded as a vital component of overall local democracy, national government may have many good reasons, as mentioned above, to regulate and constrain local financial freedom. Reasons may range from regulatory predictability and macroeconomic stability and development to concerns with regional and social inequalities and the rule of law.

In this section, four hypotheses on explanations of variations of financial autonomy are developed and tested: stakes, risks, size and culture.

H1: National governments have more at stake in local government the larger the share of local government to total government finances is. The higher the proportion of local finances to overall government finances, the more important prudent management of local finances is to the central government since, for example, local over-borrowing may disturb overall macroeconomic stability. High stakes may increase the likelihood of tight financial controls. In the subsequent analysis, the weight of local government is measured through the range of functions assigned to local government as indicated by the policy scope (PS) and effective political discretion (EPD) indices, on the assumption that the larger the range of functions, the greater the share of government funds needed to finance local government.

H2: The higher are the risks of local mismanagement, the more tightly controlled are local finances likely to be. Risks of mismanagement may of course come in many forms. Corruption poisons government operations in many parts of the world, including local government. Corruption in local government may seriously disturb the allocative efficiency of local government and thus become a concern for national governments. Presumably, central governments want to prevent corruption in local government or at least reduce the likelihood of corruption, which may entail keeping a close eye on local finances and hence reducing the space of local decision-making. There is no separate indicator of corruption in local government, so the risk of corruption is measured through Transparency International's ranking of countries according to perceptions of risks of corruption (Transparency International 2020).

H3: Small-scale local government is more tightly controlled than large-scale government. The reason for tighter control of small authorities is the assumption of lower managerial capacity and thus their greater need of guidance in financial affairs; hence the expectation that the smaller is the average size of local authorities in a country the tighter the financial controls are. Size is, furthermore, frequently an issue in discussions of local-government reforms and amalgamations are often mentioned by reformers as a precondition for greater local autonomy (Baldersheim and Rose 2010).

H4: A participatory political culture reduces the need for central corrections. This is an argument from second-generation fiscal federalism derived from the information-asymmetry problem of principal-agent models (Oates 2005). Electorates are cast as the principals and local officials as the agents. High levels of electoral participation ensure that elections become good signalling systems for voter preferences and thus help allocative efficiency (Seabright 1996). There is thus less need, for example, for earmarking of national grants. This line of reasoning represents an interesting bridge from fiscal federalism to studies of civic culture in the tradition leading from Gabriel Almond and Sidney Verba (1963) to Robert Putnam (1994) and Francis Fukuyama (2011). The information on electoral participation comes from the country experts of the LAI programme.

The hypotheses are tested through regression analysis reported in Table 6.3. Two of the four hypotheses are supported by the findings in Table 6.3: the risks and the civic-culture hypotheses. The risk of mismanagement implied by corruption is the most important driver of central-government restrictions on local financial autonomy. In other words, the higher the non-corruption score, the larger the democratic space. Non-corruption opens up both dimensions of democratic space – freedom of financial decision-making and revenue independence. A participatory civic culture pulls in the same direction – greater revenue independence and an even stronger impact on overall financial autonomy.

Interestingly, the relationship between the importance of local government and financial autonomy points in the opposite direction to that suggested by the

Table 6.3 *Drivers of financial autonomy and its components – regression analysis (OLS)*

-	Income autonomy (tax+borrow) 2020	Spending autonomy (transf + self-rel) 2020	Financial autonomy total 2020
Stakes (range of functions x discretion)	.242*	.039	.120
Risks (non-corruption score; high score = low risk)	.394**	.339**	.462***
Size (mean size of local authorities)	–.108	.146	.059
Civic culture (turnout in local elections)	.228	.279*	.284**
Adj R^2	.35	.23	.39

Notes: Levels of statistical significance: *** ,001; ** ,01; * ,05.
Beta coefficients. N=56. Data sources: Stakes – LAI variables PS and EPD multiplied; Risks – Corruption Index of Transparency International; Size – mean size of municipalities, calculations by LAI; Civic culture – turnout in local elections, collated by LAI.
Source: Authors' own.

stakes hypothesis: the relationship is a positive and statistically significant one, which suggests that local responsibility for a large range of public functions is accompanied by freedom at least in terms of income-generating powers. There is, however, no relationship to spending freedom or overall financial autonomy. At least we can conclude that high stakes do not lead national governments to tighten the regulations of local finances. To some extent the opposite may be the case.

Surprisingly also, the *size hypothesis* is not supported. The local-government scale structure is not of significance for financial autonomy. Small-scale or large-scale makes little difference to regulations and autonomy. Further research on this issue with more refined measures of local-government size may therefore be warranted.

CONCLUSIONS

The overarching issue of this chapter is the scope of local financial decision-making, which is assumed to be a driver of local democracy. Well-functioning local democracy is a precondition for allocative efficiency, which is a central concern of fiscal federalism. Financial autonomy regarding revenue raising and spending is presumed to stimulate local debates on taxation and spending priorities and thus contribute to expression and clarification of local preferences among voters and next among decision-makers. However, central governments have wider responsibilities and must take the collective interests of the nation as a whole into account and establish regulatory frameworks for local finances that both enable and restrain local autonomy. The frameworks entail compromises between several national goals, including those of local autonomy and allocative efficiency.

The analyses of this chapter have demonstrated enormous variation in terms of local financial autonomy across 57 countries. On a scale of 0–100, 26 out of 57 countries scored below 50 points while 16 countries obtained more than 70 points in 2020. Ten countries were below 30 points.

Development of financial autonomy 1995–2020 was charted for four groups of countries termed Old Europe, New Europe, Non-EU Europe and Non-European countries. As a group, the 20 countries of Old Europe were definitely ahead of the rest in terms of financial autonomy on all four indicators, while Non-EU Europe was last. This pattern was interpreted as resulting largely from variations in the intensity of exposure to normative centres of good financial governance, although the position of Non-European countries did not quite fit this interpretation. Clearly, further factors would have to be taken into account.

The 57 countries were spread out widely in terms of local democratic space. Only a minority of around 15 countries fitted clearly into the pattern termed 'rational-choice democracy' with high levels of freedom regarding spending priorities and revenues, including borrowing. The rest could be classified as either 'guided democracies', 'constrained democracies' or 'incongruent democracies'. The capacities of the three latter groups to fulfil the requirements of allocative efficiency may be questioned.

Finally, the chapter has sought to find determinants of variations in financial autonomy and its components. The hypotheses focused on variations in stakes, risks, size and civic culture as potential explanations of financial autonomy. Stakes refer to the weight of local government in the overall machinery of government, risks focus on the occurrence of corrupt practices in government, size describes the scalar structure of local government and civic culture emphasizes the role of electoral participation. Two of the four potential explanations were supported through regression analysis: risks and civic culture. The level of risks in the form of corruption is an important determinant of financial autonomy. Low levels of corruption are associated with high levels of financial autonomy and especially control over sources of income. High levels of electoral participation are also conducive to financial autonomy.

Are there any strategic lessons for enhancing local financial autonomy and thus the space of local democracy inherent in these findings? Certainly: intensifying the battle against corruption and stimulating electoral participation.

7. Assigned tasks and tasks delivered

INTRODUCTION

In certain nations, the notion of local autonomy encompasses the freedom, often referred to as 'general competence', for municipalities to undertake new responsibilities not specifically designated to other tiers of government, commonly known as residual powers. This principle is integral to a dynamic local autonomy framework, prevalent particularly in Nordic and Continental European federal models, wherein municipalities are encouraged to proactively engage in initiatives addressing predominantly local concerns. This expansive concept appears to enhance the scope of local governance and stimulate socio-political innovation. In contrast, an alternative conception of local autonomy, rooted in the Anglo-Saxon tradition, confines municipal competencies to a predefined and non-residual set of statutory tasks, adhering to the ultra vires principle (Kuhlmann and Wollmann 2019: 21–22). In other countries, intermediate concepts of local autonomy afford municipalities the flexibility to select from a spectrum of predefined tasks, varying in scope from narrower to broader sets of responsibilities.

Both in countries where municipalities are afforded the flexibility to choose among legally predefined areas of action and in those where municipalities possess 'general competence', the result is a differentiation in the degree of decentralization. Some municipalities will exploit to a greater extent, and some to a lesser extent (or not at all), opportunities for expanding the scope of action provided to them by law, either due to political choice or due to a lack of economic, human or knowledge resources and means. Furthermore, objective capabilities and political priorities will vary even within the same municipality, depending on the policy field in question. Thus, a central issue concerning the substantive autonomy of municipalities pertains to the actual ability of local self-government to formulate and implement its own policy decisions according to its priorities. An additional question is how and to what extent this ability differs across various policy fields, such as education, environment, health, etc.

These questions are addressed to some extent by the Local Autonomy Index (LAI), which comprises two variables focusing on the relevant issues. The first and most important of these is the variable incorporated into the LAI framework termed 'effective political discretion' (EPD: scale 0–4). It gauges the authoritative decision-making power of local authorities across eight distinct policy fields: education, social assistance, health, land use, public transport, housing, police and caring functions. Common municipal responsibilities applicable universally across countries, such as local road networks, parks and basic public utilities, have been deliberately excluded from consideration.

The other relevant variable employed in the LAI framework is 'policy scope' (PS, scale 0–4), which evaluates the extent of local-government involvement in service delivery and associated responsibilities across the eight fields used to measure EPD. These two variables assess facets of local autonomy in identical policy domains, revealing a robust correlation in previous LAI measurements spanning the period 1990–2014. This alignment, while anticipated, does not universally apply to all policy fields and their respective aspects. Municipalities often find themselves responsible for implementing externally determined public policies, even in their intricate details ('administrative decentralization'), with limited flexibility for localized adjustments based on contextual factors (Ladner et al. 2019: 221).

In the volume, *Patterns of Local Autonomy*, an examination of functional responsibilities across 39 countries during the period 1990–2014 revealed significant variations in PS and EPD across diverse countries and policy fields. While certain commonalities exist, the distinctive influence of national factors shapes the composition of functions constituting local government, resulting in a unique mosaic in each country. This implies that, if we adhere to the notion that 'policies shape politics' (Lowi 1972), local politics will exhibit considerable divergence from one country to another (Ladner et al. 2019: 120).

In this chapter, leveraging data spanning 30 years (1990–2020) from 57 countries, we will closely examine instances where PS and EPD exhibit significant disparities, focusing particularly on countries where this deviation is more pronounced. We anticipate that such discrepancies will be observed in several countries, and rather than being scattered, they are likely to be attributed to specific policy fields that may be consistent across several countries. The discrepancy in decision-making authority for local authorities within these fields is expected to arise from distinct characteristics inherent to concrete policy areas and some additional factors, such as national contexts.

In the present chapter, a section will follow where a theoretical and systematic analysis of municipal powers will be conducted, focusing primarily on the issue of the discretionary authority of municipalities. This analysis will encompass municipal competencies, their historical evolution, legal categorizations and the related relationships that develop among various levels of government. Additionally, specific areas of public policy will be examined that hold particular interest for the functions performed by municipalities and were subjects of empirical research forming the basis for the development of the LAI and this current book. Empirical findings will then be presented and discussed before certain conclusions are drawn.

LOCAL GOVERNMENT TASKS

The variation in municipal decision-making and discretionary powers within diverse domains of municipal competence, along with the absence of discretion in certain municipal tasks, constitutes a historical norm. Since the inception of modern local self-government, local authorities have been mandated to execute specific responsibilities on behalf of the state. Following the French Revolution, local authorities were given tasks encompassing the maintenance of civil registers (births, deaths, marriages, etc.), electoral rolls and even tasks related to conscription. The legal doctrine in France known as *dédoublement fonctionnel* called for mayors to engage in a plurality of functions, simultaneously fulfilling the dual roles of elected municipal officials and local agents of the Republic, serving as a 'deconcentrated' state organ (Meunier 2006). When undertaking duties on behalf of the Republic, mayors assumed the status of state officials, subject to directives from higher state authorities, primarily the Prefect or the Minister of the Interior. This doctrine, originating from the Napoleonic model, spread to various other nations, often integrating with indigenous legal traditions. Analogous frameworks are observable in the United Kingdom, where ostensibly autonomous entities of local self-government, such as borough councils, are compelled to execute the objectives of the central government. While inherently local self-governing units, they concurrently function as 'agents of local obligation', executing directives from the central government, particularly in areas such as education and law enforcement. Around the globe, authoritarian and hybrid regimes would go much further and turn municipalities into their local agents, in substance solely accountable to the central government (Diamond 2002).

Nearly everywhere, states take advantage of municipalities, their resources and their problem-solving capacities to make sure that wide-ranging state policies are implemented everywhere and are close to citizens and challenges (Chevallier 2019). Decentralization, in general, offers significant opportunities to improve government accountability by exerting stronger pressures both from below (demand) and above (supply), even though the relevant literature contains many examples where the potential has not been realized (Yilmaz et al. 2010).

Modern local government has a dual character, encompassing both 'deconcentration' and decentralization, acting as a nexus between central convenience and the acknowledgement that not all authority should emanate from the centre. This amalgamation can be clearly seen in the discretionary nature of certain powers vested in local-government units, subject to stringent central control and financial support while others remain autonomous. The combination yields the intricate complexity observed in contemporary local governance. Additionally, local government operates as a departmentalization of the state's functions, based on the territorial dispersion of services. This stands in contrast both to central departmental divisions and to the decentralization of functions to public corporations. In local governance, the pivotal essence lies in the territorial apportionment of power (Smoke 2015).

In the early twenty-first century, the jurisdictional prerogatives wielded by contemporary local authorities transcend those of preceding eras when their primary functions embraced municipal roads, urban policing, public assistance, the mitigation of health-related nuisances, occasional firefighting and public education. In Nordic countries, municipalities underwent a gradual transformation, evolving to constitute the cornerstone of the Scandinavian welfare-state model (Sellers and Lidström 2007), with various other nations incorporating elements thereof. Alongside contemporary social services and advanced public utilities, the competencies routinely exercised by municipalities across diverse nations encompass: educational oversight, spanning from primary to high-school levels and technical institutions (in the USA, occasionally extending to colleges and universities); the provision of public-health services; housing management and provision; urban planning, zoning and building regulation; environmental preservation and climate change initiatives; and the facilitation of immigrant integration and social inclusion. Modern municipalities, characterized not only by their territorial scope but also by their generalist, multipurpose, multisectoral and multitask nature, serve as comprehensive authorities with multifaceted responsibilities (Chevallier 2019).

The German legal doctrine offers a good example where this wide array of municipal tasks has been systematized, depending on authority (or 'service dominion') and discretion, or the character of the task (obligatory or voluntary, genuinely municipal or delegated). Generally, municipal tasks in Germany are categorized as follows:

a. Mandatory tasks without instruction (*Pflichtaufgaben ohne Weisung*): tasks provided by federal or state law (public order and safety, basic public services, schools and kindergartens, etc.). Municipalities are obligated to perform these tasks, but have discretion in deciding how to fulfil them and there is no detailed instruction from higher-level authorities.
b. Optional tasks (*Wahlaufgaben*) that municipalities can choose to undertake within their discretion but are not obligated to do so. Examples include cultural offerings, sports facilities and recreational facilities.

c. Delegated tasks (*Übertragene Aufgaben*) that states (*Länder*) delegate to municipalities, usually (but not always) providing that state authorities can prepare detailed instructions (*nach Weisung*).

For delegated tasks, expediency control is allowed in addition to legality control, and supervising authorities can intervene even within the discretionary scope of local authorities, while in the first two categories of tasks, state supervision is limited to legality control.

Municipal responsibilities are similarly categorized in other countries as well (Marcou 2010). However, the actual possibilities for exercising discretionary powers are determined by many factors other than the legal framework. Sometimes the mere indifference or incapacity of state organs can expand the discretion exercised by municipalities in practice, temporarily or over the long term. On other occasions, higher levels of government deliberately grant greater discretion to municipalities for various political, economic, administrative or social reasons (The World Bank 2009). In some cases, establishing a satisfactory routine is enough for local authorities to develop powers beyond those explicitly provided by the law. However formally bound to the higher levels' authority and regulations local authorities may be, a degree of discretion is unavoidable in practice (Chevallier 2019).

On the other hand, the formally recognized discretion of municipalities cannot bypass the fact that modern local government is an integral part of the state, and local authorities are accountable to state bodies in many ways besides the classical supervision mechanisms and rules. Municipalities are moreover obliged to respond to policy priorities and targets set by state or regional governments, implementing these policies locally, often using resources given (e.g. earmarked grants) and controlled by the state and/or other higher levels of governance (Ladner et al. 2019: 281).

Across the different OECD (Organisation for Economic Co-operation and Development) countries, it is rare for competencies to be truly exclusive. Most responsibilities are shared across levels of government, particularly between the municipal and regional levels. In practice, the issue is not a clear-cut allocation of responsibilities but rather how to manage shared functions and responsibilities The degree of responsibility sharing varies across sectors. Shared competencies can arise either through explicit legislation or through the acquisition of residual powers. The necessity for sharing responsibilities may stem from functional considerations, often seen between municipal and regional tiers in areas such as transport and infrastructure, environment and water, culture and tourism, communication and economic development. It may also arise for financial reasons, such as in the case of social services. Major areas of public-service provision, like healthcare and education, may be well suited for tiered management and provision (Allain-Dupré 2018).

The extent of responsibility sharing also depends on the specific service involved. For instance, responsibilities are more commonly shared in public transport than in childcare or elderly care, doubtless reflecting the network-industry character of the former and the consequent need for enhanced coordination (OECD 2022). Some examples of the most commonly shared responsibilities highlighted by the OECD are as follows (Allain-Dupré 2018):

- Physical infrastructure. One of the most frequently shared responsibilities involves physical infrastructure and related public investment. Nearly 60 per cent of public investment flows through subnational governments (OECD 2013), although the control over projects and fund utilization varies widely.
- Education. Education stands out as the most common major public service shared across multiple tiers of government (OECD 2022). It constitutes the largest budget item for local governments in most countries, representing an average of 25 per cent of total subnational expenditure. Central governments often establish framework legislation, while local governments are typically responsible for maintaining and constructing physical infrastructure and staff payments, although hiring or salary authority may vary. Teachers' unions are among the strongest trade unions and in some countries they tend to favour centralized governance of the education system, especially concerning employment status and payment (Chevallier 2019).
- Healthcare. Due to its high system complexity and its technical aspects, healthcare tends to be more centralized than education, with distinct roles for different levels of government but often less autonomy (OECD 2022). Funding needs and standards of quality imply controls from higher levels of government.
- Social assistance. Social assistance is more likely to be provided jointly due to its strongly redistributive nature. In the USA, federal welfare benefits and programmes are administered through states in collaboration with local governments, resulting in varying degrees of control. States have the freedom to create specific social-assistance programmes and often grant autonomy to municipalities, leading to a diverse range of programmes and coverage (Allain-Dupré 2018). In other countries, national policies extensively use municipalities for implementation, without granting equivalent discretion to the local level.
- Land use. National and regional governments primarily focus on strategic planning and providing policy guidelines for land use. While land use planning is predominantly a local task, several countries use guiding land-use

plans prepared at the regional or intermunicipal level. In some instances, countries are responsible for preparing land-use plans for areas of particular economic or environmental importance. The degree of local autonomy appears to be more influential than the degree of regional autonomy in shaping the character of a planning system (OECD 2017).

Within the framework of the LAI 2.0, there is a special focus on caring functions, which are provided jointly less often than social assistance. On the other hand, higher levels of governance define unitary standards, elaborate relevant programmes and provide funding (sometimes through earmarked grants), usually resulting in restrictions upon local discretionary power.

Based on the preceding analyses, the following would be anticipated:

- EPD is expected to be lower than PS in most of the 57 countries surveyed.
- EPD is expected to be lower in complex multi-tier government systems, such as federal or regional states.
- EPD is expected to be lower in authoritarian or barely democratic hybrid regimes that consider local authorities as local agents of the central government.
- EPD is expected to be lower in certain policy fields such as education, social assistance, health, land use and caring functions.

EMPIRICAL RESULTS

Table 7.1 shows a detailed comparison of EPD and PS values for the year 2015 across 57 countries surveyed, along with the average for the five years from 2015 to 2020. The last column of the table highlights any differences between the average EPD and PS scores during that period. The main aim of this analysis is to identify any discrepancies between the values of these two variables in each country, specifically focusing on those countries where the scores for discretionary powers of municipalities are much smaller than the scores for PS. By doing so, we can test the validity of three of the aforementioned expectations: (1) in most countries, discretionary powers are more restricted compared to the PS of municipalities, (2) discretionary powers are comparatively more limited in countries with complex federal or regional structures and (3) discretionary powers are noticeably lower than PS in countries with hybrid regimes.

Table 7.1 shows that only six countries – Bulgaria, France, Lithuania, Luxembourg, Romania and Slovakia – have no significant differences between the values of the variables. These countries have different scores on both variables and cannot be considered as a cohesive group. Therefore, drawing general conclusions for the entire group is inappropriate.

Table 7.1 *Policy scope and effective political discretion 2015, 2015–2020 mean, difference PS-EPD*

Country	PS 2015	EPD 2015	PS mean (2015–2020)	EPD mean (2015–2020)	**Difference of EPD mean from PS mean**
Albania	2.24	2.59	2.24	2.59	**+0.30**
Andorra	1.47	1.06	1.47	0.94	**+0.53**
Argentina	1.83	2.08	1.85	2.08	**+0.13**
Armenia	1.82	1.67	1.83	1.69	**−0.14**
Australia	1.35	0.71	1.35	0.71	**−0.64**
Austria	1.72	1.71	1.73	1.71	**−0.02**
Belarus	2.94	2.18	2.94	2.18	**−0.24**
Belgium	2.00	1.65	2.00	1,65	**−0.35**
Bosnia and Herzegovina	1,85	2.11	1.84	2.11	**+0.27**
Bulgaria	2.00	2.00	2.00	2.00	**-**
Canada	0.98	0.89	0.98	0.89	**−0.09**
Chile	1.29	1.59	1.29	1.59	**+0.30**
Colombia	2.65	2.59	2.65	2.59	**−0.06**
Croatia	1.19	1.13	1.20	1.13	**−0.07**
Cyprus	0.86	0.83	0.86	0.83	**−0.03**
Czech Republic	1.47	1.35	1.47	1.35	**−0.12**
Denmark	3.06	2.94	3.06	2.94	**−0.12**
Estonia	2.29	2.18	2.29	2.18	**−0.11**
Finland	3.06	3.29	3.06	3.29	**+0.23**

Country	PS 2015	EPD 2015	PS mean (2015–2020)	EPD mean (2015–2020)	**Difference of EPD mean from PS mean**
France	3.17	3.17	3.17	3.17	-
Georgia	2.18	2.24	2.37	2.24	**−0.13**
Germany	2.76	1.65	2.76	1.65	**−1.11**
Greece	1.65	2.35	1.61	2.35	**+0.74**
Hungary	1.88	1.59	1.84	1.59	**−0.25**
Iceland	2.24	2.12	2.22	2.10	**−0.12**
Ireland	0.94	0.71	0.94	0.71	**−0.23**
Israel	1.76	0.71	1.76	0.71	**−0.05**
Italy	1.82	1.47	1.80	1.47	**−0.33**
Japan	2.41	1.60	2.41	1.61	**−0.80**
Kosovo	2.00	1.35	2.00	1.35	**−0.65**
Latvia	2.12	1.94	2.12	1.88	**−0.24**
Liechtenstein	2.65	1.41	2.65	1.41	**−1.24**
Lithuania	2.47	2.47	2.35	2.35	-
Luxembourg	1.41	1.41	1.41	1.41	-
Malta	0.41	0.06	0.41	0.06	**+0.35**
Mexico	1.75	1.94	1.67	1.94	**+0.27**
Moldova	1.24	1.18	1.24	1.18	**−0.06**
Montenegro	1.53	1.29	1.22	0.98	**−0.24**
Netherlands	2.59	1.88	2.59	1.88	**−0.71**

Country	PS 2015	EPD 2015	PS mean (2015–2020)	EPD mean (2015–2020)	**Difference of EPD mean from PS mean**
North Macedonia	1.64	1.94	1.64	1.94	**+0.34**
Norway	2.35	2.47	2.35	2.47	**+0.12**
Poland	2.39	1.96	2.39	1.81	**−0.58**
Portugal	1.24	1.18	1.56	1.44	**−0.12**
Republic of Korea	1.53	0.94	1.53	0.94	**−0.59**
Romania	1.82	1.82	1.82	1.82	-
Russian Federation	1.62	0.32	1.62	0.32	**−1.30**
Serbia	2.54	2.04	2.55	2.,04	**−0.51**
Slovakia	2.00	2.00	2.00	2.00	-
Slovenia	1.51	1.24	1.54	1.26	**−0.28**
South Africa	1.24	1.00	1.24	1.00	**−0.24**
Spain	1.39	1.31	1.39	1.31	**−0.08**
Sweden	2.71	2.59	2.71	2.59	**−0.12**
Switzerland	2.33	1.34	2.33	1.34	**−0.99**
Turkey	1.50	0.56	1.50	0.56	**−0.94**
Ukraine	2.09	1.48	2.24	1.55	**−0.69**
United Kingdom	2.36	1.90	2.35	1.90	**−0.45**
United States of America	2.67	2.65	2.67	2.65	**−0.02**
Mean (N=57)	1.93	1.68	1.93	1.67	-

Source: Authors' own.

On the other hand, in 11 countries, EPD has higher values than PS. This is particularly notable in Greece, Malta, North Macedonia, Chile, Mexico and Finland. However, these countries have distinctive characteristics unique to their national context that influence this outcome.

In most countries, 40 of them to be precise, discretionary power is lower than PSe. This aligns with expectations, since municipalities take on various responsibilities on behalf of the central government and other higher governance levels. Additionally, many of these responsibilities are shared and municipalities lack complete relevant authority. The first expectation is therefore affirmed as, in most countries, EPD is smaller than PS.

The pattern also holds for the third expectation: countries with hybrid regimes, such as the Russian Federation, Turkey and Belarus, have lower discretionary power. Furthermore, significantly diminished discretionary power is noted in several federal and regional countries, including Australia, Germany, Switzerland and Italy. Conversely, slightly lower discretionary power than PS is observed in Austria, Canada, the USA and Spain. Additionally, in certain cases of federal or regional countries where EPD surpasses PS, such as Mexico, Argentina, or Bosnia and Herzegovina, the opposite trend is prevalent.

As a result, the second expectation is confirmed in some cases where complex multilevel structures are associated with lower discretionary power for the lower level, i.e. the municipality. However, this expectation is not substantiated in several cases where the difference between EPD and PS is very small. It even appears to be contradicted in two cases of federal countries in the Americas and in the specific case of Bosnia and Herzegovina.

We will now discuss specific policy areas that were examined in the empirical research framework of the LAI 2.0. Table 7.2 presents scores for PS and EPD for nine selected countries where the local self-government's discretionary power (EPD score) differed the most from the PS score. These nine countries have the lowest EPD scores compared to their relevant PS scores. Therefore, they are ideal for investigating whether the difference between PS and EPD is spread out or concentrated in some policy areas. The PS and EPD scores in Table 7.2 show the sum of sub-variables in each of the eight policy areas that were studied. This method should help us identify any significant differences between the PS and EPD variables in some policy areas, which would confirm or challenge existing literature on disparities in local discretionary power in specific policy domains.

Table 7.2 suggests that the fourth expectation (lower EPD in certain policy fields) related to education is validated in most countries, with exceptions being Germany, Australia and the Netherlands. In these countries, the municipalities' discretionary power is considerably lower than their responsibilities for providing the corresponding service. The same is observed in social assistance, except for the Russian Federation, where local self-government has no

Table 7.2 *PS-EPD difference in 2020 in eight different policy fields in selected countries*

	RUS	GER	CHE	TUR	JPN	NLD	UKR	KOS	AUS
Education PS	3.00	1.75	3.00	0.75	2.75	1.50	2.50	3.00	0.00
Education EPD	**0.00**	1.50	**1.50**	**0.00**	**1.50**	1.50	**1.50**	**1.50**	0.00
Social Assistance PS	0.00	2.25	2.00	0.75	1.00	3.00	1.00	0.50	1.00
Social Assistance EPD	0.00	**1.50**	**0.00**	**0.00**	**0.00**	**1.50**	**0.00**	0.50	**0.00**
Health PS	0.25	1.50	1.00	0.75	1.25	0.50	1.00	2.50	0.50
Health EPD	0.00	**0.75**	**0.00**	**0.00**	1.00	0.50	*1.50*	**1.25**	**0.00**
Land Use PS	1.50	2.00	2.00	2.00	1.50	2.00	2.00	1.00	2.00
Land Use EPD	**1.00**	**0.50**	**1.00**	2.00	1.50	**1.00**	2.00	1.00	**1.50**
Public Transport PS	1.00	1.00	0.50	1.00	0.50	0.00	0.50	0.50	0.25
Public Transport EPD	1.00	**0.50**	0.50	1.00	0.50	0.00	0.50	0.50	0.00
Housing PS	1.00	1.00	1.00	0.25	1.00	1.00	1.00	1.00	0.50
Housing EPD	**0.00**	0.75	1.00	0.00	1.00	**0.50**	1.00	1.00	0.50
Police PS	0.00	0.00	0.75	0.00	0.00	0.00	0.25	0.00	0.00
Police EPD	0.00	0.00	0.75	0.00	0.00	*0.50*	0.00	0.00	0.00
Caring Functions PS	3.00	2.25	1.50	1.50	2.25	3.00	3.00	0.00	1.00
Caring Functions EPD	**0.00**	**1.50**	1.50	**0.00**	**1.50**	**1.50**	**1.50**	0.00	1.00

Notes: Country abbreviations: AUS=Australia, GER=Germany, JPN=Japan, KOS=Kosovo, NLD=Netherlands, RUS=Russian Federation, CHE=Switzerland, TUR=Turkey, UKR=Ukraine. A difference of more than 0.25 points in EPD is shown in bold. Data refer in Russia to urban okrugs, in Turkey to municipalities, in Japan to cities, in Ukraine to amalgamated hromadas and cities, and in Australia to the largest state per population, New South Wales (NSW).

service-provision responsibilities, and Kosovo. Regarding caring functions, this expectation is confirmed in six countries but contradicted in Switzerland, Kosovo and Australia. The results for land use and health are not conclusive, with five countries confirming the expectation and four countries contradicting it. In summary, it can be concluded that the fourth expectation is validated in most countries for education, social assistance and caring functions, while it tends to be affirmed in two other domains, health and land use.

CONCLUSIONS

The focus of this chapter was on examining the significance of and potential reasons for any discrepancies between EPD and PS. These discrepancies imply that municipalities are administratively responsible for more issues than those for which they have discretionary power, indicating limited room for their own choices and politically oriented decisions. Although this phenomenon has traditionally involved the inevitable handling of certain state matters by municipalities, cases where local-government administration functions solely as 'administration' have expanded significantly for various reasons.

Substantially lower EPD values can raise concerns about the true local autonomy of first-tier local authorities. Limited discretionary power regarding certain tasks means that local authorities essentially transform into local agents of higher governance levels in those specific policy areas, losing their political essence while their role becomes marginalized. The phenomenon of municipal 'bureaucratization' becomes more pronounced, especially when there is a broader shift towards a hybrid regime, inherently incompatible with genuine local self-government, as confirmed by the empirical findings of this chapter.

Systematic examination and analysis of empirical data, however, have revealed that also in some democratic countries, the discretionary power of local authorities is significantly lower than the scope of responsibilities for which they are administratively accountable. While the breadth of responsibilities in these countries may initially create the impression that there exists a strong local self-government, in reality, local authorities cannot make their own choices, indicating a lack of corresponding political power. Even a high degree of fiscal autonomy can prove hollow when it cannot translate into local political decisions made by elected and politically accountable local figures.

The risk of 'bureaucratization' of a political institution is evident in several instances. On the other hand, this initial perception is nuanced when one realizes that it does not apply uniformly to all policy fields but is concentrated in specific domains that exhibit peculiarities. Yet, even for these policy areas, it should be examined whether the current situation should be accepted, especially when greater political decentralization in specific sectors, such as education, has proven to be much more effective (Daun 2004). Local self-government possesses a direct, unmediated relationship of legitimation and accountability to the local community, along with local knowledge allowing for quicker and better responses to the needs and demands for certain services, notably in the social-assistance and caring functions explored in the LAI 2.0 survey.

However, these policy areas, along with education and particularly healthcare, often require financing, quality specifications, impartiality safeguards and, sometimes, control from higher governance levels. Regarding the policy field of land use, the limitation of municipal discretionary power is related to the need for an integrated and coherent environmental policy, sustainable development and management of settlements that have formed various networks for decades. This results in multiple interdependencies concerning land use and interactions among cities that are geographically non-contiguous.

Nonetheless, the issues related to the specificity of each policy area and the subsequent implications for local autonomy could not be subjected to a deeper analysis within the scope of this chapter, which was restricted to identifying those policy fields where limitation of the first-tier self-government's discretionary power is evident. This chapter also sought to highlight the importance of interdependence that characterizes a significant part of local self-government action, inherently restricting its discretionary power. On the other hand, this interdependence might potentially operate in the opposite direction, enhancing the influence of local self-government on other governance levels and actors through cooperation and dialogue during the shared exercise of competencies: a topic worthy of further investigation. Finally, some findings indicate that in certain federal and regionalized countries, the discretionary power of municipalities may be constrained by the complexity of the multilevel governance system they develop, with these systems occasionally restricting the autonomy of first-tier governance, i.e. municipalities. However, this finding cannot lead to definitive conclusions, and it would be worthwhile to conduct further research into how a complex and multilevel governance system affects the autonomy of first-tier governance, namely municipalities.

8. Legal regimes and local autonomy: the interaction of administrative supervision and legal protection

INTRODUCTION

The subject of this chapter is the relationship between the legal standing of local authorities and the administrative supervision of their actions. As noted in the LAI 1.0 (Local Autonomy Index), local authorities can often be heard to complain that administrative supervision is so comprehensive and detailed that it undermines their autonomy and efficiency, both in terms of allocative efficiency and the cost-effectiveness of operations. Of course, the need for vertical coordination of public action across levels of government necessitates some restrictions on local autonomy. This is recognized in the European Charter of Local Self-Government (cf. art. 8 and art. 11 especially). Some of the reasons for central-government regulations are reviewed in Chapter 6 of this volume. An overarching issue is how to organize national control and coordination in ways that do not unduly limit local autonomy (Council of Europe 1999). The findings of the LAI 1.0 project suggest that there is no clear-cut or uniform solution to this problem; on the contrary, 'there are considerable inconsistencies' (Ladner et al. 2019: 97) between the legal standing of local government and the modes and intensity of administrative supervision. In most European countries, the overall long-term trend of supervision has been to move away from scrutiny of the *merits* of local-government decisions to reviews of only the *legality* of decisions.

At the same time, and also inspired by the European Charter, a series of measures to ensure the legal protection of local autonomy has been introduced more or less comprehensively in many countries. Such measures may involve constitutional guarantees as well as recourse to legal redress for local authorities in cases of disagreement with the central government.

However, the LAI 1.0 also reported attempts in several countries to introduce scrutiny of merit through 'the back door' in the form of more frequent or detailed supervision or a greater emphasis on budgetary discipline in ways that impinge upon policy directions (Ladner et al. 2019: 190).

This chapter is organized into four parts: first, a discussion on theoretical perspectives on the interaction of legal protection and supervision; second, a brief review of trends among the 57 countries regarding legal protection and modes of supervision; third, an analysis of the cases according to ensuing 'legal regimes'; and, finally, discussions and conclusions.

MEASURING AND MODELLING LEGAL REGIMES

The present analysis focuses on administrative supervision and legal protection of local government. The former is a top-down-driven control mechanism of central government and the latter a bottom-up-driven protective mechanism for local government, both of which may be constructed in manners that contribute to enhancing or reducing local autonomy.

The Council of Europe's latest recommendation on the conduct of administrative supervision (Council of Europe 2019) establishes a clear connection between control and protection:

> [...] under article 11 of the Charter, 'local authorities shall have the right of recourse to a judicial remedy in order to secure free exercise of their powers', which implies the possibility of recourse against improper exercise of supervisory powers. (Council of Europe 2019)

This chapter focuses on the interaction and combinations of legal protection and supervisory approaches and asks whether and how the two dimensions of 'legal regimes' support or thwart each other. Do they pull in the same direction or in opposite directions?

The measurement of the two mechanisms for the sake of the Local Autonomy Index consists of a four-step ladder for each of them: one is a four-step ladder of potential interventions and the other a four-step ladder of potential legal defences of local freedom of decision-making (details of LAI in the Appendix to this book).

The ladder of legal protection varies from 0 to 3, where 0 indicates no legal protection, 1 that local authorities are protected by constitutional clauses or other statutes, 2 that local authorities may additionally challenge administrative decisions of state agencies through the judicial system and 3 that there are other legal means of protection on top of that.

On the ladder of supervision, 0 indicates the most intensive format of supervision – reviews of merits and legality of decisions, 1 that reviews of accounts and spending priorities occur, 2 that supervision is limited to the legality of decisions and 3 that supervision is limited to pointing out possible illegalities without state agents having powers to suspend local decisions.

In theoretical terms, the problem of central-local coordination as seen from the point of view of central government may be stated as that of the principal-agent relationship outlined in agency theory (Jensen and Meckling 1976; Laffant 2003).

In principal-agent terms, the central government is cast as the principal that contracts one or more agents – local authorities – to carry out a task along lines and for remuneration to be agreed upon in a contract. The task may be specified through legislation and directives or agreements between central and local government, or arrived at through other channels. Even legal obligations will normally have been preceded by negotiations and information exchanges between central and local governments. In decentralized welfare states, the central government is dependent upon local authorities for the implementation of a long series of policies vital for the overall functioning of society, but even in countries with a narrower range of local-government tasks, the central government may be presumed to take an interest in how well local government functions.

The problem that plagues principal-agent relationships, according to agency theory, is that of *information asymmetry*: the agents, namely local authorities, have more information about the issues at hand than the principal has. The information problem may be handled a priori or post hoc. The a priori solution in agency theory is the contract, which in central–local relations most often means legislative duties and obligations imposed upon local government, accompanied by more or less adequate funding.

Further down the road, the principal may seek information about the agent's compliance with the contract in various ways. These are in the jargon of agency theory often referred to as *alarms* and *police patrols*. Administrative supervision may be classified as an example of police patrols: regular surveillance of local authorities in terms of their legal obligations and/or other criteria that are applied in the supervisory approach of specific countries. Alarms are also found, e.g. citizen complaints or challenges through the courts, or certain thresholds that may trigger central-government interventions.

Administrative supervision of local-government decisions is a top-down solution to the information problem regarding local-government compliance with national regulations. Supervision may be carried out in a variety of ways, from inspections and mandatory reviews of local-council decisions and budgets to dialogue and guidance (Kiuriene 2020). More or less sophisticated risk-assessment procedures may guide supervision, e.g. assessment of the likelihood of noncompliance in combination with assessment of the seriousness of the consequences of noncompliance. Nowadays, the use of digital technology seems to offer several possibilities to mitigate (if not resolve) the principal-agent information problem in some respects (Greenstone et al. 2022)

Stipulations and procedures for the legal protection of local government are inherently *bottom-up* procedures that can supplement or correct central-government information on the status and quality of local-government operations or serve as a means for renegotiating the 'contract' with the state. Local authorities may for example invoke constitutional clauses that may have been infringed by central-government dispositions, and ensuing court cases may serve to clarify local-government duties and rights in a particular issue area. In other cases, local authorities may disagree with a decision of a supervisory authority and challenge that decision in court.

Court cases may hold advantages for principals too. The inherent transparency problem of principal-agent relations can be overcome through an impartial body: the courts. This is not to say that every disagreement between local and central authorities would be better solved through the courts, but that important court cases might help transparency and mutual understanding. Local government has of course other channels for communicating with central government besides the courts, for example through the channels of access analysed in Chapter 10. These channels are political and therefore dependent upon the goodwill of the government of the day, whereas the procedures of legal protection offer more permanent means of defence in case of controversy with state institutions. The drawback is that legal channels may be rather cumbersome and costly to engage in.

Analysing central–local relations in terms of the principal-agent model is of course complicated by the fact that local authorities serve *two* principals: the local electorate as well as the central government. While responsiveness to the electorate is the basis for the allocative-efficiency mechanism so cherished in fiscal-federalism theory, it may also bring a local authority into conflict with the central-government principal. The dilemma of regulatory frameworks is to find a balance between the demands of the two principals: to further local electoral responsiveness within the rule of law and macroeconomic responsibility.

This chapter argues that reaching the goal of allocative efficiency hinges upon the balance between control and correction, i.e. between supervision and legal protection. Presumably, citizen involvement in supervision may amount to a further corrective mechanism for promoting allocative efficiency.

The analysis in this chapter investigates how the combinations of modes of legal protection and formats of supervision are distributed among the 57 countries to form legal regimes with varying degrees of local autonomy. Of particular interest is the question of to what extent the various combinations form mutually reinforcing or contradictory regulatory settings.

Table 8.1 suggests possible combinations of administrative supervision and legal protection. The upper right-hand corner is the one that offers local government the greatest degree of autonomy and may be likened to 'contracts' in the parlance of agency theory. The agent has the freedom to operate under the

Table 8.1 *Legal regimes: combinations of supervisory approach and legal protection*

		Supervisory approach (to local decisions)	
		Discretionary (Merits +)	*Limited* (Legality only -)
Legal protection (of local discretion)	*Strong* (through constitution and courts)	**Precarious autonomy 1** + -	**'Contractual'** + +
	Weak (neither option)	**Top-down governance** - -	**Precarious autonomy 2** - +

'police patrolling' of limited state supervision and at the same time recourse to legal procedures in case of disagreements. The state may, of course, install further means of control of the alarm-clock variety, but this would be not only a sign of distrust and bad faith but also an intensification of supervision that would move the legal regime into one of the other cells. Such developments are not uncommon (see below under 'cases'). The contrast to 'contracts' is 'top-down governance', which is characterized by weak legal protection and discretionary supervision and a focus on the merits of local decisions.

TRENDS

The development of legal protection and administrative supervision over time is presented in Figure 8.1. The scores are transformed to a standardized scale of 0–100. Zero (0) represents the lowest level of local autonomy and 100 the highest level. Regarding administrative supervision, a high score indicates an unobtrusive mode of supervision, i.e. limited to reviews of the legality of local-government decisions or less (cf. level 3 on the ladder indicated above).

Figure 8.1 shows a gradual augmentation of autonomy in both dimensions. The growth is most noticeable regarding legal protection (from 67 to 75 points) while supervision scores have changed from 53 to 60 points. The latter change

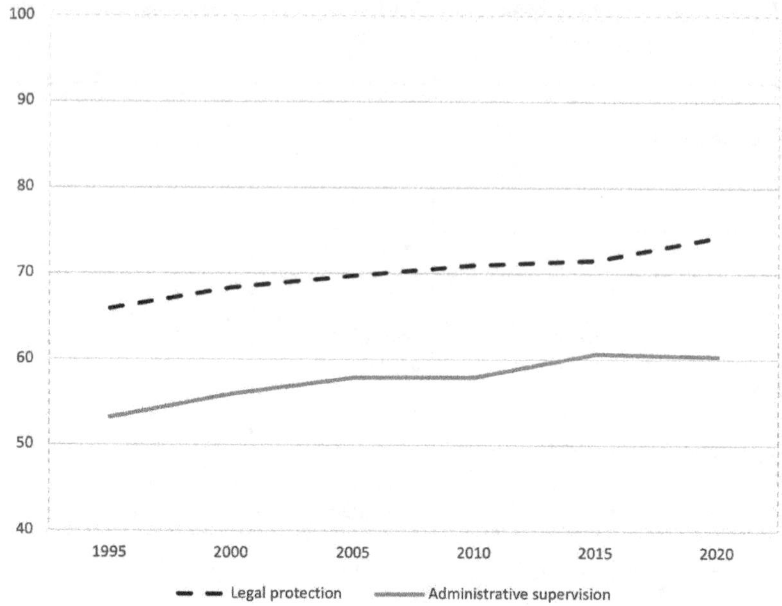

Source: Authors' own.

Figure 8.1 *Development of legal protection and administrative supervision (1995–2020, 57 countries, standardized scores)*

involves a slight decrease in freedom from 2015 to 2020. A divergence of the two curves over the last five years is also apparent, with supervision on a slightly downward trend while legal protection points more steeply upwards. In other words, supervision is becoming marginally more intense, while legal protection provides more opportunities for local government to defend local decisions through legal means, including more ways to challenge supervisory agencies.

How the two curves relate to each other country by country is shown in Figure 8.2.

Figure 8.2 shows the distribution of countries according to 'legal regimes', i.e. the simultaneous scores on indicators of supervision and legal protection. The countries can be further located by using the mid-point (50) of the scale of 0–100 as cut-off points on both axes. It appears then that there is a slight tendency for the countries to gravitate towards the upper right-hand corner of the figure. This means that a good number of countries are approaching a situation denoted 'contractual' in Figure 8.1. Spain, Estonia, South Africa

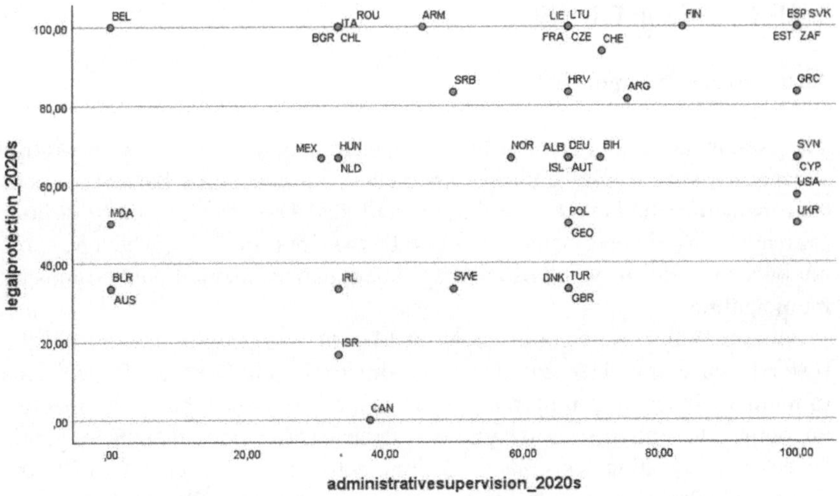

Source: Authors' own.

Figure 8.2 The legal regimes of local government by country (2020)

and Greece do so most conspicuously. There are altogether 22 cases in the 'contractual' corner, nearly 40 per cent of cases. Moldova, Australia, Belarus, Canada and Ireland are found in the opposite corner, that of 'top-down' governance or weakly developed legal constraints on national governance of local government. There are also a good number of countries in the corners denoted 'precarious autonomy'. In precarious autonomy 1 are Russia, Italy and Chile for example. In precarious 2, Denmark, Turkey and the United Kingdom are the most clear-cut cases.

In other words, less than half of the cases have regulatory frameworks that in legal terms can be said to be conducive to the overarching goal of allocative efficiency. Other goals of the national principals seem to take precedence over or are corrections on the local responsiveness of authorities, at least potentially. How the balance works in practice is investigated through the scrutiny of two cases below: Greece and Norway. Greece is a clear-cut case of the upper right-hand 'contractual' corner while Norway is a rather 'fuzzy' case near the middle of the figure.

THE CASE OF GREECE

Administrative Supervision

The oversight of municipalities in Greece encompasses, firstly, administrative supervision with legality control (expediency assessment has been abolished) over the actions and omissions of municipalities. The second primary form of oversight is fiscal supervision, exercised by the Court of Audit, which pertains not only to the legality but also to the prudent management of public funds by municipalities.

Administrative oversight is carried out by the Secretary of each one of the seven deconcentrated territorial state administrations in Greece. The decisions of municipalities have full force as soon as they are issued, but municipalities are obliged to send their most significant decisions (local regulations for public spaces, expropriation decisions, etc.) along with relevant documentation to the Secretary, who has the authority to annul them if deemed illegal. In addition to these acts, the Secretary can independently annul any other municipal act that he/she considers illegal, as well as any act that is challenged through an administrative appeal by citizens or legal entities. The Secretary's decision is not necessarily final, as the party affected by the Secretary's decision can subsequently file an appeal to a special committee, asking for the annulment of the Secretary's unfavourable decision. The Secretary's initial decision is suspended as long as the final decision of the special committee is pending. In the meantime, the initial decision of the municipality is still valid and can be implemented. Only a court can order the temporary suspension of a municipal decision. In practice, supervision authorities often refrain from annulling municipal decisions if there is no obvious, unquestionable violation of the law (Hlepas 2020).

Specifically, regarding the financial management of municipalities in Greece, the key institution for financial oversight is the Court of Audit, which, until 2017, even conducted preventive audits on the legality of all municipal expenses surpassing certain audit thresholds. Therefore, Greece scored 2.00 on this indicator. Since 2018, however, the Court of Audit has examined municipal expenses randomly and only *ex post*. Following this restriction of formal supervision, the overall score of administrative supervision has increased to 3.00 since 2019.

This restriction of formal fiscal supervision was also due to the establishment of a specialized body called the 'Observatory of Fiscal Autonomy' during the crisis in 2012. This observatory was given real-time access to all financial transactions of municipalities and is providing relevant technical and accounting support to all municipalities. The Observatory proved to be a very efficient mechanism of fiscal oversight, even though it lacked the formal powers that the traditional mechanism of the Court of Audit had. It offered a solution to the information problem of central state authorities as principals of local authorities. In addition, platforms that were created in compliance with European law, such as platforms and registers for public contracts according to the 2014/24/EU Directive on Public Procurement, have also mitigated the information problem that the state has been trying to address through stricter supervision.

Legal Protection

As legal entities of public law, municipalities have legal standing in all courts. Greece has a fully developed system of administrative justice with administrative courts of first instance, administrative courts of appeal and the Council of State. Local authorities have recourse to the judicial system to settle disputes with higher authorities, mainly through administrative courts.

Constitutional protection is provided, especially by article 102 of the Constitution. In Greece, there is no special constitutional court. However, the question of constitutionality can be raised at any court (dispersed control of constitutionality, article 93 of the Constitution). In case there are contradicting decisions of the highest courts (civil, administrative, fiscal courts) on the constitutionality of a certain norm, the Special Highest Court will resolve the question of constitutionality (article 100 of the Constitution). This court is unique in that it not only declares that a law cannot be applied because it violates the Constitution but can also declare ineffective an unconstitutional law that ceases to be in force. Therefore, a constitutionality check is possible and effective in Greece, although no constitutional court exists, and disputes between local authorities and higher authorities can be settled by courts who review the question of constitutionality ad hoc. Therefore, the overall score on legal protection is 2.5.

Municipalities are quite frequent parties in lawsuits in Greece. The relevant jurisprudence of the courts is generally restrained, and often seems to acknowledge that Parliament has a significant margin of discretion when deciding on the organization and operation of local authorities. However, in some cases, the courts have recognized the unconstitutionality of laws, as requested by local self-government. Moreover, many acts of supervisory authorities have ultimately been annulled by the courts.

THE CASE OF NORWAY

Administrative Supervision

Administrative supervision of municipalities is carried out through the offices of county governors, who are the heads of state district administrations. Formally, since 2001 supervision has been aimed at controlling only the legality of municipal decisions and service provision, but in practice supervision has become extremely detailed and extensive over the last decade. Researchers have argued that the concept of legality has been stretched through certain formulas in legal texts such as 'municipal duty to provide adequate/appropriate/ proper …etc. services', which leave local services to be judged in the light of the evolving norms of professionals (Askim et al. 2013).

Financial supervision of local government is not only a matter of scrutinizing the budgets of individual municipalities to ascertain whether budgetary dispositions are within the law. Monitoring of accounts takes place through a mandatory reporting system (KOSTRA) that makes municipal financial results publicly available and thus facilitates comparison and benchmarking across municipalities. The system is digitally available through the website of the Norwegian Statistical Service.

The new Local Government Act of 2018 included some general guidelines for the relationship between central and local government that could potentially lead to greater reticence in state agencies' supervision of local government and review of citizen complaints, i.e. the principles of subsidiarity, proportionality and financial compensation for new obligations imposed on local government. These guidelines were already acknowledged in existing government directives on central–local relations without having the status of law (Stokstad and Bock Segaard 2013). Whether turning these guidelines into law will make any difference to actual, legislative or administrative practices remains to be seen.

Based on the formal status of supervision, a score of 2 could have been justified. However, the increasing intensity of supervision and the density of regulatory decrees in recent years suggested a somewhat reduced score of 1.75.

Citizen scrutiny is not a topic covered by the scoring system. It should be mentioned, however, that modes of citizen scrutiny are widespread, for example through public hearings, user panels for specific services, citizen surveys or citizens' hours before localcouncil meetings. Ninety-five per cent of municipalities reported that they held regular hearings on municipal zoning plans (such meetings are legally mandatory), 71 per cent conduct user surveys on a regular basis and 33 per cent have instituted citizens' hour (KMDs Organisasjonsdatabase 2021). The Local Government Act also has provisions for citizen initiatives, but this is an opportunity that citizens rarely make use of.

Legal Protection

Norway scored 0 on this indicator until 2015 because there were no constitutional clauses on local government and no access for local government to adjudication or arbitration by independent bodies in cases of disputes about interpretations of legal texts regarding municipal duties. A constitutional clause on local government was adopted in 2016; the formulation is brief, vague and general;[1] whether it will have any real impact on central–local relations is uncertain; nevertheless, the clause is now there, and augments the score from 0 to 1 on the legal protection indicator.

Furthermore, the Local Government Act of 2018 recognized the right of local authorities to request adjudication in cases of disagreement with national authorities (*partsrettigheter*). Such cases arise in particular as a result of complaints from citizens over municipal decisions in their disfavour; the reviewing authority can review not only the legality of the municipal decision but also the exercise of discretion. Seen in connection with new regulations in the Act on Conflict Resolution (*tvistelova*) the new right to adjudication enables municipalities to bring such cases before the civil courts and may thus result in their having a stronger hand in processes against state agencies. The new right raises the score by another 1 point. From 2019, the overall score on legal protection was 2.

It should be noted that Norway has no constitutional court; accordingly, there is no opportunity for local authorities to bring cases before a constitutional court. Consequently, there is no score to be obtained for Norway on this item. In Norway, issues of constitutionality are reviewed by the Supreme Court. So far, however, no cases of this nature have been brought before the Supreme Court by municipalities.

A comparison of the two cases indicates, first, the complexities of the legal relations between central and local government in both cases. A web of supervisory institutions exists to enforce the seemingly simple rule of 'supervision only according to legality'. Second, there is a striking contrast in the density of modes of legal protection of local government. Institutions of legal protection are more highly developed in Greece than in Norway, where real legal protection has been introduced only in the last few years, with uncertain effects. This

[1] Section 49 of the Norwegian Constitution, second part, now states that citizens have the right to govern local affairs through locally elected bodies, and that detailed rules in this regard will be enacted through ordinary laws.

contrast is probably a reflection of different administrative traditions, Greece having been more strongly influenced by the legalistic Franco or Napoleonic tradition than Norway. Consequently, Greek local government enjoys more comprehensive legal protection than its Norwegian counterpart.

On the other hand, new systems introduced to mitigate the information problem of principals concerning municipal finance are more comprehensive in Norway. The mandatory reporting system (KOSTRA) is aimed at resolving (or at least mitigating) the information problem of both the state and the electorate/taxpayers as the two principals of local self-government. In this way, both allocative efficiency/local responsiveness and the rule of law/macroeconomic stability are promoted at the same time, through an open and comprehensive system of transparency and accountability. In contrast, the Greek system of the fiscal observatory is one-sided and exclusive, aimed only at resolving the information problem of the state government as principal, while completely bypassing the need of the second principal, namely the electorate/taxpayers, to resolve its information problem. The exclusion of transparency and accountability towards the citizenry as principal, appears, at first glance, understandable, under the particular circumstances of unprecedented economic and political turbulence in Greece during the financial crisis. At the same time, however, the influence of deeper and long-lasting features of a competitive political culture, weak social capital and an opaque public administration should not be underestimated (Hlepas 2020).

Higher Greek scores in autonomy regarding administrative supervision may reflect that Greek local government is less important than its Norwegian counterpart, for public finance and the Greek health and welfare systems. The Greek state has regulatory, planning and taxation monopolies that offer a wider range of leverage mechanisms. Since compromises are particularly difficult within the frame of the prevailing political culture, the courts are often called to resolve relevant conflicts. Litigation between different public entities is not rare, and relevant judicial systems are quite extensive.

CONCLUSIONS

The central argument of the chapter is that features of the legal regimes for the protection and supervision of local government are decisive for the realization of the goal of allocative efficiency. Legal regimes have been analysed with concepts from the principal-agent model in which administrative supervision serves to provide information for the principal – the central government to check on the fulfilment of obligations, while modes of legal protection, e.g. access to courts, serve as means of correction and renegotiation of contracts for the agents. For the 57 countries overall, the long-term development of legal regimes has been towards higher levels of autonomy. A slight reversal of the trend can be observed regarding administrative supervision from around 2015, a trend that could be related to the preceding economic crisis or even to authoritarian tendencies in several countries. Among individual countries, the level of legal autonomy varied considerably, from scores close to 0 to scores close to 100.

Combining the two dimensions yields a fourfold table where one of the corners represents the most purely 'contractual' relationships and is expected to be best suited for fulfilling the goal of allocative efficiency. Less than 40 per cent of cases were found to suit these specifications. The cases of conspicuous top-down governance were far fewer, though. Most of the remaining countries were in the groups termed 'precarious autonomy', which means either low levels of legal protection or modes of supervision beyond scrutiny of legality.

In other words, in the majority of cases, the legal preconditions for fulfilling the goal of allocative efficiency are weak or lacking.

There are, however, also trends that point in a more optimistic direction. First, in the field of legal protection of local self-government there is a slow but visible and continuous trend towards more local autonomy. Second, the information problem of principals can sometimes be mitigated or even resolved using modern technology (platforms, open data, etc.). The Norwegian example of the KOSTRA reporting system has shown that some innovative systems can resolve the information problem of principals in both directions, namely both for the state and for the local electorate. In this way, the need for traditional administrative supervision may be reduced.

Finally, we must point out that the latest version of the Council of Europe's recommendations on good supervisory practices appears to be moving beyond a purely legalistic perspective on central-government control. The latest recommendations also encourage member states to introduce *advisory* approaches and to facilitate *citizen scrutiny* as tools of supervision (Council of Europe 2019). It has not been possible within the existing framework of the LAI to cover such innovations in supervisory practices, but these will undoubtedly be important areas of investigation for the next round of the LAI.

9. Regional and local autonomy: comparing measurements of decentralization

INTRODUCTION

The vast majority of countries worldwide have a local level of government, although territorial frameworks vary significantly between geographical areas and even within them (e.g. UCLG 2008). It is also common for countries to have intermediate levels between the central and local levels, with regionalization being a significant development in democracies in recent decades (Hooghe et al. 2010). Western states have implemented decentralization reforms since the 1980s to delegate more political, administrative and fiscal responsibilities to subnational governments. In 1985, the Council of Europe adopted the European Charter of Local Self-Government to promote decentralization as the standard for territorial administration. Similarly, influential multilateral institutions such as the United Nations, the International Monetary Fund, the World Bank and the Organisation for Economic Co-operation and Development (OECD) have encouraged decentralization reforms to devolve responsibilities to levels of government closer to citizens, in order to increase the accountability of local authorities, improve policy-provision efficiency or balance central powers. Along with the normative claims, these organizations have also developed their own instruments for observing, monitoring and adjusting decentralized systems. Decentralization can indeed be either a promoted process of change or a concept used to analyse the actual organization of countries, and is variously associated with regional and local autonomy (Ladner and Keuffer 2023).

This chapter delves into the territorial organization of countries across various levels of government, exploring the distribution of power among them. It aims to answer the following questions: 1. What developments have occurred in regional and local decentralization over the past three decades? 2. How is autonomy allocated across different levels, and how can we compare multilevel systems with varying degrees of autonomy? 3. Which countries have led the implementation of decentralization or centralization reforms, and at which governmental tier? To answer these questions, the chapter begins by describing key concepts in the field of decentralization and how they have been measured in the literature. It subsequently employs fiscal-decentralization data, the Regional Authority Index (RAI) and the Local Autonomy Index (LAI) to empirically portray the situation and draw conclusions on issues related to intergovernmental relations.

CONCEPTUALIZING AND MEASURING DECENTRALIZATION, REGIONAL AUTHORITY AND LOCAL AUTONOMY

Decentralization of Countries Evidenced by Fiscal Data

Given its widespread and systemic nature, decentralization has been the subject of extensive debate and academic scrutiny. Scholars specializing in federalism were among the first to develop measures for comparing political systems based on the power vested in regional governments (e.g. Fesler 1965). However, this endeavour was not without conceptual confusion between decentralization and federalism (Elazar 1976). Federalism, on the one hand, emphasizes the constitutional choice between a unitary system, where the central government holds supreme authority and can establish or dissolve subnational units, and a federalist system, where governmental power and responsibilities are divided between the central and federal governments. Decentralization, on the other hand, assumes the presence of a central authority and situates the dispersion of power along a heuristic continuum between centralization and decentralization. Consequently, some federalist countries exhibit significantly higher levels of decentralization than others and, similarly, certain unitary countries are more centralized than others, while some are highly decentralized – sometimes even more so than federalist countries (Anderson 2008).

The concept of decentralization is broader than the distinction between federal and unitary states. Another aspect to consider is which state activities among decision-making, executing and financing are decentralized. When financing and decision-making remain at the national level while the lower level merely executes, decentralization is administrative and is referred to as executive federalism. On the other hand, political decentralization refers to situations where decision-making, executing and financing are all in the hands of subnational government. The literature commonly uses the term 'deconcentration' to describe situations where the national government is present throughout the country and carries out its tasks through its own administration, which may not necessarily be located in the capital. Conversely, 'devolution' is used when tasks are in the hands of decentralized governments (e.g. Kuhlmann and Wollmann 2019).

To measure decentralization, scholars of fiscal decentralization have either quantified the decentralization of specific activities (political, administrative or fiscal decentralization) or comprehensively classified decentralization, by collecting data on the proportion of subnational expenditures, revenues and tax-raising powers (Oates 1972). Since the 1990s numerous classification endeavours have been undertaken to assess countries' degree of decentralization, fiscal autonomy and intergovernmental relations, relying on economic databases created by the abovementioned international organizations (Wolman 2008). The most widely used indicators in fiscal decentralization that describe the significance of subnational governments in public-policy implementation are the share of subcentral-government direct expenditures in total expenditures and the share of subcentral-government revenues in total revenues (Blöchliger 2013). However, these indicators do not capture other dimensions of decentralization, such as the extent to which subnational governments have a say in how funds are spent and how relevant tasks are executed (Ladner et al. 2016).

Authority of Regions within a Country Assessed with the RAI

Studies on federalism and regionalization examine the allocation of authority between local and national levels. Federalism involves combining a central (federal) government with regional (federalist) governments within a single political system, dividing power between them. This arrangement entails decentralization and has historically been implemented to address diversity or prevent the concentration of power in the hands of a single government. By creating socially more homogeneous units that can control each other, federalism helps maintain a balance of power in a political system that includes diversity. The national building process significantly influences how competencies are distributed across different layers of the state. When central power introduces federalism and the competencies of the federalist units result from a bargaining process, residual power is likely to remain with the nation-state. Conversely, when nation-states are creatures of federalist entities, residual powers may be retained by lower levels of government (Watts 2003). In the 1990s there was increasing interest in studying regionalization as a result of the growing establishment of regional structures. These intermediate entities, not necessarily federal, are involved in the implementation of policies, applying the principle of subsidiarity, and have greater access to funding (Loughlin et al. 2012). This trend was influenced by the European Union's regional policies and a response from central governments to national movements. It was during this period that Sharpe (1993) referred to 'the rise of the meso tier'.

Hooghe et al. (2016) have investigated variations among regional authority across states, defined as the capacity to make legitimate and binding decisions for a community. In the RAI that resulted from their research, they differentiate between elements concerning the extent to which a regional unit has authority over those who live in its territory – self-rule – and the influence of regional units on shaping national decision-making – shared-rule. The most recent update of the RAI measures regional governance in 96 countries from 1950 through 2018, covering metropolitan and indigenous regions alongside conventional regions.

Autonomy of Local Governments Measured with the LAI

Local autonomy and decentralization have often been treated as closely related concepts. It is widely expected that local autonomy gives positive value to decentralization, but the nature of their relationship varies depending on the approach taken towards decentralization (Fleurke and Willemse 2004). When decentralization is viewed as a dynamic process, reforms are aimed at enhancing local autonomy, while also improving efficiency and democratizing the policy-making process. When decentralization is viewed as a static state, the degree of decentralization becomes a characteristic of the politico-administrative system and implies varying degrees of autonomy enjoyed by the local government. As we saw in Chapter 1, local autonomy has traditionally been apprehended as a relative concept that reflects the degree of freedom of local governments from higher levels of government, without consensus in the literature on how to define it. Drawing on insights from various disciplines and approaches, Ladner et al. (2019) proposed a theory-based concept of local autonomy that encompasses dimensions related to both the right of local autonomy to resist constraints from higher levels of government and the ability to pursue local interests.

As for the measurement of local autonomy, studies have developed categorical measures to compare local autonomy or local-government systems between countries. Page and Goldsmith's seminal research (1987a, 1987b) examines the limits imposed on local governments by higher levels of government from the perspective of intergovernmental relations under three headings: the range of functions, the discretion to perform these functions and access to higher levels of government. Integrating elements related to the substantial abilities of local government, Sellers and Lidström's (2007) conceptualization covers supervision of local actions and considers the importance of grants, tax autonomy and supervision, and local capacities, measured through two fiscal and three politico-administrative indicators. In these examples, however, variation in subnational government has been conceived as variation in types of nation-states. The categories are too crude to guide comparison among levels of government within and beyond states. To go beyond categorical measures, a more recent wave of research has conceptualized numerical measures based on a battery of indicators that respect the multi-dimensionality of power allocation across different political levels (Keuffer and Ladner 2021).

Among the plethora of indexes that have been created, two measures are recognized as having the most robust and comprehensive design (Harguindéguy et al. 2021): the RAI, described above, and the LAI, which measures the autonomy enjoyed by local governments through seven dimensions (see Chapter 1). In this chapter, we rely on fiscaldecentralization data, the RAI and LAI to empirically portray and compare the territorial organization of countries.

TRENDS IN FISCAL DECENTRALIZATION, REGIONAL AUTHORITY AND LOCAL AUTONOMY

In addition to their synchronic dimension, fiscal-decentralization data (expenditures and revenues), the RAI and the LAI make it possible to visualize developments in decentralization, regional authority and local autonomy over the years. Figure 9.1 compares trends over 30 years (five-year means, 1990–2020) for the 30 common countries covered by the four indicators. Each indicator and index has its own scale and cannot be compared in terms of level of autonomy. But what the figure clearly shows is an overall increase in decentralization, although not at the same rate in each index nor at the same time. The OECD's fiscal-decentralization data are quite stable over the period covered, particularly the indicator of revenue decentralization between central and subnational governments. The distribution of expenditures, on the other hand, has changed, with an increase between 1995 and 2005, followed by a decrease at the time of the economic and financial crisis of 2007–08. Both indicators, calculated as a percentage, show that subnational expenditures are more than 10 per cent higher than revenues.

If we focus more specifically on a particular lower level of government, we can see that regional authority was strengthened between 1990 and 2020, with the RAI showing a 21 per cent global increase. This occurred particularly between 1995 and 2005, influenced, in Europe, by cohesion policies and European Union enlargements. Local autonomy has also grown over the whole period covered, with the LAI showing a less intense 7 per cent increase between the 1990–94 mean and the 2015–20 mean. However, the increase occurred particularly before the 2000s and the decrease of the overall index occurring in the years following 2009 mainly in financial aspects can be seen as a consequence of the financial crisis. Standard deviations (SD) of RAI and LAI decrease, which shows respective convergence. A closer analysis of the data shows, however, that the situation is more mixed and heterogeneous.

Multilevel Arrangements: Variation in Decentralization Patterns

From a static perspective, an intriguing analysis is to compare the indices over similar periods, with five-year averages providing more robust results. Table

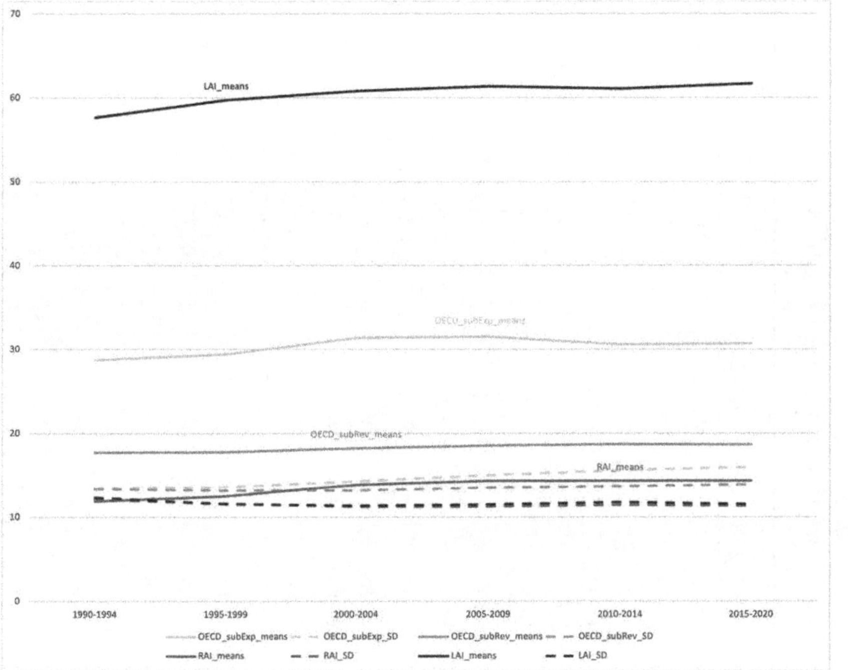

Note: N=30 over the whole timespan; for the counties that were not independent at some point in time, the first year of observation is considered. *Sources:* OECD Fiscal Decentralisation Database 2023 (https://www.oecd.org/tax/federalism/), RAI Country annual scores (2018, https://garymarks.web.unc.edu/data/regional-authority-2/), LAI, own calculations.

Figure 9.1 *Comparison of fiscal decentralization (subnational expenditures and revenues), RAI and LAI trends, means and standard deviations (five-year means, 1990–2020)*

9.1 presents country-wise results for two fiscal-decentralization ratios (subnational expenditures and revenues), the RAI, the LAI and the RAI+LAI spanning the beginning and the end of the reviewed period. OECD data underscore significant diversity, where subnational government in Canada, Denmark and Switzerland accounts for over half of total public expenditures, in stark contrast to Greece and Ireland, where the figure is less than 10 per cent. This pattern reinforces the substantial distinction between the share of expenditures and revenues, with the latter consistently smaller (averaging 20 per cent compared to 31 per cent). Notably, federalist countries like Australia, Germany, the USA, Switzerland and Canada exhibit a relatively minor difference, while

Table 9.1 *Decentralized countries as various patterns of multilevel arrangements (2015–2020 mean)*

Countries	OECD_Sub_Exp (2015–2020)	OECD_Sub_Rev (2015–2020)	RAI (2015–2020)	LAI (2015–2020)	RAI+LAI (2015–2020)
Germany	40.09	36.75	85.89	66.11	152.00
Spain	43.57	27.89	81.02	66.53	147.56
Belgium	45.22	23.39	78.22	61.44	139.66
Switzerland	56.92	48.34	60.42	76.98	137.40
USA	47.54	43.12	67.52	67.11	134.63
Bosnia and Herzegovina	-	-	82.85	51.75	134.60
France	19.35	16.23	49.88	75.63	125.51
Italy	27.52	14.32	59.41	62.36	121.76
Austria	31.49	10.26	52.44	61.78	114.22
Argentina	-	-	54.15	59.62	113.77
Canada	66.20	55.57	63.84	45.35	109.19
Sweden	49.70	32.49	27.36	76.19	103.55
Japan	-	-	41.02	61.99	103.00
Finland	39.82	28.69	16.17	85.73	101.90
Colombia	-	-	32.99	67.72	100.71
Netherlands	30.50	8.71	39.90	59.95	99.85
Norway	33.31	16.59	27.60	69.18	96.79
Mexico	39.64	17.83	48.55	44.39	92.93
Denmark	63.56	27.29	16.74	75.59	92.33

Countries	OECD_Sub_Exp (2015–2020)	OECD_Sub_Rev (2015–2020)	RAI (2015–2020)	LAI (2015–2020)	RAI+LAI (2015–2020)
Portugal	12.84	10.33	21.71	68.37	90.08
Poland	31.94	16.20	25.81	61.94	87.76
Russian Federation	-	-	49.26	37.87	87.13
Slovakia	17.09	4.75	20.16	65.93	86.10
Czech Republic	27.51	18.98	28.09	56.79	84.88
Greece	6.96	2.97	20.52	60.52	81.04
Serbia	-	-	16.96	63.84	80.80
Iceland	29.34	25.38	0.00	76.21	76.21
Romania	-	-	23.01	51.41	74.43
Croatia	-	-	21.78	50.44	72.22
United Kingdom	22.97	8.62	20.90	49.71	70.62
Ireland	8.31	3.90	25.08	43.12	68.20
Lithuania	23.10	3.28	4.56	62.03	66.59
Ukraine	-	-	16.09	48.75	64.84
Bulgaria	-	-	4.56	59.66	64.22
Turkey	-	-	19.96	44.15	64.12
North Macedonia	-	-	18.55	54.02	63.74
Hungary	13.42	8.10	9.70	45.19	63.72
Estonia	23.86	4.33	0.00	62.75	62.75
Latvia	27.26	19.04	9.12	51.91	61.03
Slovenia	18.37	11.59	7.36	53.20	60.56

Countries	OECD_Sub_Exp (2015–2020)	OECD_Sub_Rev (2015–2020)	RAI (2015–2020)	LAI (2015–2020)	RAI+LAI (2015–2020)
Luxembourg	10.62	5.64	0.00	59.04	59.04
Montenegro	-	-	0.00	58.60	58.60
Albania	-	-	4.56	53.68	58.24
Chile	-	-	11.97	45.58	57.55
Kosovo	-	-	4.56	46.70	43.57
Israel	12.66	8.72	2.28	39.01	42.97
Cyprus	-	-	0.00	40.69	40.30
Malta	-	-	-	40.30	-
Liechtenstein	-	-	-	70.69	-
South Africa	-	-	-	66.86	-
Andorra	-	-	-	59.36	-
Georgia	-	-	-	56.53	-
Australia	44.16	45.22	–	50.32	-
Republic of Korea	-	-	-	48.74	-
Armenia	-	-	-	44.50	-
Belarus	-	-	-	38.49	-
Moldova	-	-	-	35.85	-
N	31	31	47	57	47

Notes: OECD data are subnational expenditures and revenues as a percentage of general expenditures and revenues; RAI data (1990–2018) have been multiplied by 2.2 (1990–1994) and 2.8 (2015–2020) to be comparable with LAI; LAI data are the Index D7w. Ordered by RAI+LAI.
Source: See Figure 9.1.

some unitary nations display a significant gap, suggesting the implementation of deconcentration schemes or the prominence of downward transfers.

If we focus on the proportion of subnational expenditures – the most commonly employed fiscal-decentralization data – countries with the highest percentages (2015–20 mean) are mainly federalist countries (Canada, Switzerland, USA, Belgium) but also unitary Nordic countries (Denmark, Sweden, Finland). This observation substantiates the idea that certain unitary countries can surpass specific federalist counterparts in terms of fiscal decentralization. It also raises questions about the distribution of autonomy among different subnational-government levels and how the indices capture various facets of decentralization.

To address these questions, we can turn to analyses of correlation between the measures. In the first volume, the LAI and RAI were slightly positively correlated but there were 30 countries covered in common (Ladner et al. 2019). Here, based on scores for 47 countries, the results reveal that the RAI is not significantly correlated with the LAI, underscoring distinct dynamics in regional and local decentralization. This implies that RAI values are higher than LAI values in some countries and vice versa in others, or stated differently, that one subnational layer can be decentralized while the other remains less so. Of the top seven countries based on the RAI (2015–20 mean), namely Germany, Bosnia and Herzegovina, Spain, Belgium, the USA, Canada and Switzerland, only Switzerland is among the top seven countries with the highest LAI scores (2015–20 mean), together with Finland, Iceland, Sweden, France, Denmark and Liechtenstein (see Table 9.1).

Moreover, the RAI exhibits significant correlations with OECD measures for subnational level (Pearson corr. = .543, sig. = 0.002, with the shares of expenditures and Pearson corr. = .585, sig. = 0.001, with shares of revenues, N=31), whereas LAI does not. However, when exclusively considering the local level of the OECD Fiscal Decentralization Database, also available on the website, the LAI is positively correlated (Pearson corr. = .558, sig. = 0.001, with the shares of expenditures and Pearson corr. = .589, sig. = 0.001, with shares of revenues, N=30). Notably, LAI dimensions such as policy scope, political discretion and organizational autonomy are significantly correlated (financial autonomy only with local shares of revenues). This underscores that the LAI and its seven dimensions extend beyond the conventional measures of local-government spending or the amount of local tax collected by the local authorities.

More generally, these results suggest, on the one hand, that OECD data on expenditures and revenues are already taken into account in the RAI and LAI, with subnational shares being especially related to the RAI. As the authors of the fiscal-decentralization ratios stress, the use of the RAI and the LAI complements the assessment of genuine decentralization and power sharing, as fiscal-decentralization data provide only limited insights into a subcentral government's power, autonomy or discretion over fiscal resources and the functioning of intergovernmental fiscal and budgetary institutions (OECD and KIPF 2016). On the other hand, analyses of subnational measures demonstrate that regional authority and local autonomy operate independently, with one not determining the other. Consequently, the most decentralized countries, considering a multi-dimensional approach, are those that combine a high level of regional authority with a high level of local autonomy, such as Germany, Spain, Belgium, Switzerland and the USA (Table 9.1, RAI+LAI column). To better illustrate the various combinations of regional and local autonomy, the unifying quartiles of the RAI and LAI are presented in Table 9.2. At one extreme (high RAI/high LAI) we find decentralized federalist countries, such as Germany, Spain, Switzerland and the USA. At the other extreme (low RAI/low LAI) are rather centralized, unitary countries situated on different continents, such as Latvia, Chile, Israel and Cyprus.

Table 9.2 Different combinations of regional and local autonomy

-	LAI – high	LAI – medium	LAI – low
RAI – high	Germany, Spain, Switzerland, USA, France	Belgium, Italy, Austria, Argentina, Japan, Netherlands	Bosnia and Herzegovina, Canada, Mexico, Russian Federation
RAI – medium	Colombia, Sweden, Norway, Denmark, Portugal, Slovakia, Serbia	Poland, Czech Republic, Greece, North Macedonia	Romania, Croatia, UK, Ireland, Turkey
RAI – low	Finland, Iceland, Estonia	Lithuania, Bulgaria, Luxembourg, Slovenia, Montenegro, Albania	Ukraine, Latvia, Chile, Hungary, Kosovo, Israel, Cyprus

Note: Low, medium, high for RAI and LAI quartiles (2015–2020 means).

DECENTRALIZATION AND CENTRALIZATION REFORMS AT DIFFERENT LEVELS OF GOVERNMENT

The third question to be addressed is identifying countries that have implemented decentralization or centralization reforms and at which level of government. To tackle it, we have not analysed in detail the reforms launched each year in each specific country, as done elsewhere in this book (see Chapter 13).

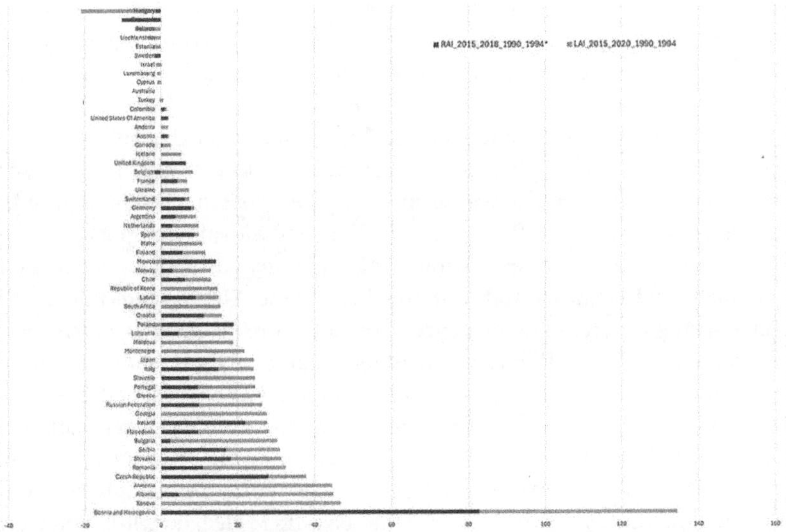

Notes: Dark: Difference between RAI 2015–2020 and 1990–1994; Light: Difference between LAI 2015–2020 and 1990–1994; N=57 (for 10 countries, no data for the RAI). For some countries where no data for the 1990–1994 mean was available, the first available has been taken into consideration; RAI data (1990–2018) have been multiplied by 2.2 (1990–1994) and 2.8 (2015–2020) to be comparable with LAI, LAI data are the Index D7w, ordered by the sum of the two measures.
Source: See Figure 9.1.

Figure 9.2 *Differences between 2020–2015 and 1990–1994 means in the RAI and LAI*

Instead, we have compared the RAI and LAI scores, respectively, between the first and last five-year means over the assessed period, for the 57 countries included in the LAI 2.0 project (Figure 9.2). For the ten countries lacking RAI data, the results indicate only whether the country has initiated decentralization reforms at the local level or centralized certain responsibilities of local government.

In line with the aforementioned trends from a dynamic perspective, the majority of countries have undergone decentralization reforms. This is evident when examining the evolution of the RAI alongside that of the LAI. The countries that have devolved the most power, decision-making responsibilities and financial resources to their subnational levels over this period are, undoubtedly, the countries of Eastern Europe, such as Bosnia and Herzegovina, Albania, the Czech Republic, Romania, Slovakia, Bulgaria and North Macedonia, especially in the 1990s when these countries implemented their decentralization processes together with their democratic transitions. Conversely, some countries have generally experienced a transfer of autonomy from subnational levels to the central government, namely Hungary, Denmark, Belarus, Liechtenstein, Estonia, Sweden, Israel, Luxembourg and Cyprus.

As elucidated in the preceding section, the decentralization landscape becomes more nuanced when scrutinizing the specific levels affected. In Bosnia and Herzegovina, the Czech Republic and Slovakia, regional authority has predominantly increased, while local autonomy has witnessed a decrease, particularly in Bosnia and Herzegovina. In contrast, Albania and Bulgaria have seen a primary increase in the degree of local autonomy. Few countries reveal a decrease in the RAI: Belgium, where local autonomy has increased, Sweden and Denmark, where local-government mergers have weakened the significance of the regional level, and Hungary – the sole country experiencing centralization of both subregional levels, notably following the reforms instituted by Prime Minister Orban's government. Among the diverse countries witnessing a decline in local autonomy over the past three decades, it is noteworthy that only Poland and Mexico have simultaneously pursued regionalization.

CONCLUSION

Multilevel governance recognizes the significance of subnational entities, such as regional and local governments, in the shaping and implementation of policy processes. The concept of multilevel governance involves complex interactions and interdependencies among various levels of government. Vertical power relations and intergovernmental relations systems become essential mechanisms for governmental effectiveness.

The wave of decentralization reforms in Western countries since the 1980s confirms the validity of multilevel governance as the landscape of contemporary political systems. These reforms have resulted in the devolution of powers to subnational governments supported by normative claims such as better levels of political accountability, policy delivery and efficiency. As reforms have become more widespread, initiatives to map and measure devolution processes have proliferated, allowing comparisons to be made across countries and over time.

Classical measures based on the fiscal-federalism approach have tended to emphasize financial indicators to gauge decentralization. Important as they are, data on expenses' and revenues' share among levels of government do not capture the whole complexity and intricacies of how vertical power is distributed and exerted. More recent multi-dimensional approaches to measure decentralization towards the regional/federalist level, i.e. the RAI and the local level, i.e. the LAI, allow for a more nuanced and precise analysis of the phenomenon. Questions related to the territorial organization of countries, the levels of autonomy of subnational governments and their evolution over time can be better answered thanks to these tools. While fiscal decentralization is a good indicator of overall decentralization, the RAI and the LAI show how countries are organized internally, to what extent decentralization processes have benefited regional or local governments, or both, and the distinction between the two. The RAI and the LAI enable more reliable cross-national and diachronic comparisons, focusing on each specific tier.

The aim of this chapter has been to gain a better understanding of decentralization processes in the 57 countries surveyed. In the first place, the analysis has shown that regional and local devolution processes have followed different dynamics, and that regional decentralization does not necessarily imply or determine local decentralization. The two processes do not correlate. Many countries have high levels of regional authority and low levels of local autonomy, and vice versa. Others have medium levels of both types of autonomy, or various combinations of low, medium and high decentralization. Diversity is the rule, and further attempts to explore the elements of this diversity would improve our understanding of the complexity of these processes.

The study has also confirmed that the LAI is a much more precise tool to gauge local autonomy than the previous indicators used by international organizations. The OECD's conventional measures for decentralization do not manage to capture the many aspects to which local autonomy extends. The variety of the LAI approach with its multiple dimensions (financial autonomy, policy scope, political discretion, organizational autonomy) provides a more realistic picture of autonomy that goes beyond spending or tax collection, and contributes to a better understanding of local autonomy.

From a diachronic perspective, the results show the breadth and depth of the decentralization processes that the countries under study have undergone in the last three decades. Central and Eastern European countries stand out as those that have carried out the most far-reaching reforms in both axes, regional and local (e.g. Albania,the Czech Republic, Romania, Slovakia, Bulgaria and North Macedonia). Others do not show significant gains in this period but present high levels of autonomy (e.g. Austria, Germany and Switzerland) indicating that they had been through a process of decentralization before. Again, there is no pattern of greater inclination towards regional or local reforms. In some countries, it is clear that changes have benefited the regional tier (e.g. Bosnia and Herzegovina, Ireland, the Czech Republic) while in others local governments have been the main recipients of reforms (e.g. Albania, South Africa, Norway, Republic of Korea). Only a minority of countries have experienced a decrease in their levels of regional or local autonomy. Denmark, Sweden and Belgium have given up regional authority. Belarus, Estonia,

Israel, Luxembourg, Cyprus, Mexico and Poland have suffered slight setbacks in local autonomy. Hungary is the country with the largest losses in both types.

The various patterns of intergovernmental arrangementspresented emphasize some macro features of the diverse territorial structures that exist. However, they say nothing about the relational mechanisms between the tiers in multilevel governance. In a future research agenda, it would therefore be interesting to go beyond a static approach to vertical distribution of power and to look at the other main pillar of multilevel governance, i.e. intergovernmental relations. It will become key to examine, for example, how service delivery is coordinated between levels. The COVID-19 pandemic has brought interesting changes and lessons, not only on fiscal issues – already present and addressed during the Great Recession – but more broadly on aspects of coordination and rescaling. In this sense, some of the LAI and/or RAI variables, such as fiscal audit, conditional transfers or access to other levels of government, are likely to play a more prominent role in future efforts to examine future decentralization and recentralization processes.

10. Pathways of access: configurations of formal and informal channels

INTRODUCTION

This chapters scrutinizes the last aspect of interactive rule: central or regional access, because local autonomy also depends on the extent to which municipal authorities gain entrance to and subsequently influence higher level decision-making. Access may come about through various channels, which can be formal and institutionalized but relatively indirect (through umbrella organizations), or informal and individualized but more direct (through designated local decision-makers). The impacts may be limited or substantial. Our contribution considers not only the breadth of such connections but also the way in which they are integrated into distinct configurations of access. These can be denoted as pathways. It therefore extends both the theoretical and the empirical coverage of the LAI 1.0 (the first version of the Local Autonomy Index; Ladner et al. 2019).

The chapter proceeds as follows. First, the access channels studied are situated against the extant literature. The second section introduces our measure of access. The third discusses the results. It describes the absence or presence of the various channels and their combinations, resulting in maximalist, intermediate or minimalist access (depending on the number of channels, illustrated by examples from our country reports). Thereafter, a more standardized measure is developed. The fourth, concluding section discusses our findings in the light of the various types of access determined.

BETWEEN INDIVIDUALIZED AND INSTITUTIONALIZED MODES OF ACCESS

The means of ingress of the municipal level into its central counterparts and its degree of impact on supralocal policy-making have traditionally been denoted as a key factor in local autonomy (Goldsmith 1995). This bottom-up impetus on intergovernmental relations stems from the political ascendancy of local office-holders to represent place-bound interests. It also tends to counterbalance top-down supervision and control from the centre. Access stands for the degree to which and the way in which local authorities penetrate and deal with central government (Ladner et al. 2016, 2023).[1]

While the literature discusses an array of mechanisms, two main modes come to the fore, each being part of a different rationale on vertical linkage. First, access can occur through direct and individualized means. Specific local decision-makers have privileged entrance to the centre, striving for their particular interests. This mode is associated with political localism based on an ethos of communalism, with local politicians tending to colonize supralocal institutions to compensate for their smaller range of functions and discretion. This can occur through dual mandate-holding, multilevel partisan networks or local anchorage of national political careers. The second alternative is indirect and institutionalized, with peak associations for the municipal sector pursuing a common interest in routinized negotiations with the centre. This reflects legal localism and an orientation towards local public services and local provision. Corporate-interest mediation through local-government associations and in intergovernmental forums confirms the larger functional and discretionary scope of municipalities (Page and Goldsmith 1987a, 1987b; 2010). The juxtaposition of both modes and their rooting in varied conceptions of local government remained prominent in further studies of central–local relations, even if the geographical reach of cases extended and qualitative categorizations gave way to quantitative scales adding nuance to the measures (Hesse and Sharpe 1991; Sellers and Lidström 2007; Loughlin et al. 2012; Do Vale 2015).

A more extensive discussion of the extant literature can be found in the volume on the first version of the LAI ('the LAI 1.0'). That version concentrated on indirect and institutionalized access (Ladner et al. 2019: 193–212). The original measure scrutinized the absence or presence of this form through consultation and/or (formal) representation further distinguishing limited from substantial influence on higher level (i.e. regional or central) policy-making. Ladner and his colleagues acknowledged the dynamics of this aspect of local autonomy. They determined an overall increase in access over their reference period (1990–2014). However, this came about through a surge in a specific time frame (around the turn of the twenty-first century) and appeared to be largely driven by developments in newer democracies. Subsequently, some form of consultation and/or representation existed in all countries by the end of that period. Consequently, an incremental shift in the amount of influence could be distinguished. Despite a growing number of countries where this turned out to be substantial, in the majority of all cases it remained limited.

[1] The European Charter of Local Self-Government also considers access as a key feature of local autonomy. It posits that local authorities must be consulted for matters which concern them directly (art. 4, § 6). It furthermore emphasizes their entitlement to cooperation and concertation in associations (art. 10, §1).

These general trends obviously differ between and within countries. The authors found 13 cases (or about 33 per cent of the total) where access could be denoted as (relatively) high. Here, consultation and/or representation came with high influence. In 19 countries (about 58 per cent) such vertical linkage was deemed medium, with the aforementioned forms of access present but of limited influence. The remaining seven instances (about 9 per cent) were characterized as low. There, consultation and/or representation was absent at least at some point in time. Compared with the beginning of the 1990s change could be determined in about 56 per cent of all cases (largely in the direction of (more influential) access).

However, the examined mode only provided part of the access picture. The previous analysis namely demonstrated the gradual routinization of indirect and institutionalized mechanisms and channels. However, many country assessments also suggested the enduring relevance of direct and individualized linkage in many instances. Therefore, 'access remains a matter of balance between theoretically often juxtaposed modes. Future research may seek to answer as to where, when and why which combinations of each appear and how they affect the entrance of local into central and regional authorities' (Ladner et al. 2019: 209).

DESIGN, DATA AND METHOD

The LAI 2.0 can probe deeper into the issue of configuration raised at the end of the previous paragraph (see also Ladner et al. 2021). The current measure considers both indirect and institutional as well more direct and individual access. It scrutinizes 'the extent to which local authorities have channels to influence higher level governments' policy-making' on a 0–3 scale. On the one hand, this covers the formal (consultation and representation) procedures, mechanisms and structures identified in the first version of the index. On the other hand, it also encompasses their informal counterparts. The measure gauges the presence (or absence) of each of these channels.

This is thus an extension of the indicator used in the LAI 1.0. It allows a more comprehensive estimation of the different channels of access, which can either be formal, informal or both. In contrast, the assessment of their extent of influence now remains more implicit (as an additional coding instruction). Similar observations (broader in scope but more implicit in influence) can be made in comparison with the indices on access in the Regional Authority Index (RAI). These imply regional representation (in the national legislature), regional consultation (on national initiatives affecting the region) and routine meetings (in which regional and national levels discuss and negotiate). For each of these channels, the RAI also considers the extent of authority (Hooghe et al. 2016).

Measurement of Access: Central or Regional Access

The extent to which local authorities have channels to influence higher level governments' policy-making **(0–3)**.

Local authorities have access to higher-level decision-making through:

- formal consultation procedures and mechanisms **(0–1)**
- formal representation structures **(0–1)**
- more informal channels (e.g. through trade unions that try to set the legislative agenda, party-political networks, dual mandate-holding, etc.) **(0–1)**

Additional coding instructions: Please clarify the channels and assess the extent of influence exercised upon the higher level.

RESULTS

First, we approach the channels in simple dichotomous terms. Table 10.1 indicates whether a certain channel can be found (somewhere) in the case under study. The total is the mere number of channels present. This can be considered as a basic index of access. Countries are ranked by their total number of channels and subsequently presented alphabetically. We refer to the most recent year of our measurement to provide the timeliest assessment.

This initial analysis will help us to explore modes of access and subsequently classify these into configurations. The latter are of particular interest in this chapter. However, caution is needed. First, as with all measures in this study, scores depend on the assessments (of presence) by the country experts. Therefore, channels should always be seen in context. They are interpreted in the subsequent parts by reference to the country reports, which also take into account the level of influence associated with a given channel (see additional coding instructions). Second, the analysis concerns the country level. It does not take into consideration whether a designated pathway is limited to one or more subunits (see Chapter 4) or explicitly scored between 0 or 1. Such deviations from the initial dichotomy can be found in 15 cases (as considered in the next empirical section). Third, when it comes to the reference year, an earlier exploration of the data suggests a highly stable picture of access values over the whole 2015–20 period (Ladner et al. 2021: 60–62). Therefore, the most recent data are preferred over the five-year mean.

The table shows that, on average, the countries included have a little more than two ways at their disposal to establish a path of access into central or regional government. Informal channels are the most prevalent (only absent in six cases), followed by formal consultation and representation (in descending

Table 10.1 *Pathways of access – presence informal vs. formal channels by country (2020)*

Country	Informal channels	Formal consultation	Formal representation	Total (0–3)
Albania	1	1	1	**3**
Australia	1	1	1	**3**
Austria	1	1	1	**3**
Bosnia and Herzegovina	1	1	1	**3**
Bulgaria	1	1	1	**3**
Estonia	1	1	1	**3**
Georgia	1	1	1	**3**
Iceland	1	1	1	**3**
Italy	1	1	1	**3**
Latvia	1	1	1	**3**
Lithuania	1	1	1	**3**
Luxembourg	1	1	1	**3**
Malta	1	1	1	**3**
Mexico	1	1	1	**3**
Moldova	1	1	1	**3**
Montenegro	1	1	1	**3**
Poland	1	1	1	**3**
Portugal	1	1	1	**3**
Romania	1	1	1	**3**
Serbia	1	1	1	**3**
Slovakia	1	1	1	**3**
South Africa	1	1	1	**3**
Spain	1	1	1	**3**
Switzerland	1	1	1	**3**
Argentina	1	0	1	**2**
Canada	0	1	1	**2**
Chile	1	0	1	**2**
Cyprus	1	1	0	**2**
Czech Republic	1	1	0	**2**
Denmark	1	1	0	**2**
Finland	1	1	0	**2**

Country	Informal channels	Formal consultation	Formal representation	Total (0–3)
France	1	0	1	**2**
Germany	1	1	0	**2**
Greece	1	1	0	**2**
Ireland	1	0	1	**2**
Japan	1	0	1	**2**
Kosovo	1	1	0	**2**
Macedonia	0	1	1	**2**
Netherlands	1	1	0	**2**
Norway	1	1	0	**2**
Republic of Korea	1	1	0	**2**
Slovenia	0	1	1	**2**
Sweden	1	1	0	**2**
Turkey	1	0	1	**2**
Ukraine	1	1	0	**2**
United Kingdom	1	0	1	**2**
Andorra	1	0	0	**1**
Armenia	1	0	0	**1**
Belarus	0	1	0	**1**
Belgium	1	0	0	**1**
Colombia	1	0	0	**1**
Croatia	1	0	0	**1**
Hungary	0	1	0	**1**
Israel	1	0	0	**1**
Liechtenstein	0	1	0	**1**
Russian Federation	1	0	0	**1**
United States of America	1	0	0	**1**
Total (% of cases present)	**51** (89.5%)	**42** (73.7%)	**34** (59.6%)	**2.23** (mean)

order of frequency). Each channel can thus be found in a clear majority of cases. All cases can make use of at least one and often two or three channels. These amounts represent the three configurations of access discussed below.

Maximalist Access: All Channels

All three channels of access are present in 24 countries (42.1 per cent). Here, local government has the most comprehensive and integrated entrance into its regional or central counterpart. This combination could be termed as *maximalist access*. It comprises a varied set of cases ranging from Albania to Switzerland. Albania has a Consultation Council for liaison between central and local government. Local government associations (even if politically fragmented) add to this form of formal influence, which is further enhanced by informal channels through party political networks. In Switzerland, municipalities are represented in Tripartite Conferences (including the cantonal and confederal levels) in pertinent policy areas (including relevant grants and allowances). These bodies manifest a wider pattern of consultation, with representatives of municipalities often taking part in expert groups or extra-parliamentary commissions. Local-government associations feature in the pre-parliamentary procedure and act as lobby organizations. Switzerland does not have a specific chamber representing municipalities at the cantonal or confederal level. Rather, an informal graduated logic prevails: municipalities are expected to address the cantons, which in turn target the confederation. This logic also applies for direct access mainly oriented at the cantonal institutions. Thus, access is more pronounced at the regional than at the national level.

South Africa turns out to be the single exception to the rule that no chamber in the national legislature directly represents municipal interests. In that country, local government is formally represented in the Upper House of the National Parliament. Its association holds ten nonvoting seats in the National Council of Provinces, and is also involved in the nomination and selection of members of the Finance and Fiscal Commission (advising the government on related issues). Finally, it is a member of a number of formal intergovernmental structures at the provincial and national levels. This formal representation is enhanced by similar consultation procedures in matters affecting the functioning of local government.

Other cases show levels and channels similar to the ones described above. Australia provides a particular example. The local level has been included in various formalized and tripartite intergovernmental fora aimed at policy reforms (such as the Council of Australian Governments, which has been in place for decades). Furthermore, an intergovernmental agreement at the beginning of the twenty-first century established a set of guiding principles for multilevel relations. The agreement included a framework for the funding and delivery and provision of services at the local level (no devolution without consultation and impact assessment). The Australian Local Government Association functions as a peak organization present in many national councils or committees. A yearly National General Assembly of Local Government provides a key event to informally engage with and influence the federal level. Unions of local government workers populate other informal channels. Examples in other countries of formalized intergovernmental fora are, in Italy and Spain, conferences between the state, region and municipalities, and in Poland the Joint Central and Local Government Committee. These bodies remain consultative but are also considered impactful. In Lithuania, the Regional Development Council was recently strengthened. Established by the municipalities, this legal entity coordinates the regional implementation of national policy, promotes development and represents regions at the national level. There are also instances in which formal representation seems limited to specific reform trajectories on local (self-)government, as in Montenegro.

Sometimes existing intergovernmental bodies are deemed uninfluential. This is the case in Mexico, where in many instances representation of local-government interests does not occur in designated structures (such as fora or bodies), but is more a matter of institutionalized consultation by, or systematic negotiations and regular meetings with, higher levels. Local government associations are often central in these procedures and mechanisms: to various extents and in different ways, this can be seen in Austria, Bosnia and Herzegovina, Bulgaria, Iceland, Latvia, Luxembourg, Malta, Moldova, Montenegro, Portugal, Romania, Serbia and Slovakia. As umbrella organizations often holding a monopoly on their sector, these associations act as favoured interlocutors recognized by central government. However, in some countries there are a number of associations. Distinctions might be based on urbanization (cities often standing apart from their ordinary municipal counterparts) but also on party-political affiliation (although this division also tends to affect unified associations). The true influence of these associations is not always self-evident and often depends on the topic and stakes.

Informal channels complement formal ones. In Austria, dual mandate-holding (with a governing party office at the provincial level) offers the main channel of informal influence. A comparable situation exists in Estonia, Luxembourg and Slovakia (at the national level) and Spain (at the regional level – even if the extent of influence is deemed low to moderate). Influence can also be achieved through informal meetings between elected representatives. Mayors (or councillors) then approach members of parliament representing the constituency the municipality is situated in. The parliamentarians may subsequently use instruments of oversight to inquire about pressing local problems. This is customary in Bulgaria. Having started one's political career at the local level can also open up informal channels. Reference to this is made in Iceland and Italy. This process may alternatively develop through internal party processes, as exemplified by Serbia and South Africa.

Intermediate Access: All But One Channel

The other countries thus display patterns with varying degrees of formal and informal characteristics. A blend of informal channels and at least one of the two formal mechanisms (consultation or representation) is present in 43 countries (or 75.4 per cent of all cases). A pathway with all but one of the channels appears in 22 countries (38.6 per cent). These lack either formal representation, formal consultation or informal channels (in descending order of frequency). Together they comprise instances of *intermediate access*.

More than half the countries in this group (N = 12) lack only representation structures. Here, local government does have at its disposal formal consultation procedures or mechanisms and informal channels. The first usually includes local government associations as stakeholders involved in the different phases of the policy-making process oriented at central legislatures and/or executives. The second pertains to party-political networks or dual mandate-holding. The interpretation in the country reports suggests differences in the relative importance or influence of both types of channels (even if both are present). In Denmark, explicit reference is made to the institutionalized system of continuous consultations between the national government and local government association. A similar pattern can be found in Cyprus, the Netherlands, Norway and Ukraine. In the Netherlands, regular consultations on matters of common interest are part of a long-standing culture of consultation. This is formally expressed in instruments such as intergovernmental agreements. Informal channels strengthen the partnership model, enhanced by recent decentralizations. In Ukraine, the lobbying efforts of (different) associations are said to have a strong voice in national policy consultations, whereas in the Czech Republic, it is argued that informal access dominates. In Finland, Germany, Greece, Kosovo, the Republic of Korea and Sweden, matters appear more balanced.

Formal consultation is wanting in other cases where formal representation and informal channels feature (N = 7). In Argentina, mayors tend to build personal networks with supralocal politicians and administrators to gain additional resources. These informal channels follow a partisan logic.[2] The federation of municipalities goes through cycles of less or more representation. A largely comparable picture emerges in Chile (where two representative associations compete). In France, there is the emblematic description of the *Sénat* as the chamber of local governments (given the composition of its electoral college). This is reinforced by other institutions of formal representation (in the

---

[2] The country report mentions that formalized consultation mechanisms do exist in a few provinces.

fields of local finances and standards evaluation). The *millefeuille territoriale* also provides ample opportunities for informal attempts to influence central decisions. In Ireland, Japan, Turkey and the United Kingdom, consultation and influence are outlined as more informal with discretion through mayors and/or parties (even if associations for corporate representation exist in most of these countries). In Turkey, formal representation comes about for district councils in metropolitan areas.

Finally, in a handful of cases (N = 3) informal channels are missing. In Canada, political parties do not operate as conduits between the local and other levels of government. Municipal elections are nonpartisan or contested by short-lived electoral organizations. Local parties tend not to be linked to their supralocal counterparts. Moreover, dual mandate-holding is lacking. The articulation of municipal interests in the political sphere is thus weakly institutionalized. Municipalities do engage with their provincial counterparts via individual or collective lobbying through official consultation processes (and on a functional basis with their federal counterparts). The first mainly occurs between administrators at different levels, the latter through local government associations (also referred to in Macedonia). In Slovenia, recognized municipal associations have to be consulted when adopting legislation that affects the local government system. Moreover, a National Council acts as the representative body of various societal interests, including territorial ones. It can offer opinions and proposals on certain issues and exercises a limited suspensive veto vis-à-vis the National Assembly.

Minimalist Access: Only One Channel

In the remaining 11 cases (19.3 per cent) only one channel appears. These situations can be denoted as *minimalist access*. Here, linkage via formal channels is usually lacking (neither consultation nor representation). Entrance into regional or national levels can thus solely be achieved through informal channels. In some of these systems, personal contacts matter heavily. Party-political networks or dual mandate-holding then provide leverage. The country reports on Andorra, Armenia, Belgium, Croatia, Israel, Russia and the United States refer to this model (mainly through party connections). To different degrees, it tends to reflect the persistence of political localism with specific local interests and particular municipal governments having central entrance (next to the local level as a whole). It can also imply that supralocal decisions on the distribution of goods or services are based on territorial affiliations.

In other countries, access is (also) assumed by local government associations engaging in negotiations and bargaining with the centre. This can occur in selected commissions or committees. In various cases, it comes close to a form of structured consultation or corporate interest representation. At times (but not always) this also has substantial influence. However, the absence of legal provisions or standard procedures keeps such interactions predominantly informal (making their authority contingent). They often depend on the invitation of central government and its openness to local interests. Armenia, Belgium, Colombia, Croatia, Israel and the United States are cases in point. In some, this informality does not preclude extensive or effective exchange in practice. In Belgium, for example, it is noted that the right combination of indirect (but non-formal) and direct access can evoke a substantial but largely unofficial mode of influence. Elsewhere, the balance appears to tilt more towards the receptiveness of the centre (e.g. in Colombia). Furthermore, corporate local interests can be expressed by a single voice or a plurality of voices. In the United States the differentiation within and between general- and special-purpose local authorities is reflected in a multitude of local government associations.

In a few instances, there is formal access through consultation but not via representation and informal channels are also missing. This is the case in Belarus, Hungary and Liechtenstein. In Hungary, the presidents of the (various) local government associations are members of the National Cooperation Council of Local Governments, a consultative body of central government. In Belarus, reference is made to 'phone rule', indicating overall top-down command and control (rather than bottom-up influence). However, in the second (territorial) chamber of the national legislature, a council exists for interaction with local self-government bodies. It has a consultative character mainly ensuring the unity of action from the top-down perspective of the state. Local government associations are weakly institutionalized.

A Standardized Measure of Access

A more refined picture with a standardized scale (0–100) for each channel can be found in Table 10.2. This takes into consideration differences between subunits and/or discrete scores between the mere absence or presence. The total corresponds with the scores on the access dimension discerned in this version of the LAI (see also Ladner et al. 2021, 2023). Data again refer to 2020. Countries are presented in descending order of the standardized extent and further on alphabetically.

In Table 10.2, countries where the total access is above the middle of the scale (> 50) are indicated in italics (N = 37 or 64.9 per cent of all cases). This form of vertical linkage between levels is thus clearly skewed to the right (further indicated by the 13 countries or 22.8 per cent of the total obtaining the maximum score). Underlined and bold respectively highlight those on (N = 3 or 5.3 per cent) or below (N = 17 or 29.8 per cent) the middle of the scale. The overall mean evidently weights the contributions of informal channels, formal

Table 10.2 *Pathways of access – standardized extent formal vs. informal channels by country (2020)*

Country	Informal channels (0–100)	Formal consultation (0–100)	Representation (0–100)	Total (0–100)
Australia	100	100	100	*100*
Austria	100	100	100	*100*
Bulgaria	100	100	100	*100*
Italy	100	100	100	*100*
Latvia	100	100	100	*100*
Lithuania	100	100	100	*100*
Malta	100	100	100	*100*
Moldova	100	100	100	*100*
Montenegro	100	100	100	*100*
Portugal	100	100	100	*100*
Slovakia	100	100	100	*100*
South Africa	100	100	100	*100*
Spain	100	100	100	*100*
Switzerland	98	100	100	*99*
Bosnia and Herzegovina	66	100	100	*89*
Iceland	50	100	100	*83*
Luxembourg	100	100	50	*83*
Albania	100	50	50	*67*
Chile	100	0	100	*67*
Cyprus	100	100	0	*67*
Czech Republic	100	100	0	*67*
Finland	100	100	0	*67*
France	100	0	100	*67*
Georgia	50	100	50	*67*
Germany	100	100	0	*67*
Greece	100	100	0	*67*
Ireland	100	0	100	*67*
Japan	100	0	100	*67*
Netherlands	100	100	0	*67*
Norway	100	100	0	*67*

Country	Informal channels (0–100)	Formal consultation (0–100)	Representation (0–100)	Total (0–100)
Poland	100	50	50	*67*
Republic of Korea	100	100	0	*67*
Slovenia	0	100	100	*67*
Sweden	100	100	0	*67*
United Kingdom	100	0	100	*67*
Serbia	62	100	37	*67*
Ukraine	77	100	0	*59*
Denmark	100	50	0	50
Kosovo	100	50	0	50
Macedonia	0	100	50	50
Turkey	100	0	31	**44**
Estonia	50	50	25	**42**
Mexico	100	7	7	**38**
Argentina	100	0	11	**37**
Canada	0	57	50	**36**
Andorra	100	0	0	**33**
Armenia	100	0	0	**33**
Belarus	0	100	0	**33**
Belgium	100	0	0	**33**
Colombia	100	0	0	**33**
Croatia	100	0	0	**33**
Hungary	0	100	0	**33**
Israel	100	0	0	**33**
Liechtenstein	0	100	0	**33**
Romania	25	50	25	**33**
Russian Federation	100	0	0	**33**
United States of America	100	0	0	**33**
Total (mean)	84	66	46	65

consultation and formal representation (in descending order of means for each aspect). Evidently, the results reflect the earlier discussion of the countries in the previous section. They also confirm that countries can hardly be placed in obvious geographical clusters or state traditions.

To check the robustness of our findings over time, we compared the 2015–20 standardized mean on (total) access for each country with that for 2010–14. This was based on the (partially) recoded data for the preceding period (Ladner et al. 2023), as the assessment of access slightly differed in this version of the index (i.e. including informal versus focus on mere presence). The analysis shows that continuity clearly trumps change. The access score has remained the same in 42 (or 74 per cent) of all countries. This dimension of interactive rule thus seems predominantly stable. It subsequently altered in the remaining 15 countries (26 per cent). In those countries, increases appear more frequent than decreases (12 or 21 per cent versus 3 or 5 per cent respectively). More longitudinal and/or aggregated evolutions can be found elsewhere (see Chapter 2 in this volume or Ladner et al. 2021, 2023).

CONCLUSION

This chapter studied the extent to which local authorities have channels to influence higher level decision-making. Access was conceived as the combination of formal, indirect and institutionalized linkage with informal, direct and individualized connections. Whereas the first referred to corporate interest mediation via consultation and/or representation, the second pertained to more privileged and personalized lobbying. Our contribution empirically scrutinized the presence of informal channels, formal consultation and formal representation. It also considered their combinations. Instances of maximalist, intermediate and minimalist channels were identified and (illustratively) discussed, after which a more standardized measure was developed (taking within-country differences or discrete scorings into consideration).

The findings of these analyses can further be summarized as in Tables 10.3a, 10.3b and 10.3c. The different categories capturing the number of channels present (cf. Table 10.1) all comprise one or more types each standing for a particular pathway of access. The last two columns display the share of cases

Table 10.3a Pathways of access by configuration of channels (2020): maximalist

Type	IF	FC	FR	% Cases (N)	Extent of access (0–100)[a]
T1	P	P	P	42 (24)	85 (Mean) 22 (Std.dev)

Table 10.3b *Pathways of access by configuration of channels (2020): intermediate*

Type	IF	FC	FR	% Cases (N)	Extent of access (0–100)[a]
T2	P	P	A	21 (12)	63 (Mean) 7 (Std.dev)
T3	P	A	P	12 (7)	59 (Mean) 13 (Std.dev)
T4	A	P	P	5 (3)	51 (Mean) 16 (Std.dev)

Table 10.3c *Pathways of access by configuration of channels (2020): minimalist*

Type	IF	FC	FR	% Cases (N)	Extent of access (0–100)[a]
T5	P	A	A	14 (8)	33 (Mean) 0 (Std.dev)
T6	A	P	A	5 (3)	33 (Mean) 0 (Std.dev)

Notes: For tables 10.3a–c:
[a] The differences in the extent of access between the various types are statistically significant ($p < .001$) and strong (eta2 = .617).
IF = informal channels; FC = formal consultation; FR = formal representation; P = present, A = absent.

that the six types pertain to and their standardized extent of access (cf. Table 10.2).

The tables extend one of the main findings of the first version of the LAI (Ladner et al. 2019): at least one channel is present in all cases. This emphasizes the sustained routinization of access as a key aspect of interactive rule in multilevel relations. However, the earlier study was confined to indirect and institutionalized channels. As already suggested, our analysis also confirms the enduring relevance of direct and individualized linkage through informal channels. These are present in all but two types (thus in almost 90 per cent of all cases). They also add nuance to the real-world combinations of channels.[3] Moreover, the prevalence of the channels and the mean value of access

[3] Considering solely formal channels would render only four types of access. More broadly, it can be noted that the presence of formal representation alone (without formal consultation and informal channels) does not occur in practice.

discussed above suggest an implicit (yet imperfect) hierarchy. When formal representation occurs, formal consultation and/or informal channels are also more likely to appear.

Remarkably, the largest group of countries can be found in type 1, where all channels are present. Here, local authorities have the most comprehensive and integrated linkage with their higher-level counterparts. This is also reflected in the mean value of the standardized extent of access, even assuming the maximum for a bit less than one in four of all cases. The second most prevalent is type 2, comprising a little over one in five cases. It combines informal channels with formal consultation. This type demonstrates access values similar to those of its subsequent third counterpart, where formal consultation in turn is missing (to the benefit of representation). The combination of both formal channels (without informal channels) in type 4 yields access just above the middle of the scale. This appears substantially lower in those types (5 and 6) where local authorities have only one channel at their disposal to influence their central counterparts. Notably, the type with only informal channels is the third most common in our comparison.

At the end of this chapter, some further caution is warranted. Our measure does not explicitly code the actual extent of influence each of these channels (or their combination into pathways) exercises on higher levels of government. The presence of more channels does not necessarily imply greater influence. Thus, each on its own or jointly can render an impact ranging from limited to substantial. This has also been highlighted in the country reports from which illustrations were drawn in our contribution. The case descriptions suggest that formalization matters, but only to a certain degree. There are instances where the municipal level is regularly consulted in central decision-making and/or actually represented in intergovernmental forums without a firm legal basis or institutionalized procedures. Under the right circumstance, this might still imply substantive influence. There are also examples where such bottom-up mechanisms are codified but remain more principle than practice, due to strong top-down centralist dynamics. Both patterns indicate that in each interaction there are two sides in the equation. The channels local authorities have thus give them entrance but do not guarantee effect. The extent to which these channels and pathways leave room for municipal interests of course depends on their ability to formulate a shared stance and/or the nature of its reception. This also holds for the informal channels of lobbying. Therefore, future research should probe further into the categories and types of access, their actual extent of influence and the conditions under which they provide effective leverage for local authorities in the relationship with their central counterparts. This will add nuance to issues of vertical access but also to the question of whether, and how, this type of access matters.

11. The impact of global crises on local autonomy

INTRODUCTION

Governments have always had to deal with crises, be they economic, health-related, dealing with mass migrations, natural disasters or of any other type. In facing these crises they have had to demonstrate their capacity to act, overcoming the many policy and politics obstacles they are confronted with. Crises tend to pose challenges to multilevel governance structures, not least the challenge of re-articulating intergovernmental relations (IGR) with the aim of functioning more effectively and more efficiently. To the extent that crises tend to create the need to coordinate public action between different levels of government, systems become embroiled in complex intergovernmental problems (Paquet and Schertzer 2020) putting IGR systems through a kind of stress test. Sometimes this leads to changes in multilevel governance, either towards greater centralization or, on the contrary, towards greater and more autonomous involvement of subnational governments in public affairs (Mello and Tovar Jalles 2024).

In the period covered by the Local Autonomy Index 1990–2020 ('the LAI 1.0'), governments had to cope with two global crises: the 2007–08 global financial crisis and the COVID-19 pandemic, two emblematic cases in which multilevel governance was affected in different ways. Analysing their impact on the autonomy of local authorities can contribute to a better understanding of IGR processes in these periods and to draw lessons for future crises.

During the global financial crisis, governments assumed a central role in shaping policy responses. Faced with a severe economic downturn triggered by the collapse of financial markets and banking institutions, governments implemented interventions to stabilize economies. The crisis highlighted the critical importance of proactive government intervention, policy coordination and a multifaceted approach to restore confidence and mitigate economic contraction. In this rediscovery, the centre of gravity in multilevel governance appeared to tilt towards the central-government level. The COVID-19 pandemic equally showcased the indispensable role of governments in public policy, requiring swift and coordinated responses to mitigate the health crisis and its socio-economic consequences. IGR became a focal point as local, regional and national authorities collaborated to implement measures including lockdowns, testing and vaccination campaigns. While the first crisis required the coordination of (inter)national responses to navigate its global financial complexities, the second was more a matter of effective cooperation, communication and resource-sharing among national and subnational governmental levels to address the challenges.

In terms of why and in particular how vertical power relations are affected in times of crises, theory on crisis management starts from the assumption that centralization is the dominant approach to decision-making (Peters 2011). This approach has both political and managerial rationales. Politically, in times of crisis the public looks for clear and assertive leadership, making prime ministers and central governments the natural focal point. In managerial terms, speaking with one voice helps in setting priorities and facilitates coherence, effectiveness and efficiency in the governmental response. Although this justification seems a rational explanation of centralized political dynamics during serious crisis episodes, there are also arguments in favour of the advantages of decentralization. One is that information and knowledge play a crucial role in improving the quality of decisions, and that centralized decision-making would hamper the provision of these resources by other (local) governments and the other actors in the network. Even though involving other parties in decision-making processes may result in slower decisions, the additional information gathered thanks to their participation can elevate the quality of the decisions made. There is therefore a compelling political logic favouring a more decentralized strategy in crisis management (Peters 2011).

This chapter will analyse the implications of the global financial crisis and the COVID-19 pandemic to local autonomy. Drawing on previous studies and on own data from 57 countries, this chapter analyses the extent to which the autonomy of local governments was impacted by the global financial crisis and the COVID-19 pandemic and the patterns of similarities and differences in countries' responses. The next section explores the changes in local autonomy that have occurred in the aftermath of the global financial crisis by looking at the stability or alteration of the seven dimensions of local autonomy. This is followed by a look at the impact of the COVID-19 pandemic on local autonomy, based on experts' assessments of its centralizing or decentralizing effects.

THE RESPONSE TO THE GLOBAL FINANCIAL CRISIS

The period immediately following the global financial crisis attracted research efforts to assess to what extent countries had strengthened or weakened the structure of local government and modulated the autonomy granted to municipalities amid periods of fiscal constraint. Studies surveying individual countries or groups of countries analysed whether the crisis had triggered recentralization tendencies or promoted decentralization dynamics. Both hypotheses were plausible. Municipalities could have been seen by central governments as active agents of sustainable economic growth, using their democratic structures. They could also have been seen as entities to pass on the burden of austerity, making them responsible for achieving spending cuts. In both cases, decentralization would have been the intergovernmental strategy to deal with the crisis. On the other hand, national governments would prefer a more centralized way of solving the pressing challenges created by the economic recession, for example, by strengthening financial supervision or setting limits on local authority borrowing.

Studies in the field have tended to support the centralization hypothesis. Not all countries were hit by the recession equally, but where it was severe, national governments intervened to varying degrees in local autonomy (Ladner 2017; Ladner et al. 2019). Taking Europe as an example, Cyprus, Greece, Ireland, Italy, Portugal and Spain were definitely much more strongly affected than the Nordic countries or Switzerland. Other countries such as Hungary, Latvia and Romania also needed financial assistance, whereas in Germany the crisis affected only parts of the country (Ladner 2017). And yet the adoption of control measures extended beyond the bailed-out countries.

Specifically focusing on countries in Southern Europe, Lippi and Tsekos report that Greece and Portugal were subjected to a comprehensive set of measures imposed by the Troika, which significantly affected the autonomy of local authorities. These measures included increased control over local finances, the imposition of hiring freezes, salary stagnation, rescaling initiatives, amalgamation processes and fiscal austerity (Lippi and Tsekos 2019). In the case of Spain, several legislative acts were implemented that reduced the autonomy of local governments by impacting financial sustainability, addressing public-debt concerns and a broader reorganization of local government through a reform of the Local Government Act. These legislative enactments encompassed coercive measures, fiscal-compliance mandates, central control over budgetary processes and the reduction of municipal functions (Navarro and Pano 2019). Italy underwent a downsizing of local governance following a letter from the European Central Bank, involving substantial cutbacks and the elimination of the second tier of governance as an autonomous unit of self-government.

Moving to other geographical areas, in Ireland the government elected in 2011 undertook the abolition of town councils (constituting the second tier) and merged neighbouring authorities, resulting in an overall reduction in the number of local governing bodies. The Netherlands underwent a rigorous rationalization programme characterized by reduced funding and a series of budget cuts for municipalities. In Germany, some *Länder* implemented a system involving supervisory commissioners for municipalities burdened with debt, coupled with the imposition of expenditure constraints. And, across most of the *Länder*, a programme was introduced to reorganize local governance through territorial upscaling initiatives and enhanced financial supervision. Several other countries, including Finland and Slovenia, experienced specific financial retrenchment through reductions in financial transfers. In Finland, central-government subsidies were curtailed, leading to deficit budgets, forcing local governments to raise property taxes. In the United Kingdom, particularly in England, the burden of austerity was largely passed on to the local level, heavily reducing central funding (Ladner 2017).

In sum, in countries where the impact was more visible, national governments tended to increase their control over local government, particularly in the areas of finance and expenditure, leading to explicit restrictions on borrowing (Ladner 2017). But control measures were also adopted in other countries. In Europe, the more strongly municipalities depended on resources from higher state levels, the more their financial autonomy was likely to be reduced. Even though large-scale amalgamation reforms as a reaction to the crisis were an exception in general terms, they were carried out in Greece, Italy and Portugal and were attempted without success in Spain.

Beyond Europe, other processes of recentralization are reported in Latin American countries but do not appear to be linked to the global financial crisis. They started before the economic recession and tended to reverse the empowerment that local authorities had developed over the previous decades. These processes were a response to a crisis of local inefficiency and corruption and to the search for territorial equality and a more homogeneous protection of rights (Cravacuore 2017).

In addition to the changes reported in the literature in the field, the Local Autonomy Index (LAI) tracks alterations towards more or less control of local authorities by higher levels of government in some countries in the period under analysis. When comparing the periods immediately before and after the financial crisis, a number of countries show decreased values in all dimensions (see Table 11.1). Although the quantitative information in our LAI database does not permit the loss of local autonomy to be definitively attributed to a response to the crisis, both evidence from the previous studies mentioned and experts' description of the country coding point to that causal relationship.

The analysis confirms the findings of the reported studies. Of the seven dimensions analysed in the LAI, financial autonomy emerges as the one most affected by the financial crisis, when local authorities saw their freedom to borrow constrained or became more dependent on transfers from other levels of government. Some countries also took backward steps in terms of non-interference after central governments stepped up their monitoring of local

Table 11.1 Countries losing local autonomy after the financial crisis

Autonomy dimensions	Countries with drops in autonomy (comparison between 2004–2009 and 2010–2015 means)
Legal autonomy	Slovenia
Political discretion	Estonia Hungary Luxembourg Spain United Kingdom
Policy scope	Hungary Spain Switzerland United Kingdom
Financial autonomy	Croatia Georgia Greece Hungary Iceland Liechtenstein Montenegro Slovenia Spain
Organizational autonomy	Latvia Romania Spain
Noninterference	Chile Czech Republic Hungary Iceland Ireland Mexico Montenegro
Access	Latvia Slovenia

Source: Own elaboration from Local Autonomy Index database 1990–2020 (57 countries).

accounts in order to maintain balanced budgets. Policy autonomy and political discretion suffered from the transfer of responsibility in some policy areas to higher levels of government. In other countries, a decline in organizational autonomy can be directly linked to specific measures taken by central authorities, such as the imposition of salary ceilings for civil servants. On the other hand, the legal autonomy and access dimensions of local autonomy, which have a more structural and long-lasting component in self-government, were only altered in exceptional cases.

THE RESPONSE TO THE COVID-19 PANDEMIC

While the global financial crisis was of a predominantly economic nature, with macroeconomic policy instruments being used, the COVID-19 pandemic brought not only a health crisis but also a sudden and profound economic and social crisis, which had to be addressed with more diverse strategies (Capano et al. 2020). These often implied trade-offs. Governments had to make difficult choices between public safety and limiting economic damage, balancing the first imperative with the potentially deleterious political and social consequences of limitations imposed on citizens' liberties (Bergström et al. 2022).

Of all the challenges facing countries in 2020, coordinating action between different levels of government was particularly prominent. COVID-19 proved to be a complex intergovernmental problem (Paquet and Schertzer 2020), requiring a high level of cooperation between all tiers of government. Analysis in the field reported that vertical coordination between levels of government was a pressing issue during crisis management, and countries responded to the pandemic differently (Bergström et al. 2022). In the European context, different types of IGR processes occurred during the first phase of the pandemic, with different levels of conflict in multilevel governance. In Norway, Germany, the Netherlands and France (after the initial phase) both central and subnational governments played a significant coordinated role, and subnational units managed to exert political influence. In France (initial phase), England and Sweden the central government assumed predominant control, allowing subnational governmental actors limited discretion and influence at the central level. In Spain, Belgium, the United Kingdom, the Czech Republic and Slovakia there was a predominantly conflicted policy process characterized by divergent views and contested rules (Bergström et al. 2022).

Local autonomy did not escape pandemic management unscathed. But the response varied. In theory, and following the assumptions of crisis management, both centralization and decentralization could occur (Peters 2011): the former because of the need to prioritize objectives in a unified rapid response due to the severity of the health impact; the latter because of the experience of local governments in health and social issues. Situations of conflict between levels of government may also have arisen, especially in the early stages of the pandemic, without any lasting impact on levels of autonomy.

The answers of country experts to an additional question in the LAI survey about the implications of COVID-19 allow us to map the impact of the pandemic on local autonomy in the 57 countries under analysis (Table 11.2). Although the evidence is based on perceptions, these perceptions are expressed

Table 11.2 *Implications of the COVID-19 pandemic on local autonomy*

Implication	Country
Local autonomy decreased (15 countries)	Albania, Austria, Belarus, Bulgaria, Croatia, Cyprus, Denmark, Estonia, Hungary, Ireland, Italy, Japan, Moldova, Poland, South Africa
Local autonomy was not impacted (31 countries)	Andorra, Argentina, Armenia, Australia, Belgium, Bosnia and Herzegovina, Canada, Chile, Colombia, France, Greece, Ireland, Israel, Latvia, Liechtenstein, Luxembourg, Macedonia, Malta, Montenegro, Netherlands, Norway, Portugal, Romania, Russian Federation, Serbia, Slovenia, Spain, Sweden, Turkey, Ukraine, United Kingdom
Local autonomy increased in health issues (7 countries)	Finland, Georgia, Germany, Kosovo, Lithuania, Republic of Korea, Slovakia
Local autonomy increased in health and other fields (2 countries)	Mexico, United States of America

Source: Own elaboration for 55 countries (Switzerland and the Czech Republic being the only ones out of 57 countries that did not respond).

by privileged observers with high knowledge of local autonomy, and it can be assumed that their assessment offers valid measurements.

These data show that, in most countries, the COVID-19 pandemic was a crisis that did not affect the autonomy of local government. Thus, in 31 countries out of 55 the pandemic appears to have triggered responses without visible impacts on the autonomy of local government. It is true that, in some of these countries, municipalities do not play a significant role in health matters, where most of the alterations of IGRs occurred. However, local autonomy increased in 9 countries and decreased in 15. Is there a pattern that helps to understand these differences?

In seven countries (Finland, Georgia, Germany, Kosovo, Lithuania, the Republic of Korea and Slovakia) the role of local government in public-health issues was further strengthened, and it is worth examining whether this role, based on LAI's survey data from 57 states, was already significant in 2020, the year the pandemic broke out, or not. We assume that if the role of local authorities in public health was already significant, the increase in local autonomy would be a reward for a successful response of the municipalities to the challenges of the pandemic, while if the role of local government was not significant, it would be a clear recognition of the need to strengthen the role of municipalities in health matters, possibly combined with a critical assessment of the performance of higher levels of governance in this area. In addition, it is worth noting that in two federal states, the United States and Mexico, the pandemic led to a general strengthening of the role of municipalities, not only in health but also in other areas.

In an attempt to point out elements that help to understand the growth of local autonomy in dealing with the COVID-19 crisis, Table 11.3 presents the following information for the nine countries where the role of local government was strengthened due to the pandemic: the alleged impact of the pandemic (0–3), the scope of responsibility and effective political discretion that municipalities had specifically for health in 2020 (0–4), the country score on the LAI in 2020 (0–100), citizens' satisfaction with the provision of local government services (0–3), the importance of local government for citizens (0–3) and trust in local politicians compared to national politicians.

The data presented in Table 11.3 indicates that the group of countries where the pandemic resulted in an increase in local autonomy is heterogeneous and diverse. Among them are countries with very high, moderate and low LAI scores, while similar variations are recorded in terms of responsibility (policy scope) and discretion (effective policy discretion) for health issues as well. Regarding satisfaction with municipal services, the importance of local government for citizens and greater trust in local politicians compared to national politicians (except for Mexico and the Republic of Korea), this group does not differ significantly from the other 46 countries covered by the survey. The relevant conclusion is that the national context was in each case the decisive factor for strengthening local government during the COVID-19 pandemic, and therefore it is necessary to turn to the specific explanations provided by national experts.

In Germany, regional peculiarities and epidemiological situations – not all regions were equally affected by the virus – made it necessary for the states (*Länder*) and districts to respond to the local situation as needed. Therefore, the policy scope for local government increased – not only regarding health services but also the opening of shops, schools and kindergartens – but discretion remained low, as general rules issued by the *Länder* must be considered. In Kosovo, local government filled gaps in state action and developed a proactive role in health in terms of protection and raising awareness on physical distance measures. In Mexico, the already bad financial situation of most municipalities worsened during the pandemic. On the other hand, *ayuntamientos* had to offer services that were not previously provided, mainly through health and economic programmes. In extreme circumstances, certain municipal authorities closed the entrance to their territories to avoid the spread of the disease, in principle violating the federal and state constitutions. Some of them even implemented martial law to force their population to remain at home. In the Republic of Korea, local governments, rather than applying the

Table 11.3 *Countries where autonomy increased with the COVID-19 pandemic*

Country	Deaths per 1 million	COVID impact (0–3)	Policy scope health 2020 (0–3)	Eff. political discretion health 2020 (0–3)	LAI 2020	Citizen satisfaction with local services (0–3)	L. govern. importance for citizens (0–3)	Rel. trust in local politicians (0–2)
Finland	2.153	2.00	3.00	2.50	85.73	2.00	3.00	2.00
Georgia	4.317	2.00	1.00	1.00	57.32	1.00	0.00	0.00
Germany	2.179	2.00	1.50	0.75	66.11	2.00	2.00	2.00
Kosovo	-	2.00	2.50	1.25	46.70	1.00	1.00	2.00
Lithuania	3.718	2.00	1.00	1.00	62.77	1.00	2.00	2.00
Mexico	2.546	3.00	0.50	1.00	40.65	0.00	3.00	0.00
Rep. Korea	700	2.00	1.50	0.50	48.74	0.00	2.00	0.00
Slovakia	3.886	2.00	0.00	0.00	65.93	2.00	3.00	2.00
USA	3.637	3.00	2.00	1.50	67.10	1.00	3.00	2.00

Note: In the USA, data for PS (policy scope) and EPD (effective political discretion) for health refer to the biggest state by population (California), and the same applies to Mexico (State of Mexico).

unitary measures issued by the central government, came up with their own tailor-made countermeasures to respond appropriately to the characteristics of regions and residents and to prevent the spread of the pandemic. For instance, Suwon City introduced a temporary COVID-19 test facility and family isolation facility, while Goyang City implemented an innovative drive-through COVID-19 test system. The central government accepted these municipal measures and expanded them nationwide. Korean municipalities also mobilized public-health centres for initial treatment and close management of self-quarantine.

Finally, in fifteen countries, the pandemic led to a reduction in the autonomy of local government, nearly all of them (except for Japan and South Africa) in Europe, including some of those heavily affected by the pandemic. It is therefore worth examining below whether the trends of limiting local autonomy in these countries are possibly related to increased death rates from COVID-19 and the subsequent perception that higher levels of governance with more resources should intervene in addressing such a crisis, while the role of municipalities should be restricted (Palermo 2021). In Table 11.4, out of 15 very different countries where local autonomy decreased, the cases of seven European countries were selected to illustrate the same features that were displayed in the previous table for countries where autonomy increased. Unlike Table 11.3, Table 11.4 does not include a column on the perceived impact of COVID-19, since the relevant score was the same for all countries where autonomy decreased, namely zero.

Again, this group of countries appears to be quite heterogeneous, in spite of the fact that all selected countries are European and EU members. Except Denmark, however, all had a high number of deaths per 1 million population, with Bulgaria ranking first in Europe and Hungary second. The high number of deaths is likely to raise concerns about the effectiveness of the healthcare system and, more generally, of the administrative system, as well as about the appropriateness of the current distribution of responsibilities among public services. Among the countries included in the Table 11.4, the lowest rate of deaths was recorded in Denmark, which was the country with the highest LAI score in this group (75.59 in 2020), while the country with the highest death rate was Hungary, the country with the lowest LAI score (45.19). Croatia had the second-lowest LAI score and the third-highest death rate. On the other hand, Bulgaria had the fourth-highest LAI score and at the same time the fourth-highest death rate in this group. While it appears that the country where local government is strongest did best in the pandemic and the country where local government is weakest did worst, this correlation cannot be confirmed in most of the countries in this group. In some cases, the pandemic could have been a welcome excuse for launching recentralization policies. Therefore, it

Table 11.4 *Selected countries where autonomy decreased with the COVID-19 pandemic*

Country	Deaths per 1 million	Policy scope health 2020 (0–3)	Eff. political discretion health 2020 (0–3)	LAI 2020	Citizen satisfaction with local services (0–3)	L. govern. importance for citizens (0–3)	Rel. trust in local politicians (0–2)
Austria	2.486	0.50	1.50	56.96	2.00	2.00	2.00
Bulgaria	5.648	0.50	0.50	59.66	1.00	2.00	2.00
Croatia	4.562	1.75	1.50	50.47	1.00	1.00	1.00
Denmark	1.511	1.50	2.00	75.59	2.00	2.00	1.00
Hungary	5.088	1.00	1.00	45.19	2.00	1.00	2.00
Italy	3.220	0.25	0.50	61.78	1.00	3.00	2.00
Poland	3.182	1.50	1.50	61.16	2.00	2.00	2.00

Note: For Croatia, PS and EPD scores for health refer to the region of Zagreb.

was also deemed necessary to examine the relevant comments from national experts for this group of countries.

At first, there was a serious deterioration in the economic situation of municipalities in all cases where autonomy decreased due to the pandemic. In Austria, it was expected in 2020 that municipalities would get no compensation from higher levels of government for their financial losses due to the pandemic. In Bulgaria, municipalities were obliged to submit an additional report on extra spending in connection with the pandemic, while the drop in revenue could be addressed through interest-free loans upon approval from central government. In Croatia, local autonomy was significantly restricted by the special regulations and guidelines issued by the central administration to address the pandemic. In Hungary, local governments were assigned extra tasks (in connection with elderly care) without resources. Central government introduced free parking in municipalities and further deprived them of important revenue sources (vehicle tax and local corporate tax). In addition, a law on 'special economic zones' was approved, which enabled tax revenues to be redirected away from investment projects at the expense of local governments. It appears that, in this country, the pandemic was perceived as a 'window of opportunity' for further decreasing local autonomy, within the framework of the ongoing central-government policies of recentralization. The same applies to Poland, where politics of recentralization already prevailed. The autonomy of local government in Poland generally further decreased with the coming of COVID-19 and the implementation of measures to contain the pandemic. The national government adopted a largely centralized response to the pandemic characterized by, among other things, the adoption of regulations and directions that provinces and municipalities must implement with little to no discretion.

CONCLUSIONS

This chapter has delved into the relationship between local autonomy and government responses to two significant global crises: the global financial crisis and the COVID-19 pandemic. The analysis, spanning 57 countries, discerned divergent patterns in the impact on local autonomy. Following the financial crisis, several nations exhibited tendencies towards recentralization, substantiated by measures that constrained localgovernments' autonomy, particularly in financial matters. In contrast, the response to the COVID-19 pandemic presented a more nuanced scenario, with a majority of countries experiencing no or minimal alterations in local autonomy. Notably, certain countries, such as Mexico and the United States, saw a broad increase in the role of municipalities during the pandemic. In other countries, this was limited to the domain of health. This diversity underscores the complex interplay between crises and multilevel governance structures.

Factors such as pre-existing roles of local governments in health, the national context and the severity of the crisis played pivotal roles in shaping these dynamics. The study underscores the need for nuanced crisis-management strategies that acknowledge the distinct contexts of each country.

The implications of crisis-induced changes in local autonomy are profound and multifaceted. The chapter has shown that crises are managed with diverse sets of strategies, depending on the type of problem to be addressed and on institutional and policy learning. The analysis of countries where local autonomy increased or decreased during the pandemic revealed a complex interplay of factors. This analysis has been limited to measuring changes in autonomy and highlighting some potential explanatory factors. But the work of critically assessing the balance between centralization and decentralization remains to be done. And it will have to take into account the role of local governments in crisis management and the long-term implications for governance structures.

12. The European Charter of Local Self-Government and its impact on local autonomy

INTRODUCTION

Among the many factors that can trigger and/or influence changes in a country's level of local autonomy, the European Charter of Local Self-Government ('the Charter') is of particular interest, not least because the 11 variables of the Local Autonomy Index (LAI) were inspired by and to some extent correspond to relevant provisions of the Charter (Ladner et al. 2019: 7–8, 49–54). This offers an opportunity to compare the evolution of national LAI scores over time with each country's response to the challenges of legally incorporating (through ratification) and correctly implementing the Charter.

Since local autonomy is recognized as a carrier of democracy and the Copenhagen criteria for EU accession include political, economic and administrative conditions, the EU reviews a candidate country's commitment to decentralization, local governance and adherence to European standards, such as the Charter, during the accession process. In addition, several EU policies underline and promote the importance of local self-government (Ladner et al. 2019: 9), which means that the EU continues to offer incentives for decentralization after full membership. The main empirical hypothesis of this chapter, therefore, is that the impact of Europeanization on both compliance with the Charter and LAI is positive. In other words, we expect that ratification of the Charter and, at a later stage, monitoring of its implementation should result in an increase in LAI scores in several countries.

More specifically, this impact is expected to be stronger in countries that started from a low or medium level of local autonomy at the beginning of the period covered by the LAI surveys (1990–2020). And, as in countries with high levels of local autonomy, this impact is expected to be weaker in countries that are not EU candidates and/or are moving away from European standards and values. These countries are also expected to display a lower level of compliance with the Charter.

While the impacts of several international treaties (especially environmental treaties) on relevant legislation and reality have been thoroughly investigated in the scientific literature (Guzman 2002), the impact of the Charter is an under-researched subject, with relevant literature usually focusing on legal issues and relevant case law (Himsworth 2015; Kalimeri 2017; Boggero 2018). This chapter will review the historical path to the Charter before turning to investigating the impact of the Charter's ratification on LAI scores. The issue of compliance control will then be analysed, before the impact of monitoring on LAI scores and compliance are examined and conclusions are drawn. The specific topic of this chapter dictates that our focus is entirely on European countries that have decided to adopt the Charter and, moreover, decided to do so during the period covered by our LAI data. In particular it means that in this chapter we leave aside non-European OECD countries, which are the subject of analysis in most of the remaining chapters of this volume.

THE LONG AND WINDING ROAD TO THE EUROPEAN CHARTER OF LOCAL SELF-GOVERNMENT

The Council of Europe (CoE) was founded in 1949. Its main statutory bodies are the Committee of Ministers (CM), having an intergovernmental character, and the Consultative Assembly (since 1994 the Parliamentary Assembly), an innovative, at that time, deliberative body with representative character, to which the national parliaments of the member states appoint parliamentarians. The CoE was the first international organization with the statutory goal of achieving European unification,[1] based on 'individual freedom, political liberty and the rule of law, principles which form the basis of all genuine democracy' (Council of Europe: article 1 of the London Treaty).

On the road to the consolidation of democracy in Europe, local self-government has been recognized, from the very beginning, as an indispensable component of democratization processes and a major remedy against the concentration of power. Before and after the Second World War, dictatorships in Europe had rejected local self-government as 'anachronistic' and promoted centralism on a technocratic-authoritarian basis.[2] The Swiss politician Adolf

[1] See Chapter I – Aim of the Council of Europe – article 1 which states: 'The aim of the Council of Europe is to achieve a greater unity between its members for the purpose of safeguarding and realising the ideals and principles which are their common heritage and facilitating their economic and social progress.' See also: https://70.coe.int/1949-statute-of-the-council-of-europe-is-signed-in-london-en.html.

[2] A similar way of thinking was presented much later, during subsequent waves of democratization in Europe. It is not incidental that in Spain, Portugal and Greece decentralization was sometimes identified with democratization (Hesse and Sharpe 1991) – as it was during the post-communist transformation of Eastern

Gasser claimed that the resilience of democracy in his country was due to vertical division of power across levels of government and strong local institutions that build up civicness.[3] Gasser was a co-founder of the Council of European Municipalities (CEM) in 1951, whose goal was 'to promote a united Europe, based on locally and regionally autonomous government and democracy' (Knemeyer 1989). Following this bottom-up mobilization of local leaders from various countries, the CoE CM and the Consultative Assembly constituted a Special Committee on Municipal and Regional Affairs in 1952.

In October 1953 more than 1,000 European mayors gathered in Versailles and jointly formulated the 'European Charter of Municipal Liberties' (CCRE-CEMR 1953), which saw the old traditions of urban authorities as a constituent part of a common cultural and democratic heritage. Although this charter had only a political and declaratory character, it contained a number of principles and rules that were to be included in the European Charter three decades later. Thus, the 1953 charter referred to citizen participation and the rule of law as fundamental conditions for municipal liberties. The latter should be enshrined in the national Constitution and protected by the courts; the organization and the boundaries of municipalities should be defined by legislation after proper consultation with the affected municipalities and/or with the local population. Municipalities should have general competence for 'every function of municipal interest', as well as be granted discretion to 'adjust the execution of general laws in local circumstances'. The power of decision in municipal affairs, and the approval and management of human and financial resources, should belong to the citizens or their elected representatives. Executive bodies of municipalities should be accountable to the local society. Administrative supervision should be limited to legality control. Municipalities should be able, through their decisions on local taxation, to ensure an income sufficient to cover their administrative costs and all expenses necessary to cover the needs of their population. If there is a proven lack of resources in some municipalities, a system of fiscal equalization should cover their needs.

In 1955 the CoE Consultative Assembly adopted Resolution 76/1955 for the convention of an annual 'Conference to be attended by representatives of all national associations of the local authorities of member countries'. Finally, the CoE 'Conference of Local Authorities' (CLA) was established in 1957,

---

Europe at the beginning of the last decade of the twentieth century (Coulson and Campbell 2006).

[3] The idea of 'power sharing' in modern democracies is as old as the Federalist Papers (Hamilton and Madison 1788); later, Thouret presented his ideas on *pouvoir municipal* in revolutionary France (Brunet 2004: 193) and Alexis de Tocqueville his ideas about collective freedom through municipal government that is close to citizens (Tocqueville 2000: 77).

including 124 elected politicians of municipalities from all member states. Coming after the creation of the CoE Consultative Assembly (in 1949), and of the European Parliament (in 1951), this was the third time that a deliberative body consisting of elected politicians and the first time that an organ representing local authorities was established at the European level. In 1961 the CM approved the CLA charter (Council of Europe Committee of Ministers 1961), which was given the right to adopt resolutions and opinions that were to be submitted to the Consultative Assembly for opinion and to the CM for action.

The same year marked the start of the process for the formulation of a charter for local self-government that would take the form of a binding international treaty including basic rules and principles for local democracy and local autonomy. Later, the CLA adopted and the Consultative Assembly approved Resolution 64/1968, whose main target was to combine human rights with municipal/local freedoms[4] and incorporate the latter into the mandate of the CoE: 'one of the essential guarantees of the rights and freedoms of man lies in the guarantee of the rights and the freedoms of local communities' (Council of Europe 1968). Further on, Resolution 64/1968 emphasized that 'an organized Europe must comprise a number of common rules legally ensuring local autonomy in the same way as the principal human rights are already guaranteed'. The perspective of using mechanisms and institutions created for the protection of human rights, and especially the European Court of Human Rights (ECtHR), and also for the benefit of 'local autonomy and freedoms' triggered worries and, eventually, reactions of governmental representatives in the CoE. The result was that the CM rejected Resolution 64/1968, pointing to the 'substantial differences' in local government and public-administration systems across the continent. A first attempt to take advantage of the existing strong mechanisms for the protection of human rights to advance local autonomy was thus successfully blocked by national governments.

Nevertheless, in close cooperation with CLA, the Consultative Assembly issued Recommendation 615, a 'Declaration of Principles on Local Autonomy' (Council of Europe 1970), which also included the freedom of association of local authorities to defend their interests. Once again, the CM refrained from adopting a major political initiative of CLA on local autonomy. However, in 1975 the CM approved an amendment of the statute of the CLA to include

[4] This combination of human rights with municipal freedoms was not a novelty, it followed a liberal tradition that was expressed in the liberal Frankfurt Constitution 1848 where a 'collective right' to municipal autonomy was established, while several prominent liberals, such as John Stuart Mill, Toulmin Smith and, of course, Alexis de Tocqueville had underlined this combination: 'Without municipal institutions a nation might give itself a free government, but it has not the spirit of liberty' (Tocqueville 2000)

elected representatives of regions and rename CLA the 'Conference of Local and Regional Authorities in Europe' (CLRA); this was a time when regionalization and regional disparities were topical issues both at national and European levels. Soon afterwards, in 1980, the first international CoE treaty addressing local authorities was adopted, namely the 'European Outline Convention on Transfrontier Co-operation between Territorial Communities or Authorities', enshrining a long-term strategy of instrumentalizing transfrontier cooperation among local authorities for the benefit of reconciliation and Europeanization.

In the meantime, the CLRA had decided (in 1978) to promote the development of a charter for local and regional authorities with the legal form of a binding international treaty. In 1981 the Hermegnies Experts' Committee completed a draft charter incorporating selected good examples from national frameworks while also introducing innovative elements of a new supranational framework for local authorities. Drawing lessons from previous pitfalls, the experts refrained from earlier ideas of an additional protocol to the European Convention on Human Rights (ECHR) on the protection of local autonomy, since such an option would call the ECtHR to review the proper implementation of such a protocol and it was clear that most state governments would vehemently oppose such an endeavour (Galette 1982).

The draft charter adopted the idea of flexibility, following the example of the European Social Charter (ESC). In line with this model, parties to the treaty would not be obliged to accept all provisions of the new Charter. A minimum number of 20 paragraphs (out of 30 in total) should be accepted, including a minimum of ten paragraphs that should be selected out of a core comprising 14 paragraphs that would enshrine the fundamental principles of local autonomy. Following the ESC model, the draft charter did not opt for a mechanism of judicial review like the ECtHR, but for a political mechanism to review compliance. According to relevant procedures, the intergovernmental body of the CM would eventually decide whether state parties had violated the Charter.

Following further development by the Steering Committee for Regional and Municipal Matters (CDRM) that increased the discretion given to state legislation in several provisions while safeguarding the Charter's character as a binding international treaty, the final draft was approved by the CM, and in 1985 the Charter was open to signature for member states. It took nearly three decades (also because many European countries first joined the CoE in the 1990s) until, in 2013, all member states had ratified the Charter.

In 1994 the CM adopted a statutory resolution establishing the Congress of Local and Regional Authorities of Europe (the CLRAE) as a body representing local and regional authorities within the CoE (Committee of Ministers 1994). This body took the place of the corresponding 'Conference' (1975–93) and dedicated a significant part of its activities to implementation of the Charter.

IMPACT OF THE CHARTER'S RATIFICATION ON THE LAI

Ideally, the impact of the Charter should have been visible in a period before and after the adoption of the Charter. There were four subsequent 'waves' of ratification of the Charter. The first was in the 1987–93 period and involved several countries of Western and Southern Europe. The second, in 1994–99, included several countries of Central and Eastern Europe. The third wave, around 2000–05, concerned the South Caucasus and several Balkan countries, but also some West European 'latecomers' (Belgium, Switzerland). Finally, the fourth wave of 2006–14 included some microstates (like Monaco), but also Montenegro, Serbia and France.

The hypothesis is that ratification of the Charter has been an important driver of the strengthening of local autonomy, sometimes in combination with the perspective of EU membership. But how to define the key moment that might be used for empirical verification of our claim regarding the Charter's impact on levels in the LAI? Potentially, we may consider three points in time: the year of signature, the year of ratification and the year of the Charter's entry into force. Signing the Charter was in practice extended from 1985 to 2005, i.e. throughout 20 years. But ratification was in some cases delayed even to 2008 and entry into force to 2009. Typically, these three points are very close in time to each other, usually falling in the space of one year. But in some cases, the process was lengthier. Table 12.1 presents all 12 cases in which the difference between the moment of signature and entry into force was three years or more. In the most extreme case, that of France, the difference between the moment of signing and entry into force was 22 years, from 1985 to 2007. The process was barely shorter in Belgium (19 years). The next country in that ranking is Portugal, with a significantly smaller timespan of six years, from 1985 to 1991.

In our empirical verification, we concentrate on the year of the Charter's entry into force, checking whether LAI scores had changed either directly before or after. However, similarly, we checked the impact of the year of ratification, obtaining almost identical results (the difference concerned only one country, in which the year of ratification was too early to conduct the empirical test, bearing in mind the availability of our data). It is not possible to define the period before and after the Charter's entry into force, which should be taken into consideration in a fully objective way. On the one hand, the period should be sufficiently long, since implementation of changes in intergovernmental relations often requires some time. On the other hand, taking into account a too-long period would make it impossible to distinguish the impact of the Charter from other, unrelated factors. Signing a binding international treaty like the Charter usually requires several months of consultation, deliberation

Table 12.1 Time of adoption of the Charter – countries with extended process of adoption

Country	Signature	Ratification	Entry into force
Belgium	1985	2004	2004
France	1985	2007	2007
Georgia	2002	2004	2005
Ireland	1997	2002	2002
Latvia	1996	1996	1999
Lithuania	1996	1999	1999
Montenegro	2005	2008	2009
Netherlands	1988	1991	1991
Portugal	1985	1990	1991
Romania	1994	1998	1998
Serbia	2005	2007	2008
Slovenia	1994	1996	1997

and bargaining with both internal and external actors before the official decision takes place. A complex set of stakeholders is involved, including local-government associations, trade unions, political parties, various ministers, national and subnational bureaucracies and relevant experts. Ratification often follows shortly after signature and relevant preparatory procedures start before signature in parliament. The prospect of signing the Charter can be an important incentive for reforms. We therefore opted to take into account a two-year period before the signing of the Charter, which appears reasonable according to our experience. A first monitoring of the Charter's implementation is normally scheduled for the fifth year after its adoption (and repeated every five years thereafter). In the meantime technical support is provided by the CoE, and relevant political dialogue within the framework of several European institutions takes place in Strasbourg and elsewhere. In this regard we followed the CLRAE's estimate (and practice) that a five-year span is appropriate for evaluation of the Charter's implementation and its impact on local autonomy in a country. We took into account increases in LAI scores of at least 3 points on the index's 0–100 scale (a change we consider moderate) or at least 5 points (a change we consider significant). While we relied on intuitive definition of thresholds, we wanted to exclude minimal changes in an index, which might be considered as no larger than an error of measurement.

The results of our test for individual countries are presented in Tables 12.2a, 12.2b, 12.2c and 12.2d. At first glance, it appears that in most of the countries

Table 12.2a *Changes in the LAI scores shortly before or after the Charter's entry into force: increase both before and after the Charter's entry into force*

Country	N–2	N	N+5
Albania	12	15	57
Lithuania	48	56	61
Slovakia	58	61	68

Note: (N – the year of entry into force).

Table 12.2b *Changes in the LAI scores shortly before or after the Charter's entry into force: increase only before the Charter's entry into force*

Country	N–2	N	N+5
Estonia	62	70	70
Latvia	47	52	52
Montenegro	61	67	62
Serbia	55	68	69

Note: (N – the year of entry into force).

that implemented the Charter in their legal system, the moment of its entry into force was correlated with an increase in LAI scores, either during the few years preceding or immediately following its implementation.

But the hypotheses we formulated in the introductory section of this chapter are more detailed. They suggest that an increase in LAI scores in relation to implementation of the Charter is more likely to occur if:

- The initial level of the LAI is low.
- The country considered was in the process of accession to the EU (in any stage of this process) in the year in which the Charter came into force in that country. This condition concerns nearly all countries of post-communist Central and Eastern Europe, but also Finland, which joined the EU in the late 1990s.[5]

[5] Two remaining new EU member states of that wave of EU enlargement (Austria and Sweden) finished their process of implementing the Charter before the period covered by LAI data.

Table 12.2c *Changes in the LAI scores shortly before or after the Charter's entry into force: increase only after the Charter's entry into force*

Country	N–2	N	N+5
Armenia	42	42	45
Bulgaria	36	36	59
Croatia	50	49	52
Finland(*)	79	79	82
Malta	38	38	41
Moldova	16	16	29
North Macedonia	36	36	50
Poland	65	67	70
Romania	35	37	48

Notes: (N – the year of entry into force). (*) – N–1 instead of N–2 was considered due to lack of earlier data.

In order to verify the first claim we grouped LAI scores in the second year before the Charter's entry into force in three clusters:

- Very low or low – up to 50 (on a standardized 0–100 scale)
- Average – from 51 to 60
- High or very high – over 60

The claim finds confirmation in data presented in Tables 12.3a and 12.3b.

The hypothesis is confirmed especially in the case of changes during the first five years after the Charter's entry into force. In countries with a low initial LAI value, a modest or significant increase affected 60 per cent of countries in this group. In countries with average or high initial LAI levels, less than 25 per cent of cases showed such an increase.

Interestingly, all countries in which we can observe an increase in LAI scores, either in the years immediately before or shortly after ratification of the Charter can be identified as countries in different stages of EU accession. This applies to countries that joined the EU in subsequent waves of enlargement (in 1995, 2004, 2007 and 2013) and to others that are currently candidate states (Western Balkans) or are still at an earlier stage of EU integration (Moldova, Armenia).

Table 12.2d *Changes in the LAI scores shortly before or after the Charter's entry into force: no increase in LAI scores before or after the Charter's entry into force*

Country	N–2	N	N+5
Belgium	59	59	59
Bosnia and Herzegovina	47	47	48
Czech Rep.	60	62	57
France	75	75	75
Georgia	34	34	34
Hungary	68	68	62
Iceland(*)	75	76	78
Ireland	44	44	44
Netherlands(*)	50	51	52
Portugal(*)	59	60	60
Slovenia	55	55	55
Switzerland	77	77	77
Ukraine	40	42	43
United Kingdom	50	50	50

Notes: (N – the year of entry into force). (*) – N–1 instead of N–2 was considered due to lack of earlier data.

The data in Tables 12.3a and 12.3b clearly indicate that while the period before the Charter's ratification and entry into force has a lower impact on changes in the LAI than the period immediately after ratification, it is nevertheless significant. Such early changes in the LAI are not surprising: several countries tried to prepare their intergovernmental systems for ratification and implementation of the Charter. Changes in the LAI in the years after the Charter's formal entry into force may be interpreted either as an endogenous desire to offer greater local autonomy after ratification or as a result of various formal and informal advice received from the CoE. We will return to these external influences in the following sections of this chapter.

AN INTERNATIONAL TREATY WITHOUT A WATCHDOG? IN SEARCH OF A PROPER MECHANISM FOR COMPLIANCE REVIEW

Attempts to mobilize the ECHR to protect local democracy and local autonomy were unfolding in parallel with the elaboration of the Charter and continued

Table 12.3a Change in LAI scores in the years before the Charter's entry into force and the initial level of LAI (number of countries)

Initial level of LAI	Decrease	No change	Modest increase	Significant increase
Very low or low	0	10	1	2
Average	0	4	1	1
High or very high	0	7	0	2

Note: Modest increase – at least 3 points on a 0–100 scale; significant increase – at least 5 points on a 0–100 scale.

Table 12.3b Change in LAI scores in the years after the Charter's entry into force and the initial level of LAI (number of countries)

Initial level of LAI	Decrease	No change	Modest increase	Significant increase
Very low or low	0	6	3	6
Average	1	3	0	1
High or very high	2	6	2	0

Note: Modest increase – at least 3 points on a 0–100 scale; significant increase – at least 5 points on a 0–100 scale.

even after its ratification. One of the earliest attempts (in 1972) was legal action taken by some Austrian communities and their councillors to contest their dissolution, the loss of community property and temporary territorial administration by state commissars. The European Commission on Human Rights (ECmHR) ruled that the existence and the operation of LAs have nothing to do with freedom of association (article 11 ECHR). In addition, it was decided in the same case that no provision of the ECHR protects LAs, thus precluding *ratione materiae* the access of LAs to the system of this treaty. Another attempt (in 1987) by the Swiss municipality of Rothenturm, which complained against damage to municipal property caused by the military, failed: the ECmHR ruled that municipalities are not nongovernmental organizations and do not have *locus standi* according to article 34 ECHR, thus precluding *rationae personae* the access of LAs to the ECHR system. Several further attempts by LAs and local politicians or inhabitants were also unsuccessful (Kalimeri 2017: 200–211).

Due to this failure, the protection of local self-government at the European level mainly depends on the Charter and relevant monitoring mechanisms. Ideally, a suitable monitoring process would be described in the relevant treaty, as part of its stipulations, because monitoring is an important tool: skilfully applied, it shows how far a state has come as well as what remains to be done. However. there is no provision in the Charter describing a monitoring process, but only an obligation of the parties to forward relevant information to the CoE (which can, of course, be of cardinal importance for monitoring) is imposed by article 14.

In general, ensuring compliance with multilateral international treaties involves various mechanisms designed to encourage states to fulfil their treaty obligations. The effectiveness of these mechanisms can vary depending on the nature of the treaty, the commitment and the agendas of the states, the influence of nonstate and substate actors and the available enforcement mechanisms and tools (Simmons 2010). Some of these are: monitoring and reporting; special treaty bodies and committees (sometimes issuing recommendations or engaging in dialogue); peer review (when states review each other's compliance): dispute resolution (international courts or tribunals, negotiation, mediation, arbitration); national legislation and implementation (adopting domestic legislation and engaging domestic courts and other institutions); sanctions and countermeasures: diplomatic pressure; public pressure and civil-society advocacy; capacity-building and technical assistance.

Sanctions and international courts are often considered to be more efficient than other mechanisms of compliance. International courts have the additional advantage of influencing or even defining the prevailing interpretation and understanding of a treaty's rules and principles, even though the normative impact of the relevant public discourse and the dominant notions of appropriateness or even of the treaty's text as such should not be underestimated (Howse and Teitel 2010). In the case of the ESC (which was a model for the Charter, see above), next to political dialogue, monitoring and reporting, an important mechanism is the Collective Complaints Procedure, which allows specific organizations such as trade unions and employers' organizations to submit complaints to the European Committee of Social Rights. The latter is an independent expert body which is responsible for monitoring the implementation of the ESC.

Due to the lack of equivalent provisions in the Charter, the CoE initially used the theory of implicit power that had been developed by the Hague International Court (Boggero 2018: 52) based on the Vienna Convention on the Law of Treaties (1969) and especially on articles 26 (*pacta sunt servanda* – agreements must be kept) and 31 (*bona fide* – in good faith). Since the promotion of democracy is a core statutory task of the CoE and local self-government is widely (and explicitly in Charter) recognized as a pillar of democracy, CoE bodies would have legitimate power to perform monitoring activities. Resolution 223/1991 (CLRAE 1991) on democratization in Eastern Europe and the integration between Western and Eastern Europe provided for the establishment of a Group of Independent Experts (GIE), which delivers legal assistance and draft monitoring reports, and for the introduction of the Collective Complaints Procedure, which can trigger fact-finding missions and special reports.

The Collective Complaints Procedure was introduced in 1996 (CLRAE 1996), while the instrument of regular monitoring reports was comprehensively regulated in 2000 (CM 2000), even though monitoring reports had already been drafted and approved since 1995. In 2010, the CLRAE introduced a set of rules and guidelines that systematized monitoring activities (CLRAE 2010). Monitoring reports have, in the meantime, reached the total number of 141 adopted reports monitoring all 47 countries, while urgent fact-finding missions on situations of concern and special reports are far less frequent (ca. 15 cases).

Monitoring reports assess the level of compliance with the Charter in the country concerned and draft recommendations for improvement that can be adopted by the CLRAE, while in some cases resolutions are issued, assessing the overall situation of local and regional democracy in a country and highlighting issues where action is needed. Publicity on report findings and a 'post-monitoring' political dialogue with the country concerned have triggered reforms and changes in many cases, sometimes combined with a road map prepared by CLRAE defining the main steps to be taken to implement the recommendations.

DO MONITORING ACTIVITIES HAVE AN IMPACT ON LOCAL AUTONOMY?

The question is: to what extent do monitoring activities and the subsequent political dialogue and cooperation with the CLRAE have a visible impact on the LAI. In other words: are recommendations from monitoring visits taken seriously by governments? We have not been able to prove a causal link between monitoring and concrete actions increasing LAI scores, but the time coincidence of these two facts points to the impact of recommendations on the national system of multilevel governance.

The data in Table 12.4 suggest that monitoring missions matter. In 11 out of 42 monitored countries LAI scores increased within a few years after at least one monitoring mission. Increases of LAI values directly before monitoring missions were sporadic only. But all in all the empirical evidence confirms

Table 12.4 Charter monitoring and changes in LAI values

Country	Monitoring	N–2	N	N+4	Monitoring	N–2	N	N+4	Monitoring	N–2	N (till 2020)	N+4 (or till 2020)
Albania	2006	50.66	47.89	47.89	2013	50.86	47.89	53.68	2021	53.68	-	-
Armenia	No	-	-	-	2014	45.0	45.0	45.0	2020	44.12	46.08	-
Austria	No	-	-	-	2011	61.79	61.70	62.74	2020	62.42	56.96	-
Belgium	No	-	-	-	2014	58.33	58.33	61.44	2022	61.44	-	-
Bosnia-Herzegovina	No	-	-	-	2012	49.0	49.0	49.0	2014	49.0	49.0	51.91
Bulgaria	No	-	-	-	2011	61.31	63.31	59.66	2021	59.66	-	-
Croatia	No	-	-	-	**2007**	**46.2**	**45.15**	**53.03**	2016	53.83	50.41	50.47
Cyprus	2005	40.49	40.47	40.44	2016	40.41	40.69	40.69	2021	40.69	-	-
Czech Republic	No	-	-	-	2012	60.88	61.98	56.79	2021	56.79	-	-
Denmark	2005	70.58	70.58	71.95	***2013***	***71.95***	***71.95***	***75.59***	2022	75.59	-	-
Estonia	2000	66.57	66.57	61.80	2010	61.80	61.80	62.75	2017	62.75	62.75	62.75
Finland	1999	75.96	75.96	75.96	**2011**	**75.96**	**75.96**	**85.73**	2017	85.73	85.73	85.73
France	No	-	-	-	No	-	-	-	**2016**	**63.56**	**75.63**	**75.63**
Georgia	No	-	-	-	**2013**	**30.24**	**30.24**	**57.32**	2018	54.95	57.32	57.32
Germany	No	-	-	-	2012	71.02	71.23	66.11	2022	66.11	-	-
Greece	2002	40.55	41.19	41.19	***2008***	***41.19***	***41.19***	***45.72***	**2015**	**45.08**	**59.60**	**61.39**
Hungary	2000	56.53	56.53	56.53	2013	56.53	48.75	45.11	2021	45.11	-	-

Country	Monitoring	N–2	N	N+4	Monitoring	N–2	N	N+4	Monitoring	N–2	N (till 2020)	N+4 (or till 2020)
Iceland	No	-	-	-	2010	75.23	75.23	76.37	2017	76.37	76.37	75.41
Ireland	No	-	-	-	**2013**	**34.19**	**34.19**	**43.12**	No	-	-	-
Italy	2007	61.71	61.71	62.81	2013	62.81	64.65	62.00	2017	62.00	62.00	61.78
Latvia	2008	53.96	53.96	46.91	2011	53.32	49.47	52.17	2018	52.17	51.66	51.66
Lithuania	No	-	-	-	2012	61.16	61.16	62.13	2018	62.13	60.21	62.77
Malta	2002	30.31	30.31	30.31	***2011***	***35.59***	***35.59***	***40.30***	2017	40.30	40.30	-
Montenegro	No	-	-	-	No	-	-	-	2015	–	58.41	57.86
Netherlands	***1999***	***53.90***	***55.00***	***57.09***	2005	57.09	55.09	58.18	2014	58.18	57.46	59.95
North Macedonia	2007	56.83	56.83	56.83	2012	56.83	56.83	54.02	2021	54.02	-	-
Norway	No	-	-	-	2003	69.30	70.23	70.23	2015	70.23	66.67	70.84
Poland	2002	71.94	71.62	71.65	2015	71.61	65.87	61.16	2019	61.16	61.16	61.16
Portugal	2003	54.19	56.96	56.96	**2012**	**56.96**	**56.96**	**65.98**	2020	70.76	70.76	-
Republic of Moldova	2005	33.22	27.73	29.17	***2012***	***31.74***	***31.74***	***35.85***	2019	34.57	37.13	38.41
Romania	No	-	-	-	2011	55.26	56.70	51.35	2023	-	-	-
Russian Federation	2004	-	-	-	2010	41.0	41.0	38.0	2019	37.88	37.86	37.85
Serbia	No	-	-	-	2017	63.60	63.61	64.39	No	-	-	-
Slovak Republic	No	-	-	-	*2006*	*54.52*	*55.99*	*58.71*	**2016**	**58.71**	**65.93**	**65.93**

Country	Monitoring	N–2	N	N+4	Monitoring	N–2	N	N+4	Monitoring	N–2	N (till 2020)	N+4 (or till 2020)
Slovenia	No	-	-	-	***2011***	***49.79***	***47.23***	***52.96***	2018	52.96	53.44	53.44
Spain	2002	59.45	59.47	59.50	**2013**	**53.83**	**55.67**	**67.15**	2021	67.19	-	-
Sweden	2005	71.51	71.51	71.51	***2014***	***71.51***	***71.51***	***76.19***	2022	76.83	-	-
Switzerland	No	-	-	-	2010	76.81	76.36	77.10	2017	76.98	76.98	76.98
Turkey	2005	37.29	37.28	37.20	**2011**	**37.20**	**37.20**	**44.15**	2020	44.15	44.15	-
UK	No	-	-	-	2014	46.41	46.42	49.04	2022	49.72	-	-
Ukraine	No	-	-	-	2013	44.72	44.73	49.71	No	-	-	-

Notes: In the table we count the difference of LAI between N–2 and N+4 (till 2020), where N is the year when the monitoring report and relevant recommendations were approved by the CLRAE.
'No' means that either no earlier monitoring report has been approved after ratification or that such monitoring report(s) were approved within five years after ratification and cannot be clearly distinguished from the effect/impact of ratification. Or that no monitoring report has been approved after the previous one.
Bold italics – *LAI score increase of at least 3.*
Bold – *LAI score increase of at least 5.*

that recommendations stemming from monitoring may have a real impact on changes in the legal system of countries that ratified the Charter.

However, it seems clear that the impact of ratification and the Charter's entry into force is greater than that following monitoring visits. The difference should come as no suprise. The ratification and consequent implementation of the Charter represents a big change in a country's intergovernmental system, while monitoring is a more routine element of formal procedures. For several countries of Eastern Europe in particular, joining various European institutions was an important element of fulfilling their aspirations to become 'fully European', so it is no wonder that they were prepared to modify their legal system to achieve the goal.

CONCLUSIONS

Our analyses confirm the practical importance of the Charter. Several of its paragraphs are formulated in a very general way, leaving wide room for national interpretations. The general, not to use the label 'vague', character of some recommendations of the Charter might suggest that it remains a general declaration of intentions, without real impact on national multilevel governance frameworks. But our results suggest that this is not the case: despite the general character of several paragraphs, the adoption of the Charter has had a positive impact on the evolution of the LAI in several countries. The moment of ratification and entry into force (which is in most cases identical or almost identical) is especially important for the reforms resulting in increased LAI values, but monitoring visits organized after the formal adoption of the Charter may have a correcting impact as well.

Empirical observations confirm the hypotheses we formulated in the introductory section of this chapter. First, the impact of the adoption of the Charter is especially visible in the case of countries with low or very low LAI levels at the beginning of the process. Second, the increase in LAI scores correlated in time with the adoption of the Charter is more visible in the countries that are in the process of European integration, especially those applying for EU membership.

13. Rapid changes in local autonomy: a race away from the bottom or a fall from a great height?

INTRODUCTION

The bulk of this volume has assessed local autonomy from a contemporary perspective. The most up-to-date scores (2020 or the 2015–20 means) served as the basis for a cross-sectional view describing and explaining similarities and differences between (sub)national political systems. Comparing across space allows us to discern patterns and configurations of local autonomy. However, variation may also be established over time by taking a diachronic outlook (see also Chapter 2). Apart from being a static feature of a given country at a certain moment, local autonomy can also be conceived as dynamic, evoking questions of stability and change (Fleurke and Willemse 2004).

It is to the latter approach (*dynamics*) and course (*change*) that this chapter turns. The central questions are as follows. Where, when and how can changes in local autonomy be determined over the last 30 years? In which aspects and dimensions and why? In addressing these, our contribution focuses on a particular kind of changes: those that are radical (i.e. significant in extent) and rapid (i.e. swift in progress). They can be seen as the most pronounced and critical manifestations of the broader category of changes.

The chapter proceeds accordingly. First, the dynamics of local autonomy are theoretically situated in the debate on institutional reform. Changes may or may not stem from the functional subset of such reforms. Second, we outline our operationalization of rapid changes. Third, the chapter empirically describes the where, when and how of such changes in the 57 countries and three decades covered by this study. We discuss shifts in the general index value as well as the specific dimensions and aspects of local autonomy these pertain to. Pertinent rapid changes are illustrated with country examples. In the fourth and final section, our findings are summarized and discussed in view of the extant literature.

FUNCTIONAL INSTITUTIONAL REFORMS VERSUS CHANGE IN LOCAL AUTONOMY

Adaptations over time in local government systems (especially of the type this chapter turns to) are often interpreted in the light of institutional reforms. These can be denoted as a form of *polity policy* intended to impact on the political or administrative setting in which authoritative decision-making occurs. Reforms thus imply deliberate attempts at structural alteration via targeted interventions. Substantially, these can also pertain to aspects or dimensions of local autonomy, often set in the context of external functional reforms modifying the boundaries of jurisdictions, implying the redistribution of responsibilities, competencies or resources and involving supralocal levels of government (Kuhlmann and Wollmann 2019).

The extant literature discerns two waves of local government reform with functional corollaries comprising issues central to our topic. These waves intended to alter the responsibility profiles and decision-making powers in vertical intergovernmental relations. The first (from the 1990s onwards until the turn of the twenty-first century) predominantly tended towards decentralization. It entailed the dispersion of power away from the centre through (a combination of) deconcentration, delegation and devolution (standing for an ascending degree of subcentral discretion). These moves were most prominent on the agenda in the newer democracies of that era. Particularly in Central and Eastern Europe, a strong belief emerged in the idea of (local level) decentralization (as an antidote to the preceding autocracy) – even if (functional) practices strongly differed between countries and went hand in hand with various levels and modes of local autonomy (Coulson and Campbell 2006; Swianiewicz 2014). Fewer activities (particularly at the local level) appeared in their older counterparts. Here, functional reforms occurred earlier on and/or mainly at the regional tier (Vetter and Kersting 2003; Kersting et al. 2009).

Against these critical junctures clear path dependencies emerged. Nevertheless, at the turn of the millennium, local government assumed a broad range of tasks, functions and responsibilities in most contexts. This stemmed either from long-standing traditions of local autonomy or more recent decentralization programmes. In most instances, local government was also endowed with (or obtained) a power of general competence. Together, these tendencies moved local government beyond the mere delivery of centrally defined public services and provisions, opening avenues towards the steering of place-bound economic, social or environmental well-being. At the same time, they also opened the way to more interaction, interconnection and interdependency between tiers towards the default of multilevel governance (Denters and Rose 2006; Hendriks et al. 2012).

The second wave, which emerged in the wake of the 2008 financial and economic crisis and subsequent austerity measures, was a mix of further decentralization and also recentralization. Institutionalized patterns regularly persisted. In countries with a tradition of centralized systems, supervision and control were often tightened (mainly in financial matters), limiting discretion for the local level. Where there was a tradition of decentralization, the crisis tended to trigger experiments with deregulation, hoping the local level would come up with innovative solutions to tackle the challenges (Hlepas 2016; Swianiewicz 2020). In some countries, recentralization sharpened through the rise of populist politics and the subsequent turn towards a more or less illiberal polity. This manifested most sharply in Hungary after the breakthrough of the Fidesz party in 2010 (Hajnal and Rosta 2019; Mazur 2020). The governing party imposed sweeping subnational governance reforms strengthening the centre (its political stronghold). Its offices took over a significant share of public functions and enhanced their legal supervision on the subnational level (with the latter steadily losing financial clout and discretion). In Poland, the emergence of PiS (Law and Justice) entailed a more creeping form of centralization, without fundamentally dismantling subnational self-government. Moreover, this centralization appeared more sectoral than horizontal. It limited competencies and capacities in selected areas over hollowingout institutional guarantees or imposing more overall central supervision (Sześciło 2019). In several other countries in turn, decentralization reforms also tended to correlate with the ratification of the European Charter of Local Self-Government (ECLSG) (see Chapter 12).

However, such diverging directions confirm that pre-existing institutional conditions and contextual circumstances shape the fate of reforms and how and to what extent they generate effects (Bouckaert and Kuhlmann 2016). Territorial governance thus rescales within limits. Exogenous and endogenous parameters facilitate or constrain voluntarism or proactive strategies to bring about change through de- or recentralization. These set the opportunity structure for shifts in discretion (Pasquier 2021). Moreover, while changes in local autonomy may well result from these institutional reforms, they do not necessarily do so. Reforms are not always sufficient to bring about changes, partly because of the contingencies outlined above. Also, as a broad force decentralization (and its counterpart) does not necessarily coincide with more municipal autonomy. As Fleurke and Willemse argue (2004: 525): 'Deliberate decentralization can increase local autonomy but […] encompasses more.' Changes, if present in turn, are not necessarily driven solely by purposeful ventures of central or regional actors. They may stem from more diffuse and incremental processes ultimately bringing about a gradual shift in (certain aspects or dimensions of) local autonomy.

Therefore, in this chapter change and reform are analytically disentangled even if the former is likely to materialize as a result of the latter. Such a perspective was also taken with regard to the first version of the Local Autonomy Index ('LAI 1.0') when considering variation over time (1990–2014). The findings confirmed that 'the degree of local autonomy [...] has not remained unchanged over the last quarter of a century' (Ladner et al. 2019: 237). The dominant trend turned out to be one of increase reflecting an upward move on the scale for quite a large number of countries. This appeared most pronounced in countries with a low or medium initial degree of local autonomy. However, also decreases could be noted as well as instances where autonomy did not alter much over the period covered. In the latter, the starting level of discretion already tended to be high (here also, the past matters). Thus in sum, there appeared no outright convergence as the 'overall picture [...] oscillates between stability and change' (Ladner et al. 2019: 243).

The second chapter of this volume already outlined how these trends and tendencies altered or preserved extending the time coverage to 2020. It also added nuance to the canvas adopting a differentiated outlook. In this chapter, we have a more particular concern, focusing on the most pronounced changes – those that are both radical and rapid. We begin by outlining such changes.

DEFINING RAPID CHANGES

In most of the countries covered by our investigation, LAI scores increased during the three decades between 1990 and 2020. Among the 57 countries studied, the value of the LAI was higher in 2020 than in 1990 in 42 instances (73.7 per cent of all cases), had not changed in three (5.3 per cent) and turned out to be lower in only 12 countries (21 per cent). In Table 13.1 we divide the values on the index into five classes (Ladner et al. 2021: 71):

Table 13.1 LAI values in 1990 and 2020

LAI	Number of countries in 1990	Number of countries in 2020
Very low (up to 40)	18	5
Low (40–50)	15	14
Average (50–60)	9	10
High (60–70)	8	17
Very high (over 70)	6	10

Note: For countries for which 1990 data is not available, the earliest available score is taken.

- very low – up to 40
- low – between 40 and 50
- average – between 50 and 60
- high – between 60 and 70
- very high – over 70.

The number of countries with a very low value on the index decreased dramatically between 1990 and 2020, while the number of those with (very) high index values increased to almost double.

In several countries the change could be termed as significant. In 24 instances the index increased by more than 10 points (against the standardized 0–100 scale), and in two countries it decreased by more than 10. Such radical changes were most frequent in post-communist Central and Eastern Europe (16 out of 26 cases).

However, in this chapter we concentrate on a specific subset of cases in which such significant changes came about during a relatively short period. These rapid changes are defined here as those which meet two conditions:

(i) a change in the LAI value of at least 10 points within no more than three years;
(ii) a change in the LAI value of at least 5 points within just one year.

MAPPING RAPID CHANGES

We identified 17 countries in which these conditions were met during decentralization moves leading to an increase of the LAI index. In two of these countries such a situation even appeared twice during the 1990–2020 period. There is also one case of a rapid decrease in LAI values. The full list of identified cases is displayed in Table 13.2.

In the remainder of this chapter we aim to answer the following questions:

- When did such radical changes take place? Were they concentrated in any particular period or allocated evenly across the whole 1990–2020 timespan of our study?
- Where did these changes occur? Can we discern any geographical concentrations of countries in this regard?
- What was the nature of those changes, i.e. which dimensions and aspects of local autonomy did they most often involve?

Table 13.3 summarily presents the period in which such radical changes occurred. It shows that numerous decentralization shifts took place in the last

Table 13.2 List of countries with rapid LAI changes

Country	Timespan of rapid changes	LAI value: at the beginning of the rapid-change period	LAI value: at the end of the rapid-change period	Magnitude of change
Albania	1999–2002	15	55	40
Montenegro	2002–2004	39	67	28
Russia	2002–2003	17	41	24
South Africa	1995–1996	54	74	20
Bulgaria	1996–2000	39	59	20
Georgia	2013–2017	34	54	20
Colombia	1990–1991	49	68	19
Italy	1999–2002	48	64	16
Serbia	2004–2007	54	68	14
Romania	1998–1999	37	51	14
N. Macedonia	2001–2002	36	50	14
Kosovo	2007–2010	34	47	13
Moldova	1997–1999	16	29	13
N. Macedonia	2004–2005	50	61	11
Japan	1997–2001	48	59	11
Italy	1990–1991	41	52	11
Korea	1994–1995	35	46	11
Chile	1990–1992	31	42	11
Hungary	2011–2015	62	43	-19

decade of the twentieth century and the first few years of the twenty-first. In the following years, cases of rapid increases in LAI scores were very rare. The only noted case of fast recentralization took place at the beginning of the 2010s.

Over half the cases identified in Table 13.3 concern countries in post-communist Central and Eastern Europe. In most of them the starting point during the 1989–91 political transformation was an extremely centralized system with a minimal level of autonomy for local authorities. Quite often during that early period of transformation, decentralization was practically identified with democratization (Campbell and Coulson 2006). Greater local autonomy thus became a key principle in the set-up of the novel political system. It is hardly surprising, therefore, that starting from that very low level of local

Table 13.3 *Period of the beginning of rapid changes in LAI values*

Region	1990–1995	1996–2000	2001–2005	2006–2010	2011–2015	2016–2020
Central and Eastern Europe	-	Albania, Bulgaria, Moldova, Romania	N. Macedonia, Montenegro, Serbia	Kosovo	Georgia, Hungary (*)	-
Western Europe	Italy	Italy	-	-	-	-
Beyond Europe	Chile, Colombia, Korea	Japan, South Africa	Russia	-	-	-

Note: (*) rapid recentralization. All other cases included in the table concern increases in the LAI score.

autonomy several of these countries showed a rapid increase in LAI values. More precisely, in some of the earlier countries in the region to transform (e.g. Poland, the Czech Republic or Slovakia), the major decentralization was actually implemented as early in 1990, just before it could be annotated by our index. Such countries could be termed the early adopters of decentralization. In others the process had to wait until the mid-1990s (Albania, Moldova, Bulgaria and Romania) or even the first years of the new millennium (North Macedonia, Montenegro, Serbia, Kosovo and Georgia). In terms of increasing local autonomy, these cases were lagging behind, or playing catch-up.

Interestingly, Central and Eastern Europe is also the region in which we identified the only country (Hungary) where such a rapid change was going into opposite direction, that of recentralization (i.e. a fast decrease in LAI values). In other regions, alterations in LAI values that meet our definition of rapid change were relatively rare. In Western Europe we note only one case – Italy – in which such changes were noted twice: in the early and then the late 1990s. The few remaining cases of rapid change were identified mostly in the OECD (Organisation for Economic Co-operation and Development) countries of Latin America and Asia.

If we look at its magnitude, we notice that the most dramatic change has occurred in Albania, where the LAI increased by 40 over just three years (see Table 13.1). There are only a few other countries in which the LAI has changed by over 20 (in 0–100 scale) over such a relatively short period. One of them is Montenegro where the index increased by 28 within three years (2002–04). Another is Russia (change by 24 within just one year), but it is worth stressing that the LAI in that country remained on a low level even after that rapid increase. The third country is Italy, in which an increase occurred from 41 to 64. However, this massive change was the result of two waves of reforms, which altogether actually took 12 years. Hence, it cannot be classified under the label of rapid change.

In Table 13.4 we reinvoke our classification of the LAI into five categories, from very low to very high. It is very clear that most of the rapid changes began at a moment when LAI values were very low and ended with them still very low to low. Montenegro is the only case in which the values changed from very low to high during a short period. A similar change can be noted in North Macedonia, but it took longer and required two subsequent waves of rapid changes. The only two countries in which rapid change started from an average LAI level were Serbia and South Africa. We found no cases of rapid decentralization occurring in a country with an already high or very high LAI value. Rapid changes thus appear more as a race away from the bottom than towards the top. Moreover, when it comes to the latter, a ceiling effect seems to be at play. When local autonomy is already relatively pronounced, jumping to even higher ground becomes difficult. However, as the case of Hungary

Table 13.4 Magnitude of LAI change during rapid changes

LAI value at the beginning of the change	LAI value at the end of the change: very low (up to 40)	LAI value at the end of the change: low (40–50)	LAI value at the end of the change: average (50–60)	LAI value at the end of the change: high (60–70)	LAI value at the end of the change: very high (over 70)
Very low (below 40)	Moldova	N. Macedonia (1), Kosovo, Chile, Korea, Russia	Albania, Bulgaria, Romania, Georgia	Montenegro	-
Low (40–50)	-	-	Italy (1), Japan	N. Macedonia (2), Italy (2), Colombia	-
Average (50–60)	-	-	-	Serbia	South Africa
High (60–70)	-	Hungary	-	-	-
Very high (over 70)	-	-	-	-	-

Note: (1) and (2) refer to the first and second waves of decentralization reforms in Italy and North Macedonia.

demonstrates, a fall from a great height remains possible. From a high degree of local autonomy before the change began, the country ended up in the low category.

What were these rapid moves actually changing? Did they concentrate on functional matters (handing over new tasks and responsibilities to local governments, or increasing decisional discretion)? Or did they increase financial autonomy through changes in the revenue structure or borrowing autonomy of local authorities? Or did they rather change local authorities' political position in relation to the state? Table 13.5 summarizes the direction of the main changes. The column identifying functional matters refers to policy scope and effective policy discretion in the LAI. The next column (financial matters) summarizes changes in four variables (fiscal autonomy, financial self-reliance, structure of transfers and borrowing autonomy). In the columns on functional responsibilities and financial autonomy we take into account the extent to which the relevant sub-index changed during the specified period. The change may reflect either an increase in the value of one of the variables (i.e. policy scope or policy discretion) or parallel increases of more than one variable from which the sub-index is composed. The remaining five columns refer to individual variables used in the construction of the index.

As is visible in Table 13.5, the changes discussed in this chapter are very diverse in nature. In some countries (e.g. Romania or North Macedonia in 2004–05) they involve just one aspect – i.e. financial autonomy. In a few other cases (e.g. Kosovo, Serbia, North Macedonia in 2001–02 or Japan) they involve two different aspects, with institutional depth appearing most often. But we can also find examples of comprehensive decentralization shifts that involve four or even five aspects at the same time (e.g. Albania, Colombia, Korea, Russia and South Africa).

If we analyse the columns in Table 13.5, it appears that rapid changes are more frequent in some aspects than others. They relatively seldom involve substantial changes in the allocation of functions or discretion in their provision or delivery, which appear in only three cases (Albania, Columbia and Russia) plus in one case of recentralization (Hungary). Equally rare are changes in legal protection of local authorities (Kosovo, Moldova and Colombia).

On the other extreme we find changes in institutional depth (12 out of 19 analysed changes), which is a measure of the general autonomy of municipal governments in defining tasks that they can deal with. Most often (half of these cases) the change was relatively minor, implying that the discretion of local government was changing from a narrow to a wider range of predefined tasks (hence, not the maximal interpretation of local self-government). But in three cases (Albania, Montenegro and Italy) the change in the score was not only very rapid but also far-reaching. That represents a move from a situation in which local government can perform only a strictly defined set of functions to a general competence in which they can deal with any function not clearly assigned to other levels of government.

Almost equally frequent changes involved two other aspects, which appeared in ten of the cases analysed. The first is access, i.e. the existence of (in)formal channels to influence policies concerning local government formulated in higher tiers of public authorities. In most of these cases our country experts assessed that change as incremental. The score increased by 1 only (from 0 to 1, from 1 to 2 or from 2 to 3).[1] Only in three cases (Albania, Bulgaria and Kosovo) was the change from 0 to 2 in the scale. The second frequent aspect of rapid changes concerns one or more variables related to financial autonomy. Changes in the local financial system affected all four measures used in our index with similar frequency. The total score of financial autonomy could potentially vary from 0 (no autonomy in any of four variables) to 13 (maximal

[1] In this paragraph we refer to the scale of initial scores as discussed in Chapter 10.

Table 13.5 Dimensions of rapid changes in LAI

Country	Period of the change	Functional	Financial	Institutional depth	Organizational autonomy	Supervision	Legal protection	Access
Albania	1999–2002	*	*	*	-	-	-	*
Bulgaria	1996–2000	-	*	*	-	-	-	*
Georgia	2013–2017	-	-	-	*	*	-	-
Kosovo	2007–2010	-	-	*	-	-	*	-
N. Macedonia	2001–2002	-	-	*	-	-	-	*
N. Macedonia	2004–2005	-	*	-	-	-	-	-
Moldova	1997–1999	-	-	*	*	-	*	-
Montenegro	2002–2004	-	*	*	-	-	-	*
Romania	1998–1999	-	*	-	-	-	-	
Serbia	2004–2007	-	*	-	-	-	-	*
Hungary	2011–2015	#	#	-	-	#	-	-

Country	Period of the change	Functional	Financial	Institutional depth	Organizational autonomy	Supervision	Legal protection	Access
Italy	1990–1991	-	-	-	*	*	-	*
Italy	1999–2002	-	-	*	-	*	-	*
Chile	1990–1992	-	*	*	*	-	-	-
Colombia	1990–1991	*	*	*	-	*	*	-
Japan	1997–2001	-	-	*	-	*	-	-
Korea	1994–1995	-	-	*	*	*	-	*
Russia	2002–2003	*	*	-	*	*	-	*
South Africa	1995–1996	-	*	*	*	*	-	*

Note: * refers to decentralization (LAI increase) and # to recentralization (LAI decrease) reforms.

autonomy in all variables). In practice, the most radical changes were implemented in four Balkan countries. In Montenegro the score of financial autonomy rose by 6 points between 2002 and 2004. The same magnitude of change appeared in North Macedonia between 2004 and 2005. A similar increase could also be noted in Romania (a rise of 5 points between 1998 and 1999) and in Albania (also a 5-point increase between 1999 and 2002).

COUNTRY CASES OF RAPID CHANGES

The cases discussed below represent the diversity of rapid changes. Four come from Europe and one from beyond (Chile). Of those in Europe, three are situated in Central and Eastern Europe, which reflects the geographical distribution of rapid change occurrence, as discussed in the previous section. Three of the four represent a rapid increase (Bulgaria, North Macedonia and Romania) in local autonomy and the other (Hungary) the only instance of a swift decrease. The remaining European case (Italy) is the only Western country exhibiting the type of changes central to this chapter. The discussion is based on the applicable country reports (LAI 1.0 and 2.0) and additional literature.

Hungary

In Hungary, political dynamics played a strong role in the post-2010 period. With a parliamentary supermajority, Fidesz imposed radical reforms in the (subnational) state structure that negatively affected local autonomy. Increased political control by the aforementioned party drove recentralization (Hajnal 2016). Newly established and highly supervised central government offices took over a significant proportion of public tasks formerly under the responsibility of the local level. This also translated into a steady decline of local government revenues and an increasing dependence on conditional transfers. The reform also strengthened the legal supervision over local self-government units (Hajnal and Rosta 2019). The underlying concept was that local governments must administer public affairs and exercise authority *for* and *supervised by* the central level (Bober and Kozina 2020). This is visible in the negative shift in the functional, financial and supervision dimensions of local autonomy.

North Macedonia

North Macedonia exemplifies decentralization reform as an important element constituting the social and political order in times of transition. Municipal amalgamations introduced together with a relatively radical decentralization package were essential in the 2001 Ohrid Framework Agreement ending the civil war between Macedonian and Albanian ethnic groups (Kreci and Ymeri

2010). As a result of that reform, the Albanian minority got the right to use its own language in local offices, and increased competencies of local authorities established self-governance of local communities of different ethnic structures. Subsequently, local government spending (as a share of total public spending) more than doubled within a few years after the 2002 agreement (Lyon 2012).

In its Basic Principles, the Framework Agreement declared: 'The development of local self-government is essential for encouraging the participation of citizens in democratic life, and for promoting respect for the identity of communities' (Official Gazette 2001, art. 1.5). It called for the transfer of 11 new municipal competencies, along with a revised law on local-government financing to ensure sufficient resources and fiscal autonomy. Those suggestions have been (partially) implemented through legislation passed by parliament during the following few years.

Romania

Romania exemplifies an increase of local autonomy clearly connected to the European integration process. The necessity for further economic and administrative decentralization was reinforced by the requirements for public-administration reform in the context of EU-membership negotiations (Dobre 2012). The system was revised to meet these requirements, including key principles of the ECLSG ratified in 1997: local self-government and decentralization, financial autonomy, eligibility of local authorities, citizen participation, and the appropriateness and legality of local authorities' decisions.

Until 1998 the most important local taxes were the personal and corporate property tax and the vehicle tax. Following the introduction of Law 189/1998 on Local Public Finances, revenues from income tax became the most important local source. The range of the tax rate is in all cases defined by national law, but within this range local authorities are free to define the rate individually. The year 1998 also brought a right of borrowing, which was again related to meeting the requirements of the ECLSG, as well as the increased role of general-purpose grants as opposed to specific, discretionary transfers.

Italy

In Italy, the two periods of rapid changes (at the beginning and the end of the 1990s) form part of an almost never-ending process of institutional reforms remapping local government through a trial-and-error approach of reallocation, reshaping and rescaling (Bolgherini and Lippi 2016). In that sense, the type of changes reported in this chapter are but the melting tip of an iceberg.

In the first period, statutory autonomy was updated in terms of organization (Magnier 2003). Starting in the early 1990s Italian municipalities obtained more discretion in choosing their internal structure, establishing legal entities and municipal enterprises. Also, administrative supervision loosened, moving towards merely ensuring legality control (away from covering financial details). Furthermore, consultation and/or representation set in as channels of access but with limited influence. The second period brought a substantial increase in institutional depth. With subsidiarity as a leading constitutional principle, municipalities acquired a general power of competence. This period also built on the former. The abrogation of some administrative controls resulted in rather limited practices of supervision. The influence of access increased via local-government associations and joint intergovernmental conferences. Together, these two waves of reforms meant not a mere quantitative but a deep qualitative difference, encompassing the principles of organization of the state, and conferring a new significance on many of the different innovations (Magnier 2003; Bolgherini and Lippi 2016).

Chile

Chile can be considered among the most centralized countries in its region: municipalities are rather a form of territorial administration than of local government. Whereas the Constitution has formally recognized local autonomy since the beginning of the 1990s, municipalities can only choose from a narrow predefined scope of tasks. This implies some exclusive and several shared functions (monitored by the central state). Such limitations also translate into financial autonomy. Chilean municipalities do not have the capacity to establish rate bases of any tax. They thus act more as a collection level. However, the financial transfer system is largely unconditional. Most grants come from the development fund aimed at investment projects or capital transfers. Changes occurred in specific years where the level of conditional grants relatively increased. In that sense, changes were perhaps more swift than substantial. Also, own sources continue to form a substantial share of income and can be complemented by conditional borrowing. The main change in organizational autonomy involves the determination of the local executive. The first local elections in the country took place at the beginning of the 1990s. Historically appointed by the centre, mayors now became elected – at first, indirectly, by the municipal council, but directly by the citizens in the next electoral cycle (Chatry et al. 2017).

CONCLUSIONS: MORE 'EARLY RACE AWAY' THAN 'LATE GREAT FALL'

Intergovernmental relations are usually stable and changes in local autonomy do not occur very often. If they appear the process of change usually unfolds slowly and takes a relatively long time. However, in this chapter we concentrated on exceptions to this rule. We identified no fewer than 17 countries in which significant changes in LAI scores occurred in a relatively short period – a maximum of three years. Only one of those cases involves a drop in the LAI value: Hungary is the sole example of recentralization. The other 16 cases all involve an increase in local autonomy. Referring to the subtitle of this chapter, only one case fell. But it did so from a fairly great height (from high to low local autonomy before and after the rapid change). The recent illiberal turn spurred enhanced political control from the centre, limiting local discretion.

The great majority of cases analysed in this chapter (11 out of 17) are countries of post-communist Central and Eastern Europe. The changes in regime and subsequent political transformation in the region were the most spectacular examples of swift decentralization over the last few decades. This does not mean that these are countries with the highest scores on the LAI. Spectacular change was relatively easy to achieve due to the very low level at the starting point. In these instances, the increase could rather be termed as an early race away from the bottom.

In the introductory section we briefly reviewed the results of earlier analyses describing trends in local autonomy until 2014. The current extension to the 2015–20 period has largely confirmed the earlier picture (even if the previous analysis adopted a more lenient frame on change not limited to those of a significant and swift nature). Almost all cases of rapid changes in local autonomy took place in earlier years, most often in the last decade of the twentieth century and in the first years of the new millennium. Only two of our cases – Georgia and Hungary – enter the extended period of analysis. As mentioned, one of these cases (Hungary) involves a reversal – recentralization – rather than an increase in local autonomy. Our analyses show that rapid changes also occur on continents beyond Europe.

Against the general trend of increasing local autonomy, the specific nature of rapid changes is highly diversified. In some countries we see a change focused on a single aspect of local autonomy while in others the change is more comprehensive, involving several aspects. Interestingly, local-government access to central level policy-making is one of the aspects which changed most often. This suggests that local governments are not only passive recipients of decisions made on a central level, but also become a more important element of their respective states, at least being systematically consulted or represented in national policy-making.

14. The potential influences of local autonomy on local government legitimacy

INTRODUCTION

Local autonomy has been advocated by numerous significant European and international organizations as a prerequisite for 'good governance', aimed at bolstering the legitimacy of local government (UCLG 2008; UN-Habitat 2009; OECD 2004). Decentralization reforms to increase the autonomy of the level of government situated closer to the citizens are frequently recommended to enhance citizen participation in the democratic process, the efficiency of service delivery, cross-functional coordination and the accountability of decisions. In the European context, the European Charter of Local Self-Government, for example, has actively safeguarded and promoted principles of decentralization and local autonomy since its adoption by the Council of Europe in 1985. Beyond Europe, the OECD (Organisation for European Co-operation and Development) has issued guidelines to policy-makers, emphasizing decentralization as a means to achieve outcomes such as democracy, efficiency, transparency and regional and local development (OECD 2019).

Nevertheless, adverse impacts from decentralization and local autonomy have also been highlighted (Wolman 2008; Kuhlmann and Wayenberg 2015). These include concerns about decreasing stabilization and macroeconomic policy (Musgrave and Musgrave 1976), rising inequality and corruption, and a decline in economic efficiency and growth (Rodríguez-Pose and Ezcurra 2011). Perhaps due to the uncertainties surrounding the implications of local autonomy and decentralization, coupled with the complexity of these concepts and the challenges of gathering comparable data across diverse countries, the normative values of local autonomy have not frequently undergone empirical testing in a comparative framework in the literature, except for studies that focused only on a very specific expected consequence in a particular context. For instance, Gendźwiłł (2021) demonstrates a positive impact of local autonomy on local voter turnout, measured by aggregate turnout rates in local elections across 21 European countries from 1990 to 2014. In our first volume, we explored various aspects, albeit within the European context, while not concentrating extensively on a singular central element of the political system influenced by autonomy (Ladner et al. 2019) . Comparative studies on the consequences of decentralization, where local autonomy is expected to have a positive value, abound, but often fail to distinguish between subnational levels of government and do not consider whether governments have a say in how tax revenues are utilized (Vetter 2007).

Against this framework, the aim of this chapter is to address the impacts of local autonomy for various aspects of democratic legitimacy. We rely on varied kinds of local-government activities as dependent variables, measured both in the framework of the LAI 2.0 (Local Autonomy Index) project and in external databases, and local autonomy dimensions as independent variables. The perspective adopted consists in not considering local autonomy as a 'hurrah word' (Page 1982: 39), a notion that would inevitably entail positive consequences. This 'freedom to' approach (Pratchett 2004: 365), on the contrary, involves going beyond the normative rationales of local autonomy by empirically testing whether the policies of autonomous local governments affect the daily lives of citizens, i.e. whether local autonomy matters or not.

This chapter is structured as follows: having mentioned the supposed positive and negative impacts of local autonomy and decentralization listed in the literature, the next section discusses the theoretical assumptions regarding the effects of local autonomy on democratic legitimacy. The results section will focus on analyses of the links between, first, dimensions of local autonomy and additional data from the LAI 2.0, and then between the LAI and external data. The chapter will conclude with a discussion and contextualization of the results.

THEORETICAL ASSUMPTIONS OF THE EFFECTS OF LOCAL AUTONOMY ON DEMOCRATIC LEGITIMACY

Local autonomy has generally been apprehended in the literature as a relative concept, defined as the discretion local governments have to act in 'freedom from' (Pratchett 2004: 363) control by higher levels of governments. As explained in the opening chapter of this book (see Chapter 1), the proposed theory-based and multi-dimensional concept of local autonomy aligns with this formal approach. From this perspective, the extent of local autonomy theoretically corresponds to the degree of decentralization of a politico-administrative system, assuming decentralization is a static state (Fleurke and Willemse 2004), and based on the literature the assumed general consequences can be highlighted without differentiation.

This chapter also introduces another theoretical insight into the concept of local autonomy, as identified by Pratchett (2004: 364), namely the 'freedom to' approach, which draws on the interpretation by Goldsmith (1990: 31):

'Conventionally local autonomy is defined as the discretion local governments possess to act, free from control by higher levels of government. The usage here is much different. Local autonomy is defined as the ability of local governments to have an independent impact on the well-being of their citizens.' Pratchett (2004) also considers that local autonomy represents a potential for local government, constrained by a central set of laws, political factors and economic capacities. However, he goes a step further in analysing how local government, with its residual ability, can respond to the preferences and collective needs of citizens in implementing public policies locally. In this approach, the actual consequences and the underlying normative rationales of local autonomy take precedence in the analysis, rather than local autonomy being seen as a positive value in itself.

Across various disciplines, there is a vigorous debate about the advantages and disadvantages of decentralization. It is noteworthy that the presumed positive and negative impacts of decentralization, indirectly linked with those of local autonomy, have been more thoroughly questioned both theoretically and empirically in the literature – especially through fiscal-decentralization studies – than local autonomy, which appears to be relatively unquestioned (Ladner et al. 2019).

The issues of the consequences of decentralization are as follows (Kuhlmann and Wollmann 2019: 164, in Ladner and Keuffer 2023: 70):

- Effectiveness and efficiency: The first advantage of decentralization results from the better match between the services delivered and citizen preferences due to the spatial closeness to the citizens and know-how regarding local needs and service targets (Mill 1991 [1835]). Compared to higher levels of government, the local-governments' proximity to citizens enables them to deal with fewer information asymmetries and constitutional constraints on providing different levels of public services in different jurisdictions and on promoting innovation and experimentation (Oates 1999). However, effectiveness may decrease because of a lack of technical expertise and professional specialization. In addition, competition between small units to prevent dissatisfied citizens from 'voting with their feet' (Tiebout 1956) by leaving their jurisdiction may increase efficiency, whereas the duplication of structures may decrease economies of scale and states as a disadvantage.
- Horizontal and vertical coordination: Improved cross-functional coordination stands against greater conflict intensity due to permanent cross-functional coordination efforts and to distorted perception regarding individual government responsibilities (Scharpf 1985). Policy stability by local veto

players and counterbalance of central power is opposed to the lack of congruence between revenue and spending and coordination benefits.

- Democratic participation: By giving an effectivity to decisions taken by local democratic institutions, local autonomy resulting (or not) from decentralization may foster citizen interest and participation, leading to the development of a sense of citizenship and of political awareness (Tocqueville 1994 [1835]) and acting as a training ground for democracy. Taking this one step further, it may conversely increase 'pork-barrel policies' (Prud'homme 1994) as well as the difficulty of finding skilled, motivated persons ready to take on increasing responsibilities and complex projects.
- Accountability and transparency of decisions: Decentralization may lead to an increase of local politicians' accountability, responsibility and transparency due to the stronger democratic control (Jones and Stewart 1982). Conversely, it may increase corruption and 'capture' (Bardhan and Mookherjee 2006) as well as lead to greater and more inefficient bureaucracy.
- Uniformity and equity: More flexible and more adequate offerings, adaptability to the local situation and preferences in decentralized systems as opposed to legal uncertainty due to different applications of the law and lack of equal living conditions (Buchanan 1950).

The anticipated positive outcomes of a decentralized system on specific aspects are counterbalanced with assumed negative impacts on others, requiring a balance. Whether the positive or negative impacts predominate also depends on other variables and may vary from one country to another. In line with the well-known democratic dilemma, there can be a trade-off between efficiency and democracy, with some countries prioritizing citizen effectiveness while others emphasize system capacity (Dahl 1994). Building on institutionalism theory, Scharpf (1970) distinguishes between two rationales that can be applied to the merits and drawbacks of local autonomy. The first involves citizens' involvement in political decision-making, focusing on input in the political system, such as votes, interest or citizen participation. The second centres on the ability to govern effectively for the people, concentrating on the output of the political system, including actual decisions and actions of governments.

To add to input and output legitimacy, Haus and Heinelt (2004) introduce throughput legitimacy. This concept describes legitimation as achieving transparency in decision-making procedures, as well as accountability of decision-makers towards local citizens. Elaborating on democratic legitimacy, Vivien Schmidt (2013: 4) defines the normative criteria as follows: 'input legitimacy refers to the participatory quality of the process leading to laws and rules as ensured by the "majoritarian" institutions of electoral representation. Output legitimacy is instead concerned with the problem-solving quality of the laws and rules and has a range of institutional mechanisms to ensure it.' Taking the European Union (EU) as an example, the author suggests that modern democratic theory lacks procedural governance practices and introduces an additional legitimacy criterion, throughput: 'Throughput legitimacy builds upon yet another term from systems theory, and is judged in terms of the efficacy, accountability and transparency of the EU's governance processes along with their inclusiveness and openness to consultation with the people' (Schmidt 2013: 2). As local autonomy is a prerequisite for respecting good governance practices at the local level, throughput legitimacy is a subsequent potential consequence of local autonomy. This third rationale relates to how procedural governance practices are carried out by the government for the citizens and focuses on the accountability and transparency of decisions.

In summary, it can be generally assumed that local autonomy can be viewed as the theoretical prerequisite for greater input legitimacy (quality of democracy), output legitimacy (efficiency of services delivery) and throughput legitimacy (development of procedural governance practices).

ANALYSES OF LOCAL AUTONOMY DIMENSIONS AND SUPPLEMENTARY LAI 2.0 DATA, 2020

In order to explore some of the abovementioned theoretical considerations and assumptions, we first look into some of the additional data that was collected during our LAI 2.0 project. The codebook for the additional questions can be found in the Appendix. The nature of the data, i.e. survey of experts at the end of the country-profile documents, only allows us to tell whether there are any signs that local autonomy points towards better governance outcomes on aspects of input, output and throughput legitimacy. Also, the data we have in our hands only concerns the situation in 2020. Finally, due to the specific nature of our data, we must limit our analysis to country-level results and turn a blind eye to the fact that there are possible intra-country differences with respect to both the independent and dependent variables. Against this framework, this section only presents correlations without moving further into more detailed analysis. A subsequent section will delve deeper into some of our exploratory findings here, handling externally sourced data and providing more refined regression models.

Tables 14.1a, 14.1b and 14.1c present bivariate correlations between the LAI and its seven underlying dimensions on one side, and the additional data variables sourced from the country profiles on the other. Here some interesting observations can be highlighted. It appears that the overall LAI correlates strongly and significantly with much of the additional data we have acquired:

Table 14.1a Correlations between the Local Autonomy Index, its seven dimensions and additional data measuring input-related aspects of legitimacy

	Satisfaction with local democracy	Turnout at local elections	Trust in local politicians
LAI	**0.458****	**0.223**	**0.299***
Legal autonomy	−0.007	0.055	0.031
Access	0.158	0.016	0.104
Policy scope	0.191	−0.097	0.168
Political discretion	0.335*	−0.006	0.293*
Financial autonomy	0.361**	0.426**	0.154
Organizational autonomy	0.324*	0.040	0.230
Noninterference	0.309*	0.181	0.166
N	56	56	56

Note: * p<0.05. ** p<0.01. Values for 2020. Pearson correlations.

Table 14.1b Correlations between the Local Autonomy Index, its seven dimensions and additional data measuring output-related aspects of legitimacy

	Importance of local government	Satisfaction with service delivery	Implications of COVID-19 pandemic
LAI	**0.434****	**0.402****	**0.128**
Legal autonomy	0.116	−0.136	0.101
Access	0.294*	0.118	−0.103
Policy scope	0.029	0.235	0.179
Political discretion	0.273*	0.259	0.050
Financial autonomy	0.446**	0.378**	0.024
Organizational autonomy	0.214	0.348**	0.222
Noninterference	0.144	0.156	0.077
N	55	56	56

Note: * p 0.05. ** p<0.01. Values for 2020. Pearson correlations.

Table 14.1c *Correlations between the Local Autonomy Index, its seven dimensions and additional data measuring throughput-related aspects of legitimacy*

	Trust compared to national politicians	Turnout compared to national elections
LAI	**0.012**	**0.154**
Legal autonomy	–0.010	0.305*
Access	0.057	0.060
Policy scope	–0.019	0.076
Political discretion	0.046	0.128
Financial autonomy	0.036	0.042
Organizational autonomy	–0.103	0.053
Noninterference	0.008	0.025
N	54	55

Note: * p<0.05. ** p<0.01. Values for 2020. Pearson correlations.

satisfaction with local democracy, trust in local politicians, importance of local government and satisfaction with local service delivery. In our design of looking into linkages between local autonomy and input-, output- and throughput-related aspects of legitimacy in political systems, these results provide a first positive argument for local autonomy towards better quality of democracy and improved government effectiveness, respectively elements of input and output legitimacy. On the throughput-legitimacy side, we currently do not observe any significant correlation between the LAI and the available dependent variables, but we could argue that the lack of negative correlations suggests that the expected negative consequences of decentralization do not occur. In the next section, we will see whether these initial considerations remain the same when using external data.

When we delve into some of the underlying dimensions of local autonomy, we can clearly see the importance of financial and organizational autonomy, and to a lesser extent political discretion. Financial autonomy is the only dimension that correlates highly and significantly with local turnout, where other dimensions and even the LAI hardly correlate at all, given the low or even negative coefficients, with high p values to boot. Organizational autonomy also correlates with local democracy and service-delivery satisfaction, but financial autonomy is a more significant dimension, based on the observations so far. Also, legal autonomy correlates with local turnout exceeding national turnout. We may suppose that when the judicial status of municipalities is well anchored in the legal framework, it is procedurally validated by the population, which can increase participation at the local level. All things considered, the overall LAI demonstrates itself as the strongest variable, which is also why in the remainder of the chapter our focus is on the overall index as the independent variable.

ANALYSES OF LAI AND EXTERNAL DATA, 2015–20 MEANS

Our additionally collected data allowed us to explore segments of relationships between local autonomy and aspects of input-, output- and throughput-related legitimacy. However, a more in-depth look into some of these aspects is warranted, for which it is necessary to delve into other datasets that reach beyond the scope of our own proprietary research. In this section we use data sourced from the most relevant datasets available outside of our own LAI 2.0 project, which can be operationalized into usable measurements. Precisely because there are astonishingly few empirical studies linking local autonomy and positive influences on various (local) governance outcomes, there is a necessity for these analyses. Again, as was the case with our own additional data, we limit ourselves to country-level analysis since, for most of the dependent variables especially, we do not possess separated subnational data on such a large comparative scale.

Our focus is on more recent developments of local autonomy (2015–20) and potential influence on governance and legitimacy outcomes, as earlier years have been covered in a previous volume (Ladner et al. 2019). The values of the variables were compiled into means covering the entire six-year period. Before examining the various results, it is necessary to present how the dependent variables were operationalized and what specific data were used for this purpose.

First, regarding the aspects of input legitimacy, we focus on what we deem to be four essential components: satisfaction with democracy, political participation, trust in local government and overall quality of democracy. For satisfaction with democracy, we use Christopher Claassen's (Claassen and Magalhães 2022) Democratic Satisfaction dataset. The measurements on political participation and the overall quality of democracy stem from the Democracy Barometer (Engler et al. 2020). Trust in local government is a measure less commonly found in a large comparative design, which is why our best option here lies in the Eurobarometer data (Standard Eurobarometer, 2021).

Second, output-related aspects of legitimacy, which mostly focus on results, efficiency and performance, can be measured in a variety of ways. Some of the indicators are very broad and very often influenced by a huge array of other explanatory variables. We took measurements on corruption control, political stability, happiness and overall government effectiveness. Three out of these four output-related aspects of political systems are from the Worldwide Governance Indicators (WGI; Kaufmann and Kraay 2023), developed by the World Bank. Based on the WGI definitions, first, corruption control 'reflects perceptions of the extent to which public power is exercised for private gain, as well as "capture" of the state by elites and private interests'. Second, political stability measures 'perceptions of the likelihood of political instability and/or politically motivated violence, including terrorism'. Third, WGI's measurement of government effectiveness 'reflects perceptions of the quality of public services, the quality of the civil service and the degree of its independence from political pressures, the quality of policy formulation and implementation, and the credibility of the government's commitment to such policies'. Finally, to test the impact of local autonomy on the well-being of citizens, we used the World Happiness Report (Helliwell et al. 2020), a United Nations initiative, which also combines various economic and social indicators in an aggregated fashion.

Third, the concept of throughput legitimacy is theoretically divided into four aspects (Schmidt and Wood 2019; Caby and Frehen 2021): accountability, transparency, inclusiveness and openness. In our design, accountability is measured by the effective control of political officials through horizontal and vertical accountability mechanisms, as defined by the Democracy Matrix (Lauth and Schlenkrich 2021). We opted for the Democracy Barometer's (see above) measurements on transparency, inclusiveness and openness. For inclusiveness, we considered the Democracy Barometer's 'equality in participation' as a variable assessing to what extent various concerned groups are integrated into the decision-making process. Openness, here, is restrictively measured by the openness of elections. Alternatively, as a wider proxy measurement, we also used the Voice and Accountability indicator as defined by the WGI (Kaufmann and Kraay 2023): 'the extent to which a country's citizens are able to participate in selecting their government, as well as freedom of expression, freedom of association, and a free media'. As a proxy, this measurement can equally be used to assess inclusiveness.

As control variables, we used OECD membership first, as it covers a major proportion of countries under scrutiny in the LAI study, and because joining the organization implies adhering to a number of standards, including certain efforts towards decentralization and building good governance structures (OECD 2019). Second, we included a variable on the mean size of local governments in the countries under scrutiny (see Appendix), to control for theoretical considerations on the ideal size of municipalities and the impact on democracy and efficiency (Dahl and Tufte 1973; Denters et al. 2014).

Moving on to results, Tables 14.2a, 14.2b and 14.2c show the correlations between the LAI, its dimensions and our selection of dependent variables. Here we observe some strong significant linkages between local autonomy

Table 14.2a *Correlations between the Local Autonomy Index, its seven dimensions and variables measuring input-related aspects of legitimacy*

	Satisfaction with democracy	Effective participation	Trust in local government	Quality of democracy
LAI	**0.427****	**0.259**	**0.469****	**0.535****
Legal autonomy	−0.168	−0.119	−0.214	−0.165
Access	0.106	0.255	−0.009	0.092
Policy scope	0.183	−0.049	0.382*	0.380*
Political discretion	0.169	−0.095	0.338*	0.453**
Financial autonomy	0.609**	0.531**	0.547**	0.533**
Organizational autonomy	0.291*	0.154	0.335*	0.411*
Noninterference	0.098	0.007	−0.038	−0.012
N	55	46	36	37

Note: * p<0.05. ** p<0.01. Mean values 2015–2020. Pearson correlations.

Table 14.2b *Correlations between the Local Autonomy Index, its seven dimensions and variables measuring output-related aspects of legitimacy*

	Corruption control	Political stability	Happiness	Government effectiveness
LAI	**0.524****	**0.440****	**0.345****	**0.495****
Legal autonomy	−0.173	0.096	−0.255	−0.089
Access	0.113	0.266*	0.009	0.131
Policy scope	0.264*	0.019	0.170	0.178
Political discretion	0.251	0.237	0.150	0.182
Financial autonomy	0.634**	0.451**	0.558**	0.622**
Organizational autonomy	0.369**	0.303*	0.274*	0.358**
Noninterference	0.208	0.178	−0.002	0.215
N	57	57	55	57

Note: * p<0.05. ** p<0.01. Mean values 2015–2020. Pearson correlations.

and diverse aspects of democratic legitimacy. More specifically, on the input side, local autonomy is strongly associated with democratic satisfaction, trust in local government and overall quality of democracy. Output-wise, the LAI is positively linked with all dependent variables under scrutiny. Finally, only two throughput-related aspects seem to correlate with local autonomy: accountability and inclusiveness/openness as measured broadly by the WGI. As was the case in our previous section on additional data, some dimensions (mainly financial and organizational autonomy) also correlate with many dependent variables, but the overall index tends to show the strongest and most significant values. In sum, many of these bivariate correlations seem promising but do not allow us to draw conclusions about the impact of local autonomy on legitimacy, which is why we proceeded with a series of linear regressions to confirm or reject some of our assumptions.

The expectations that local autonomy really has an impact on the entire set of correlating dependent variables are somewhat tempered when we run our multivariate models. Tables 14.3a, 14.3b and 14.3c show the results of our linear regression models with its controls. When controlling for the average size of municipalities and OECD membership, we observe a significant impact, in many cases, with higher standardized Beta coefficients than the LAI. One explanation could be that both groups share a substantial amount of countries, and as we already reported a certain degree of multicollinearity, higher-ranked countries on the LAI often seems to rank highly across other measurement

Table 14.2c *Correlations between the Local Autonomy Index, its seven dimensions and variables measuring through-put-related aspects of legitimacy*

	Transparency	Accountability	Equality in participation	Openness of elections	Inclusiveness
LAI	**0.308**	**0.537****	**0.184**	**0.040**	**0.558****
Legal autonomy	−0.324*	0.028	−0.019	0.329*	0.001
Access	−0.230	0.325*	0.077	0.081	0.300*
Policy scope	0.454**	0.080	0.201	0.062	0.071
Political discretion	0.429**	0.336*	0.230	0.144	0.298*
Financial autonomy	0.254	0.529**	0.102	−0.258	0.588**
Organizational autonomy	0.348*	0.350**	0.097	0.123	0.373**
Noninterference	−0.132	0.287*	−0.044	0.004	0.319*
N	38	55	45	45	57

Note: * $p<0.05$. ** $p<0.01$. Mean values 2015–2020. Pearson correlations.

scales of legitimacy and good governance. This, however, does not erase the importance of local autonomy in reaching these goals of increased legitimacy across all three conceptual aspects. Furthermore, many of these models display good explanatory value if we look at the high adjusted R squared numbers. The remainder of the models need further research on what factors influence their outcomes, especially in the throughput-legitimacy area.

Table 14.3a Linear-regression models – LAI and aspects of input-legitimacy

	Satisfaction with democracy	Effective participation	Trust in local government	Quality of democracy
LAI	**0.266***	0.192	0.266	**0.436****
Mean size of local government	0.055	−0.012	0.006	−0.004
OECD membership	0.413**	0.161	0.466**	0.328*
R^2 adj.	0.292	0.024	0.340	0.328

Note: * p<0.05. ** p<0.01. Means 2015–2020. Standardized Beta coefficients.

Table 14.3b Linear-regression models – LAI and aspects of output-legitimacy

	Corruption control	Political stability	Happiness	Government effectiveness
LAI	**0.369****	**0.360****	0.088	**0.323****
Mean size of LG	0.028	−0.084	−0.101	0.035
OECD membership	0.451**	0.207	0.624**	0.503**
R^2 adj.	0.425	0.192	0.415	0.441

Note: * p<0.05. ** p<0.01. Means 2015–2020. Standardized Beta coefficients.

Table 14.3c *Linear-regression models – LAI and aspects of throughput-legitimacy*

	Transparency	Accountability	Equality in participation	Openness of elections	Inclusiveness
LAI	0.188	**0.331****	0.217	0.097	**0.408****
Mean size of LG	−0.079	0.117	0.142	−0.185	0.041
OECD membership	0.379*	0.535**	−0.058	−0.184	0.441**
R^2 adj.	0.170	0.524	−0.011	−0.007	0.459

Note: * $p<0.05$. ** $p<0.01$. Means 2015–2020. Standardized Beta coefficients.

CONCLUSION

This chapter has shown that local autonomy, including its different dimensions, measured on an aggregated country-level basis (from 2015 to 2020), is positively related to many measurements of input-, output- and throughput-related aspects of legitimacy. Most often, it is our combined index that is positively related to these diverse measurements, but financial and organizational autonomy almost consistently play an important role. At this stage, the findings (correlations and regression models) are compatible with the general assumptions.

We have examined the relationship between local autonomy and aspects of democratic legitimacy from various angles using a wide array of data sourced either from our own project or from external sources. In a first section, we made use of additional data that we collected using a short survey at the end of the country profiles that were sent to the expert coders. These results were limited to 2020 and used project-specific scales to assess what we did not find in other datasets, at least at the desired large comparative scale. The subsequent section used secondary sourced data that is more quantitative in nature, spanning from 2015 to 2020. Here, we ran regression models to empirically test our introductory assumptions, based on the literature. Both sections are important as they are complementary: using different types of data, from different sources, measuring different aspects of legitimacy. The fact that our evidence shows a lot of significant relationships throughout the variety of expert assessments, scales and data collection/processing methods, but also a lack of observations contradicting our assumptions, allows us to generally indicate a positive contribution of local autonomy towards systems that function more democratically.

Indeed, increased local autonomy may lead to improved quality of democracy, higher satisfaction with democratic institutions, better corruption control, political stability and higher government effectiveness, which confirms some of the more general positively tinted consequences of decentralization that we mentioned above. Additionally, to a certain extent, local autonomy also fosters more procedural (i.e. throughput) legitimacy by increasing the likelihood of stronger accountability and more inclusiveness and openness, albeit through rather approximate measurements of these concepts. The inclusion of throughput-related legitimacy is essential and necessary, for practical reasons, as better governance and legitimacy is attained not only through improving input and output aspects of political systems (Schmidt 2013; Caby and Frehen 2021), but also theoretically, because procedural aspects fall beyond the realm of input and output and are less prone to be affected by socio-economic factors. Examining the triad of legitimacy aspects, especially throughput, is a primary contribution to the literature on local autonomy and democratic governance.

Examining the impact of local autonomy on aspects of democratic legitimacy poses a significant challenge due to the scarcity of data related to these aspects, especially from a broader international perspective. Available indicators such as political interest, trust and participation primarily focus on general political aspects or national-level political institutions. Because our study did not initially include variables of this nature at the level of objective detail, we must, while recognizing inherent limitations, depend on available data. Nonetheless, given the theoretical consideration outlined at the beginning of this chapter, we posit that certain characteristics measured at the national level may have some relevance to the local level, despite potential disconnections. The difficulties mentioned above are intensified by temporal bounds that our data is limited to: the additional survey data extracted from the country profiles only measures values for 2020 and we limited the remainder of our analysis to mean values from 2015 to 2020. We suggest a more detailed additional codebook to better grasp the intricacies related to local democracy, efficiency and procedural validity, which could subsequently provide more substantial and precise evidence to support or reject our current findings and conclusions. Bastianen and Keuffer (2024) delve deeper into the LAI data as a time series and use different datasets and more refined and controlled analysis models to test some assumptions related to local autonomy and impacts on legitimacy.

OECD membership as a concomitant variable was used for control purposes in our research, but it seems to have a major impact on various legitimacy-related outcomes. This finding calls for more in-depth research on the practice of joining supranational organizations and adhering to their governance standards, more so than the influence of local autonomy. With regard to our current research, it does validate and enable efforts by international organizations to promote efforts towards decentralization.

Returning to the issues of autonomy and those more broadly related to decentralization, the absence of certain linkages in our results could signify that some of the positive consequences cannot be confirmed at this point, but it could also highlight some potential issues. Decentralization can increase both transparency and accountability but can also shift corrupt behaviour to the local level. The mixed results (i.e. increased corruption control but no significant link with transparency) allow both sides of the argument to remain valid. Another example: the absence of a significant relationship between the LAI and turnout/trust in our regressions could possibly indicate a risk of pork-barrel politics. Other impacts and issues of local autonomy inferred from the positive and negative consequences of decentralization were not tested in this chapter due to lacking data. Testing these assumptions, and those we only scratched the surface of, warrants our call for more extended research.

Again, it is important to remember that the relationship between local autonomy and the various indicators of legitimacy and performance is most likely two-sided or circular, with many concomitant variations needing to be added. Increasing local autonomy may provide a preconditional framework that favours these sought-after outcomes, but better socio-economic factors and stronger democratic institutions with more trustworthy and accountable local governments may also encourage the move towards greater autonomy. A simple increase in local autonomy is not a panacea to improve the functioning of local governments. It might help in particular conditions to begin sound capacity-building, but it also comes with idiosyncratic risks. The intricacies are in dire need of more quantitative and qualitative research that falls beyond the intended scope of this chapter.

All things considered, based on our findings, we can confirm a certain amount of positively related impacts of local autonomy on aspects of input, output and throughput legitimacy. This chapter therefore underlines the importance of taking into account local government and local autonomy in the study and pursuit of good democratic governance.

Appendix

LAI 2.0 PROJECT CODING INSTRUCTIONS FOR THE COUNTRY EXPERTS

Codebook LAI 2.0

Start with the most recent year (2020) and work backward. Find out whether there have been reforms which change the score. If there are no written sources available you may have to get in contact with officials or colleagues. Please, state the source when the score stems from such sources.

Half-scores are not permitted. Exceptions: policy scope and effective political discretion (please see coding instructions by fields of service below), organizational autonomy and legal protection.

Table A.1a Self-rule

Institutional depth	*The extent to which local government is formally autonomous and can choose the tasks they want to perform* Additional coding instructions: The coding has to comply with the legal framework in the respective countries. This means that the coding refers to the status of local government according to the constitution and other relevant legislation. Whether a municipality is responsible for the different tasks and/or has the financial resources is not the question here. If there are deeply contradictory regulations, this should be reflected in the coding and also mentioned in the notes.	**0–3**	0 local authorities can only perform mandated tasks 1 local authorities can choose from a very narrow, predefined scope of tasks 2 local authorities can choose from a wide scope of predefined tasks 3 local authorities are free to take on any new tasks (residual competencies) not assigned to other levels of government
Policy scope	*Range of functions (tasks) where local government assumes responsibility for the delivery of the services (whether it is provided by municipal personnel or through other arrangements)* Additional coding instructions: Here we want to know whether local government assumes responsibility for the delivery of these tasks and services. How much they can decide is part of the next question. Half points can be used if local government is only partly involved (*i.e.* coding instructions by fields of services below).	**0–4**	Not at all, partly, or fully responsible for: Education (0–3) Social assistance (0–3) Health (0–3) Land use (0–2) Public transport (0–1) Housing (0–1) Police (0–1) Caring functions (0–3)

Effective political discretion	*The extent to which local government can make final decisions over these functions* Additional coding instructions: Here we want to know whether municipal decision-makers are required by law to consult with, seek the permission, consent or cooperation of regional and national agencies before final decisions can be made or not. Half points can be used if local government can only partly decide (*i.e.* coding instructions by fields of services below).	**0–4**	No, some, or real authoritative decision-making in: Education (0–3) Social assistance (0–3) Health (0–3) Land use (0–2) Public transport (0–1) Housing (0–1) Police (0–1) Caring functions (0–3)
Fiscal autonomy	*The extent to which local government can independently tax its population* Additional coding instructions: For this dimension the level of contribution of the tax for local authorities (how much the tax actually yields) has to be clarified in the explanations.	**0–4**	0 local authorities do not set base and rate of any tax 1 local authorities set base or rate of minor taxes 2 local authorities set rate of one major tax (personal income, corporate, value added, property or sales tax) under restrictions stipulated by higher levels of government 3 local authorities set rate of one major tax (personal income, corporate, value added, property or sales tax) with few or no restrictions 4 local authorities set base and rate of more than one major tax (personal income, corporate, value added, property or sales tax)

Financial transfer system	*The proportion of unconditional financial transfers to total financial transfers received by the local government*	**0–3**	0 conditional transfers are dominant (unconditional = 0–40% of total transfers) 1 there is largely a balance between conditional and unconditional financial transfers (unconditional = 40–60%) 2 unconditional financial transfers are dominant (unconditional = 60–80%) 3 nearly all transfers are unconditional (unconditional = 80–100%)
Financial self-reliance	*The proportion of local government revenues derived from own/local sources (i.e. taxes, fees, charges over which local government has influence)* Additional coding instructions: A shared tax collected by central government and over which local government has no influence individually (cannot e.g. set base or rate), has to be regarded as financial transfer. Please, make a note in your country report if this is the case.	**0–3**	0 own sources yield less than 10% of total revenues 1 own sources yield 10–25% 2 own sources yield 25–50% 3 own sources yield more than 50%

Borrowing autonomy	*The extent to which local government can borrow* Additional coding instructions: When borrowing under restrictions applies (code 1 or 2), please make a note in your country report as to which restriction(s) apply: a. golden rule (e. g. no borrowing to cover current account deficits) b. no foreign borrowing or borrowing from the regional or central bank only c. no borrowing above a ceiling, absolute level of subnational indebtedness, maximum debt-service ratio for new borrowing or debt brake mechanism d. borrowing is limited to specific purposes	**0–3**	0 local authorities cannot borrow 1 local authorities may borrow under prior authorisation by higher-level governments and with borrowing restrictions imposed by higher-level authorities 2 local authorities may borrow without prior authorisation but with restrictions imposed by higher-level authorities 3 local authorities may borrow without authorisation or restriction imposed by higher-level authorities

Organizational autonomy	*The extent to which local government is free to decide about its own organization and electoral system* Additional coding instructions: If the status of staff (e.g. possibility to hire contract workers) is largely determined by national norms a maximum score of 0.25 is obtainable	**0–4**	**Local executives and election system (0–2):** <u>(0–1) local executives are elected by the municipal council or directly by citizens</u> <u>(0–1) local government can decide core elements of the political system (electoral districts, number of seats, electoral system)</u> **Staff and local structures (0–2):** *Local authorities:* Hire their own staff (0–0.05) Fix the salary of their employees (0–0.05) <u>Choose their organizational structure and status of staff (0–0.05)</u> Establish legal entities and municipal enterprises (0–0.05)
Self-rule	-	**0–28**	The overall self-rule enjoyed by local government in X country (the sum of all the indicators above)

Note: Underlined are the changes compared to Codebook LAI 1.0.

Table A.1b Interactive rule

Legal protection	*Existence of constitutional or legal means to assert local autonomy*	**0–3**	(0–1) constitutional clauses or other statutory regulations protect local self-government (0–1) local authorities have recourse to the judicial system through constitutional courts to settle disputes with higher authorities (0–1) local authorities have recourse to the judicial system through administrative courts or ordinary courts to settle disputes with higher authorities or other means that protect local autonomy exist (e.g. listing of all municipalities in the constitution or the impossibility to force them to merge)
Administrative supervision	*The extent to which administrative supervision of local government is (un)obtrusive*	**0–3**	0 administrative supervision reviews legality as well as merits/ expediency of municipal decisions 1 administrative supervision covers details of accounts and spending priorities 2 administrative supervision only aims at ensuring compliance with law (legality of local decisions) 3 there is very limited administrative supervision (e.g. the higher authorities cannot suspend a decision)
Central or regional access	*The extent to which local authorities have channels to influence higher level governments' policy-making* Additional coding instructions: Please clarify the channels and assess the extent of influence exercised upon the higher level.	**0–3**	(0–1) local authorities have access to higher-level decision-making through formal consultation procedures and mechanisms (0–1) local authorities have access to higher-level decision-making through formal representation structures (0–1) local authorities have access to higher-level decision-making through more informal channels (e.g. through trade unions that try to set the legislative agenda, party political networks, dual mandate holding, etc.)
Interactive rule	-	**0–9**	The overall interactive rule enjoyed by local government in X country (the sum of all the three indicators above)

LA	-	**0–37**	The combined autonomy of local authorities (the sum of all indicators)

Note: Underlined are the changes compared to Codebook LAI 1.0.

Additional Coding Instructions by Fields of Services

Range of functions (tasks) where local government assumes responsibility for the delivery of the services (whether it is provided by municipal personnel or through other arrangements).

You can use half of the points if local government assumes only a part of the responsibility – 0.5 in Land use and 0.25 in Education, Social assistance, Health, Public transport, Caring functions and Police.

Table A.1c *Policy scope (0–4)*

Fields	Services	Codes
Education (0–3)	• Preschool (age 1–6) • Primary school (age 6–15) • Secondary school (age 15–18)	For each of the services: +0.5 point if local government assumes full responsibility for infra-structure and/or the delivery of services +0.5 point if local government assumes full responsibility for personnel, including staffing and salaries
Social assistance (0–3)	• Economic assistance (distress relief) • Work training/rehabilitation • Integration of refugees	For each of the services: +0.5 point if local government assumes full responsibility for the organisation and/or delivery of services +0.5 point if local government assumes full responsibility for personnel, including staffing and salaries
Health (0–3)	• Primary health • Hospitals • Dental services	For each of the services: +0.5 point if local government assumes full responsibility for infra-structure and/or the delivery of services +0.5 point if local government assumes full responsibility for personnel, including staffing and salaries
Land use (0–2)	• Building permits • Zoning	+1 point if local government assumes full responsibility for administering building permits +1 point if local government assumes full responsibility for administering zoning
Public transport (0–1)	• Bus transport services • Railway transport services	+0.5 point if local government assumes full responsibility for bus transport services +0.5 point if local government assumes full responsibility for railway transport services

Fields	Services	Codes
Housing (0–1)	• Housing and town development • Social housing	+0.5 point if local government assumes full responsibility for housing and town development +0.5 point if local government assumes full responsibility for social housing
Police (0–1)	• Public order • Traffic police	+0.5 point if local government assumes full responsibility for public order +0.5 point if local government assumes full responsibility for traffic police
Caring functions (0–3)	• General caring services • Services for special groups • Child protection	For each of the services: +0.5 point if local government assumes full responsibility for infra-structure and/or the availability of the service +0.5 point if local government assumes full responsibility for personnel, including staffing and salaries

Table A.1d *Effective political discretion (0–4): the extent to which local government can make final decisions over these functions*

Fields	Services	Codes
Education (0–3)	• Preschool (age 1–6) • Primary school (age 6–15) • Secondary school (age 15–18)	For each of the services: 0 if local government has no authoritative decision-making 0.5 if local government has some authoritative decision-making 1 if local government has real authoritative decision-making
Social assistance (0–3)	• Economic assistance (distress relief) • Work training/rehabilitation • Integration of refugees	For each of the services: 0 if local government has no authoritative decision-making 0.5 if local government has some authoritative decision-making 1 if local government has real authoritative decision-making
Health (0–3)	• Primary health • Hospitals • Dental services	For each of the services: 0 if local government has no authoritative decision-making 0.5 if local government has some authoritative decision-making 1 if local government has real authoritative decision-making
Land use (0–2)	• Building permits • Zoning	For each of the services: 0 if local government has no authoritative decision-making 0.5 if local government has some authoritative decision-making 1 if local government has real authoritative decision-making
Public transport (0–1)	• Bus transport services • Railway transport services	For each of the services: 0 if local government has no authoritative decision-making 0.5 if local government has some authoritative decision-making 1 if local government has real authoritative decision-making

Fields	Services	Codes
Housing (0–1)	• Housing and town development • Social housing	For each of the services: 0 if local government has no authoritative decision-making 0.5 if local government has some authoritative decision-making 1 if local government has real authoritative decision-making
Police (0–1)	• Public order • Traffic police	For each of the services: 0 if local government has no authoritative decision-making 0.5 if local government has some authoritative decision-making 1 if local government has real authoritative decision-making
Caring functions (0–3)	• General caring services • Services for special groups • Child protection	For each of the services: 0 if local government has no authoritative decision-making 0.5 if local government has some authoritative decision-making 1 if local government has real authoritative decision-making

With these additional questions on the potential causal mechanisms and effects of local autonomy, we want to collect a current perception. More concretely, it means that it would be great if you could give us your answers to these questions directly here (i.e. no coding sheet), without considering any possible asymmetries in your country (i.e. national level only) or any changes over time (i.e. 2020 only). Any interesting (legal) indication may be also mentioned/added.

To better understand how an external shock may cause a change in local autonomy in a given country, a question is asked about the implication of the COVID-19 pandemic.

The effects of local autonomy concern the satisfaction with local government service delivery, the importance of local government for citizens, the satisfaction with local democracy, the turnout at local elections and the trustworthiness of local politicians.

Table A.2 Codebook of additional variables

Variable	***Description***	**Scale**	Codes
Implication of COVID-19 pandemic	*The extent to which the autonomy of local government has been impacted by the COVID-19 pandemic*	**0–3**	0 local government autonomy has generally decreased with the COVID-19 pandemic 1 local government autonomy has not been impacted by the COVID-19 pandemic 2 local government autonomy in health has increased with the COVID-19 pandemic 3 local government autonomy in health and in other fields related to the COVID-19 pandemic has increased
Satisfaction with local government service delivery	*The extent to which the citizens are satisfied with local government service delivery*	**0–3**	0 citizens are generally not satisfied at all with local government service delivery 1 citizens are generally moderately satisfied with local government service delivery 2 citizens are generally mostly satisfied with local government service delivery 3 citizens are generally entirely satisfied with local government service delivery

Variable	*Description*	Scale	Codes
Importance of local government	*The extent to which local government has an important role in the daily life of citizens*	**0–3**	0 local government is not important at all in the daily life of citizens 1 local government is somewhat important in the daily life of citizens 2 local government is important in the daily life of citizens 3 local government is very important in the daily life of citizens
Satisfaction with local democracy	*The extent to which the citizens are satisfied with local democracy*	**0–4**	0 citizens are not at all satisfied with local democracy 1 citizens are rather not satisfied with local democracy 2 citizens are neither dissatisfied nor satisfied with local democracy 3 citizens are rather satisfied with local democracy 4 citizens are entirely satisfied with local democracy
Turnout at local elections	*Electoral turnout at local elections (approximately, last general elections)*	**0–4**	0 no elections 1 between 1 and 25 % 2 between 26 and 50 % 3 between 51 and 75 % 4 between 76 and 100 %

Variable	Description	Scale	Codes
Electoral participation on local level compared to electoral participation on national level	*The extent to which electoral participation on local level is higher than on national level*	**0–2**	0 electoral participation on local level is generally lower than electoral participation on national level 1 electoral participation on local and on national level are very much the same 2 electoral participation on local level is generally higher than electoral participation on national level
Perception of trustworthiness of local politicians	*The extent to which local politicians are trustworthy*	**0–4**	0 local politicians are not at all trustworthy 1 local politicians are rather not trustworthy 2 local politicians are moderately trustworthy 3 local politicians are rather trustworthy 4 local politicians are very much trustworthy
Perception of trustworthiness of local politicians compared to national politicians	*Whether local politicians are more trustworthy than national politicians*	**0–2**	0 local level politicians are generally less trustworthy than national politicians 1 local and national politicians are similar in terms of trustworthiness 2 local level politicians are generally more trustworthy than national politicians

Table A.3 *Descriptive statistics of additional variables*

Additional variable	Mean	Median	SD	Min	Max
Implication of the COVID-19 pandemic	0.93	1.00	0.74	0.00	3.00
Satisfaction with local government service delivery	1.49	1.75	0.71	0.00	3.00
Importance of local government	2.07	2.00	0.85	0.00	3.00
Satisfaction with local democracy	2.30	2.50	0.97	0.00	4.00
Turnout at local elections	2.66	3.00	0.82	0.00	4.00
Electoral participation on local level compared to electoral participation on national level	0.56	0.00	0.69	0.00	2.00
Perception of trustworthiness of local politicians	2.23	2.00	0.91	0.00	4.00
Perception of trustworthiness of local politicians compared to national politicians	1.52	2.00	0.69	0.00	2.00

Table A.4 Size and number of local governments

Country	LG_1990	LG_2000	LG_2010	LG_2020	Change_ LG_ 2020_1990	MeanSize LG_1990	MeanSize LG_2000	MeanSize LG_2010	MeanSize LG_2020	Change_ MeanSize_ 2020_1990
Albania	374	374	373	61	**-313**	8788	8259	7810	46520	**37733**
Andorra	-	7	7	7	**0**	7787	9341	12065	11038	**3251**
Argentina	2179	2187	2261	2173	**-6**	14970	16859	18040	20882	**5913**
Armenia	-	930	915	482	**-448**	3804	3301	3145	6148	**2343**
Australia	823	621	538	518	**-305**	20735	30842	40951	49589	**28854**
Austria	2317	2358	2356	2094	**-223**	3314	3398	3550	4258	**945**
Belarus	1672	1672	1495	2637	**965**	6094	5969	6348	3564	**-2530**
Belgium	589	589	589	581	**-8**	16923	17404	18498	19890	**2967**
Bosnia and Herzegovina	-	71	71	72	**1**	62865	52833	52190	45567	**-17298**
Bulgaria	274	262	264	265	**-9**	31819	31184	28014	26141	**-5678**
Canada	4446	3820	3585	3476	**-970**	6228	§	9485	10934	**4705**
Chile	334	341	345	345	**11**	39744	44992	49457	55409	**15665**
Colombia	-	1088	1101	1101	**62**	31860	36425	41074	46215	**14355**
Croatia	172	546	556	556	**384**	27775	8184	7726	7279	**-20496**
Cyprus	380	380	379	78	**-302**	2017	2482	2936	15479	**13462**
Czech Republic	4100	6251	6250	6258	**2158**	2520	1641	1676	1710	**-811**
Denmark	275	275	98	98	**-177**	18694	19417	56609	59504	**40810**

Country	LG_1990	LG_2000	LG_2010	LG_2020	Change_ LG_ 2020_1990	MeanSize LG_1990	MeanSize LG_2000	MeanSize LG_2010	MeanSize LG_2020	Change_ MeanSize_ 2020_1990
Estonia	255	247	226	79	**-176**	6154	5656	5891	16849	**10695**
Finland	460	452	342	310	**-150**	10840	11452	15682	17841	**7001**
France	36693	36683	36685	35090	**-1603**	1587	1661	1773	1921	**333**
Georgia	1004	1004	69	64	**-940**	4783	4061	54880	58031	**53248**
Germany	15978	13735	11882	10789	**-5189**	4971	5986	6882	7715	**2744**
Greece	5923	1033	1034	332	**-5591**	1722	10461	10756	32276	**30554**
Hungary	3089	3158	3175	3178	**89**	3358	3233	3150	3068	**-290**
Iceland	213	124	77	69	**-144**	1196	2268	4130	5311	**4114**
Ireland	113	114	114	31	**-82**	31097	33379	40001	161120	**130023**
Israel	239	264	253	255	**16**	19498	23822	30133	36145	**16647**
Italy	8094	8097	8094	7904	**-190**	7008	7032	7324	7535	**527**
Japan	3223	3217	1727	1717	**-1506**	38312	39429	74157	73288	**34977**
Kosovo	-	30	33	38	**8**	62067	56667	53808	46720	**-15346**
Latvia	573	558	118	119	**-454**	4648	4243	17776	15979	**11332**
Liechtenstein	11	11	11	11	**0**	2617	3017	3272	3467	**850**
Lithuania	58	60	60	60	**2**	63756	58326	51621	46578	**-17177**
Luxembourg	118	118	116	102	**-16**	3236	3697	4370	6199	**2963**
Macedonia	34	123	80	81	**47**	58712	16543	25884	25721	**-32992**
Malta	67	68	68	68	**1**	5286	5737	6096	7725	**2439**
Mexico	2403	2452	2466	2479	**76**	34933	40334	46266	52010	**17077**

Country	LG_1990	LG_2000	LG_2010	LG_2020	Change_ LG_ 2020_1990	MeanSize LG_1990	MeanSize LG_2000	MeanSize LG_2010	MeanSize LG_2020	Change_ MeanSize_ 2020_1990
Moldova	959	649	893	898	**-61**	3096	4505	3187	2915	**-181**
Montenegro	20	21	21	24	**4**	30319	28807	29497	25905	**-4414**
Netherlands	672	537	431	355	**-317**	22249	29656	38551	49130	**26881**
Norway	448	435	430	356	**-92**	9468	10324	11370	15111	**5643**
Poland	2383	2491	2479	2477	**94**	15993	15359	15346	15321	**-671**
Portugal	305	308	303	308	**3**	32732	33409	34328	33460	**728**
Republic of Korea	260	232	223	226	**-34**	164882	202621	217343	229118	**64236**
Romania	2948	2951	3181	3181	**233**	7870	7605	6365	6063	**-1807**
Russian Federation	-	112	20339	17723	**17611**	1321155	1308901	7023	8131	**-1313025**
Serbia	145	145	145	145	**0**	52317	51837	50286	47643	**-4674**
Slovakia	2826	2883	2891	2890	**64**	1875	1869	1865	1889	**14**
Slovenia	62	203	221	212	**150**	32228	9798	9270	9906	**-22322**
South Africa	-	842	283	257	**-585**	43706	53406	180979	230773	**187067**
Spain	8108	8111	8115	8131	**23**	4794	5002	5740	5824	**1030**
Sweden	284	289	290	290	**6**	30137	30699	32338	35702	**5565**
Switzerland	3021	2899	2596	2202	**-819**	2223	2478	3014	3922	**1699**
Turkey	2061	3244	2966	1947	**-114**	26163	19495	24385	43317	**17155**
Ukraine	10572	11595	11622	9525	**-1047**	4908	4241	3947	4634	**-275**

Country	LG_1990	LG_2000	LG_2010	LG_2020	Change_ LG_ 2020_1990	MeanSize LG_1990	MeanSize LG_2000	MeanSize LG_2010	MeanSize LG_2020	Change_ MeanSize_ 2020_1990
United Kingdom	540	468	434	404	**-136**	106014	125839	144623	166374	**60360**
United States of America	84955	87525	90056	90075	**5120**	2938	3224	3435	3658	**720**
Total	**220083**	**219260**	**235747**	**225204**	**5121**	**2586785**	**2578607**	**1646317**	**1994421**	**-592365**

Note: For 2020–1990 changes the first data available was taken into account.

References

Allain-Dupré, D. (2018). Assigning responsibilities across levels of government. OECD Working Papers on Fiscal Federalism, No. 24.

Allain-Dupré, D., Chatry, I., and Moisio, A. (2020). *Asymmetric Decentralization: Trends, Challenges and Policy Implications*. Paris: OECD.

Almond, G. A. and Verba, S. (1963). *The Civic Culture: Political Attitudes and Democracy in Five Nations*. London: Sage Publications.

Anderson, G. (2008). *Federalism: An Introduction*. Oxford: Oxford University Press.

Askim, J., Baldersheim, H., Klausen, J. E., Renå, H., Smith, E., and Zeiner, H. (2013). *Hvordan påvirker det statlige tilsynet kommunene og det lokale selvstyret?* Oslo: NIBR-rapport 2013:20

Baldersheim, H. and Rose, L. (Eds.) (2010). *Territorial Choice: The Politics of Boundaries and Borders*. Basingstoke: Palgrave Macmillan.

Baldersheim, H. Houlberg, K., Lidström, A., Hlynsdottir, E.-M., and Kettunen, P. (2019). *Local Autonomy in the Nordic Countries*. A report for the Norwegian Association of Local and Regional Authorities. Universitetetet I Agder.

Bardhan P. and Mookherjee D. (2006) Decentralization, corruption and government accountability: An overview. In S Rose-Ackerman (Ed.), *International Handbook on the Economics of Corruption* (pp. 161–188). Cheltenham, UK and Northampton, MA, USA: Edward Elgar Publishing.

Bastianen, A. and Keuffer, N. (2024). Are the normative rationales of local autonomy related to democratic legitimacy justified? Evidence from 57 countries in Europe and beyond (1990–2020). *Local Government Studies*. http://dx.doi.org/10.1080/03003930.2024.2378128.

Bennett, R. (1993). European local government systems. In R. Bennett (Ed.), *Local Government in the New Europe* (pp. 28–47). London: Belhaven Press.

Bergström, T., Kuhlmann, S., Laffin, M., and Wayenberg, E. (2022). Special issue on comparative intergovernmental relations and the pandemic: How European devolved governments responded to a public health crisis. *Local Government Studies*, 48(2), 179–190.

Blöchliger, H. (2013). Measuring decentralisation: The OECD Fiscal Decentralisation Database. In J. Kim, J. Lotz, and H. Blöchliger (Eds.), *Measuring Fiscal Decentralisation: Concepts and Policies* (pp. 15–35). Paris: OECD and Korea Institute of Public Finance.

Bober, J. and Kozina, A. (2020). Local government in the V4 countries: Heady, stability or retreat? In S. Mazur (ed.), *Public Administration in Central Europe: Ideas as Causes of Reforms* (pp. 210–228). London: Routledge.

Boggero, G. (2018). *Constitutional Principles of Local Self-Government in Europe*. Leiden: Brill.

Bolgherini, S. and Lippi, A. (2016). Italy: Remapping local government from re-allocation and re-shaping to re-scaling. In U. Sadioglu and K. Dede (Eds.),

Theoretical Foundations and Discussions on the Reformation Process in Local Governments (pp. 265–287). Hershey, PA: IGI Global.

Bolgherini, S., Klotz, G., and Lennart Fromm, U. (2021). Context-driven local autonomy: The importance of differentiated assessments in asymmetric countries. *Revue internationale de politique comparée*, 28(1), 207–255.

Bouckaert, G. and Kuhlmann, S. (2016). *Local Public Sector Reforms in Times of Crisis.* London: Palgrave Macmillan.

Brunet P. (2004). *Vouloir pour la nation. Le concept de la représentation dans la théorie d'Etat.* Paris: Bruylant LGDJ-Montchrestien.

Buchanan, J. M. (1950). Federalism and fiscal equity. *American Economic Review*, 40(4), 583–599.

Buchanan, J. M. (1965). An economic theory of clubs. *Economica*, 32(125), 1–14

CCRE-CEMR – Council of European Municipalities and Regions (1953). The Charter of Municipal Liberties. https://www.ccre.org/img/uploads/piecesjointe/filename/charter_municipal_liberties_en.pdf.

CLRAE (Conference of Local and Regional Authorities of Europe) (1991). Resolution 223 on the role of local and regional authorities in integration policy between Western and Eastern Europe. https://search.coe.int/congress/Pages/result_details.aspx?ObjectId=090000168071a539.

CLRAE (Congress of Local and Regional Authorities of Europe) (1996). 3rd Session Resolution 34 on monitoring the implementation of the European Charter of Local Self-Government. https://rm.coe.int/on-monitoring-the-implementation-of-the-european-charter-of-local-self/1680719cee.

CLRAE (Congress of Local and Regional Authorities of Europe) (2010). Resolution 307. Revised Procedures for monitoring the obligations and commitments entered into by the Council of Europe member states in respect of their ratification of the European Charter of Local Self-Government (ETS No.122). https://rm.coe.int/CoERMPublicCommonSearchServices/DisplayDCTMContent?documentId=090000168071aa43.

Caby, V. and Frehen, L. (2021). How to produce and measure throughput legitimacy? Lessons from a systematic literature review. *Politics and Governance*, 9(1), 226–236.

Campbell, A. and Coulson, A. (2006). Into the mainstream: local democracy in Central and Eastern Europe. *Local Government Studies*, 32(5), 543–562.

Capano, G., Howlett, M., Jarvis, D. S., Ramesh, M., and Goyal, N. (2020). Mobilizing policy (in)capacity to fight COVID-19: Understanding variations in state responses. *Policy and Society*, 39(3), 285–308.

Caramani, D. (2023). *Comparative Politics* (6th edition). Oxford: Oxford University Press.

Chatry, I., Melchor, O., Michalun, M., Ruiz, A., and Zapata, I. (2017). *Making Decentralization Work in Chile: Towards Stronger Municipalities. Main Findings and Recommendations.* Paris: OECD.

Chevallier, J. (2019). *Science Administrative* (6th edition). Paris: Themis Droit.

Claassen, C. and Magalhães, P. C. (2022). Effective government and evaluations of democracy. *Comparative Political Studies*, 55(5), 869–94.

Clark, G. L. (1984). A theory of local autonomy. *Annals of the Association of American Geographers*, 74(2), 195–208.

Collier, D., LaPorte, J., and Seawright, J. (2008). Typologies: Forming concepts and creating categorical variables. In J. Box-Steffensmeier, H. Brady and D. Collier (Eds.), *The Oxford Handbook of Political Methodology* (pp. 152–171). Oxford: Oxford University Press.

Collier, D., LaPorte, J., and Seawright (2012). Putting typologies to work: Concept formation, measurement, and analytic rigor. *Political Research Quarterly*, 65(1), 217–232.

Council of Europe (1999). Supervision and Auditing of Local Authorities' Action, Local and Regional Authorities in Europe No. 1966. Strasbourg.

Council of Europe (2019). Recommendation CM/Rec (2019) 3 of the Committee of Ministers to Member States on Supervision of Local Authorities' Activities. Adopted by the Committee of Ministers on 4 April 2019 at the 1343rd meeting of the Ministers' Deputies. Strasbourg.

Council of Europe, CM (Committee of Ministers) (1961). Resolution (61)20 of the Committee of Ministers of the Council of Europe: 'Charter of the European Conference of Local Authorities'. https://www.cvce.eu/en/obj/resolution_61_20_of_the_committee_of_ministers_of_the_council_of_europe_13_september_1961-en-7c3f04ae-aa63–4a99–9396–04f4a60e6a0f.html.

Council of Europe, CM (Committee of Ministers) (1994). Statutory Resolution (94) 3Relating to the Setting up of the Congress of Local and Regional Authorities of Europe. https://rm.coe.int/09000016804efe6c.

Council of Europe, CM (Committee of Ministers) (2000). Statutory Resolution (2000) 1 Relating to the CLRAE.

Council of Europe. Consultative Assembly (1968). Resolution 64 on a Declaration of Principles on Local Autonomy. https://search.coe.int/congress/Pages/result_details.aspx?ObjectId=0900001680718fec.

Council of Europe. Consultative Assembly (1970). Recommendation 615 (1970) on a 'Declaration of Principles on Local Autonomy'. http://assembly.coe.int/nw/xml/XRef/Xref-XML2HTML-en.asp?fileid= 14649&lang=en.

Cravacuore, D. A. (2017). La recentralización municipal en América Latina. In A. Zicardi and D. A. Cravacuore (Eds.), *Los gobiernos locales y las políticas de vivienda en México y América Latina* (pp. 35–48). México: Universidad Nacional Autónoma de México.

Dahl, R. A. (1994). A democratic dilemma: System effectiveness versus citizen participation. *Political Science Quarterly*, 109(1), 23–34.

Dahl, R. A. and Tufte, E. (1973). *Size and Democracy.* Stanford, CA: Stanford University Press.

Däubler, T., Müller, J., and Stecker, C. (2018). Assessing democratic representation in multilevel democracies. *West European Politics*, 41(3), 541–564.

Daun, H. (2004). Privatisation, decentralisation and governance in education in the Czech Republic, England, France, Germany and Sweden. *International Review of Education*, 50, 325–346.

Denters, B. and Rose, L. (2006). Towards local governance. In B. Denters and L. Rose (Eds.), *Comparing Local Governance: Trends and Developments* (pp. 246–262). Basingstoke: Palgrave Macmillan.

Denters, B., Goldsmith, M., Ladner, A., Mouritzen, P. E., and Rose, L. (2014) *Size and Local Democracy.* Cheltenham, UK and Northampton, MA, USA: Edward Elgar Publishing.

DiMaggio P. J. and Powell, W. W. (1983) The iron cage revisited: Institutional isomorphism and collective rationality in organisational fields. *American Sociological Review*, 48(2), 147–160.

Diamond, L. (2002), Elections without democracy: Thinking about hybrid regimes. *Journal of Democracy*, 13(2), 21–35.

Do Vale, H. (2015). Comparing and measuring subnational autonomy across three continents. *Lex Localis – Journal of Local Self-Government*, 13(3), 741–764.

Dobre, A. M. (2012). Romania: From historical regions to local decentralization via the unitary state. In J. Loughlin, F. Hendriks and A. Lidström (Eds.), *The Oxford Handbook of Local and Regional Democracy in Europe* (pp. 685–714). Oxford: Oxford University Press.

Elazar, D. J. (1976). Federalism vs. decentralization: The drift from authenticity. *Publius*, 6(4), 9–19.

Engler, S., Leemann, L., Abou-Chadi, T., et al. (2020). *Democracy Barometer. Codebook Version 7.* Aarau: Zentrum der Demokratie.

European Commission (2022). Eighth Report on Economic, Social and Territorial Cohesion. Luxembourg: Publications Office of the European Union. KN-01–22–027-EN-N.

Fesler, J. W. (1965). Approaches to the understanding of decentralization. *The Journal of Politics*, 27(3), 536–566.

Fiorillo, F., Giuranno, M., and Sacchi, A. (2021). Asymmetric decentralization: Distortions and opportunities. *Economia Politica*, 38(12), 625–656.

Fleurke, F. and Willemse, R. (2004). Approaches to decentralization and local autonomy: A critical appraisal. *Administrative Theory and Practice*, 26(4), 523–544.

Fukuyama, F. (2011). *The Origins of Political Order.* New York: Farrar, Straus and Giroux.

Galette A. (1982). The Draft Charter of Local Self-Government Submitted by the Conference of Local and Regional Authorities of Europe. *German Yearbook of International Law*, 25, 309–353.

Gendźwiłł, A. (2021). Local autonomy and national–local turnout gap: Higher stakes, higher turnout? *Regional & Federal Studies*, 31(4), 519–539.

Gendźwiłł, A., Kjaer, U., and Steyvers, K. (Eds.). (2022). *The Routledge Handbook of Local Elections and Voting in Europe.* London: Routledge.

Goldsmith, M. (1990). Local autonomy: Theory and practice. In D. S. King and J. Pierre (Eds.), *Challenges to Local Government* (pp 15–36). London: Sage Publications.

Goldsmith, M. (1995). Autonomy and city limits. In D. Judge, G. Stocker, and H. Wolman (Eds.), *Theories of Urban Politics* (pp. 228–252). London: Sage Publications.

Goodspeed, T. J. (2002). Bailouts in a federation. *International Tax and Public Finance*, 9, 409–421.

Greenstone, M., Guojun H., Ruixue J., and Tong L. (2022). Can technology solve the principal-agent problem? Evidence from China's war on air pollution. *American Economic Review: Insights*, 4(1), 54–70.

Guérard, S. (2016). Local autonomy in Europe: Myth or reality? Is the ideal image of local autonomy as it is described and promoted by the Council of Europe (The Congress of Local and Regional Authorities) realistic? In S. Guérard and A. Astrauskas (Eds.), *Local Autonomy in the 21st Century: Between Tradition and Modernization* (pp. 39–60). Institut Universitaire Varenne: Collection Kultura.

Gurr, T. R. and King, D. S. (1987) *The State and the City.* London: Macmillan.

Guzman, A. (2002). A compliance-based theory of international law. *California Law Review*, 90(6), 1823–1887.

Hajnal, G. (2016). New wine in old bottles? Assessing Hungary's post-2010 public administration reforms. In G. Hammerschmid, S. Van de Walle, R. Andrews, and P. Bezes (Eds.), *Public Administration Reforms in Europe: The View from the Top* (pp. 96–104). Cheltenham, UK and Northampton, MA, USA: Edward Elgar Publishing.

Hajnal, G. and Rosta, M. (2019). A new doctrine in the making? Doctrinal foundations of subnational governance reforms in Hungary (2010–2014). *Administration & Society*, 51(3), 404–430.

Hamilton, A. and Madison, J. (1788). Federalist No. 51: The structure of the government must furnish the proper checks and balances between the different departments. New York Packet 1788. https://guides.loc.gov/federalist-papers/text-51–60.

Hansen, T. and Klausen, J. E. (2002). Between the welfare state and local government autonomy. *Local Government Studies*, 28(4), 47–66.

Harguindéguy, J.-B. P., Cole, A., and Pasquier, R. (2021). The variety of decentralization indexes: A review of the literature. *Regional & Federal Studies*, 31(2), 185–208.

Haus, M., Heinelt, H., and Stewart, M. (Eds.) (2004). *Urban Governance and Democracy: Leadership and Community Involvement*. London: Routledge.

Heinelt, H. and Hlepas, N. (2006). Typologies of local government systems. In H. Bäck, H. Heinelt, and A. Magnier (Eds.), *The European Mayor: Political Leaders in the Changing Context of Local Democracy* (pp. 21–42). Wiesbaden: VS Verlag.

Heinelt, H., Hlepas, N., Kuhlmann, S., and Swianiewicz, P. (2018a). Local government systems: Grasping the institutional environment of mayors. In H. Heinelt, A. Magnier, M. Cabria, and H. Reynaert (Eds.), *Political Leaders and Changing Local Democracy: The European Mayor* (pp. 19–78). Cham: Palgrave Macmillan.

Heinelt, H., Magnier, A., Cabria, M., and Reynaert, H. (Eds.) (2018b). *Political Leaders and Changing Local Democracy. The European Mayor*. Cham: Palgrave Macmillan.

Helliwell, J. F., Layard, R., Sachs, J., and De Neve, J.-E. (2020). *World Happiness Report 2020*. New York: Sustainable Development Solutions Network

Hendriks, F., Loughlin, J., and Lidström, A. (2012). European subnational democracy: Comparative reflections and conclusions. In J. Loughlin, F. Hendriks, and A. Lidström (Eds.), *The Oxford Handbook of Local and Regional Democracy in Europe* (pp. 715–742). Oxford: Oxford University Press.

Hesse, J. and Sharpe, L. J. (1991). Local government in international perspective: Some comparative observations. In J. Hesse (Ed.), *Local Government and Urban Affairs in International Perspective: Analyses of Twenty Western Industrialized Countries* (pp. 603–621). Baden-Baden: Nomos-Verlagsgesellschaft.

Himsworth, C. (2015). *European Charter of Local Self-Government: A Treaty for Local Democracy*. Edinburgh: Edinburgh University Press.

Hlepas, N. (2016). Is it the twilight of decentralization? Testing the limits of functional reforms in the era of austerity. *International Review of Administrative Sciences*, 82(2), 273–290.

Hlepas, N. (2020). Local government and regional administration. In K. Featherstone and D. Sotiropoulos (Eds.), *The Oxford Handbook of Modern Greek Politics* (pp. 187–202). Oxford: Oxford University Press.

Hooghe, L. and Marks, G. (2016). *Community, Scale, and Regional Governance. A Postfunctionalist Theory of Governance, Volume 2*. Oxford: Oxford University Press.

Hooghe, L., Marks, G., and Schakel, A. (2010). *The Rise of Regional Authority: A Comparative Study of 42 Democracies*. London and New York: Routledge.

Hooghe, L., Marks, G., Schakel, A., Chapman, H., Osterkatz, S., Niedzwieckiand, S., and Shair-Rosenfield, S. (2016). *Measuring Regional Authority: A Postfunctionalist Theory of Governance, Volume 1*. Oxford: Oxford University Press.

Howse, R. and Teitel, R. (2010). Beyond compliance: Rethinking why international law really matters. *Global Policy*, 1(2), 127–136.

Ivanyna, M. and Shah, A. (2014). How close is your government to its people? Worldwide indicators on localization and decentralization. *Economics: The Open-Access, Open-Assessment E-Journal*, 3(8), 1–62.

Jensen, M C. and Meckling, W. H. (1976). Theory of the firm: Managerial behavior, agency costs and ownership structure. *Journal of Financial Economics*, 3(4), 305–360.

Jones, G. W., & Stewart, J. D. (1982). The value of local autonomy — A rejoinder. *Local Government Studies*, 8(5), 10–15. https://doi.org/10.1080/03003938208433030.

KMDs Organisasjonsdatabase (2021). *Sluttrapport 2021. Rapport 13:2021.* Oslo: Ministry of Local Government and Regional Affairs.

Kalimeri, V. (2017). *Le Conseil de l'Europe et les collectivités territoriales. Contribution a l'étude de l' autonomie locale.* Paris: L'Harmattan.

Kaufmann, D. and Kraay, A. (2023). *Worldwide Governance Indicators, 2023 Update.* www.govindicators.org.

Kersting, N., Caulfield, J., Nickson, A., Olowu, D., and Wollmann, H. (2009). *Local Governance Reforms in Global Perspective.* Wiesbaden: VS Verlag.

Keuffer, N. (2016). Local autonomy, a multifaceted concept: How to define it, how to measure it and how to create a comparative local autonomy index? Paper presented at the International Congress of the International Political Science Association (IPSA), Poznań, Poland.

Keuffer, N. and Ladner, A. (2021). Local and regional autonomy: Indexes and trends. In M. Callanan and J. Loughlin (Eds.), *A Research Agenda for Regional and Local Government* (pp. 19–34). Cheltenham, UK and Northampton, MA, USA: Edward Elgar Publishing.

King, D. S. and Stoker, G. (Eds.) (1996). *Rethinking Local Democracy.* Basingstoke: Palgrave Macmillan.

Kiuriene, V. (2020). Administrative supervision of local self-government in the Baltic states: A comparative view. *Journal of Education Culture and Society*, 6(2), 394–410.

Knemeyer, F. L. (1989). *Die Europäische Charta der kommunalen Selbstverwaltung.* Baden-Baden: Nomos.

Kreci, V. and Ymeri, B. (2010). The impact of territorial re-organisational policy interventions in the Republic of Macedonia. *Local Government Studies*, 36(2), 271–290.

Kuhlmann, S. and Wayenberg, E. (2015). Institutional impact assessment in multi-level systems: Conceptualizing decentralization effects from a comparative perspective. *International Review of Administrative Sciences*, 82(2), 233–254.

Kuhlmann, S. and Wollmann, H. (2019). *Introduction to Comparative Public Administration: Administrative Systems and Reforms in Europe* (2nd edition). Cheltenham, UK and Northampton, MA, USA: Edward Elgar Publishing.

Ladner, A. (2017). Autonomy and austerity: Re-investing in local government. In C. Schwab, G. Bouckaert, and S. Kuhlmann (Eds.), *The Future of Local Government in Europe: Lessons from Research and Practice in 31 Countries* (pp. 23–52). Baden-Baden: Nomos.

Ladner, A. and Keuffer, N. (2021). Creating an index of local autonomy: Theoretical, conceptual, and empirical issues. *Regional & Federal Studies*, 31(2), 209–234.

Ladner, A. and Keuffer, N. (2023). Decentralisation and autonomy: A picture of big differences. In F. Teles (Ed.), *Handbook on Local and Regional Governance* (pp. 65–81). Cheltenham, UK and Northampton, MA, USA: Edward Elgar Publishing.

Ladner, A., Keuffer, N., and Baldersheim, H. (2016). Measuring local autonomy in 39 countries. *Regional & Federal Studies*, 26(3), 321–357.
Ladner A., Keuffer N., Baldersheim H., Hlepas N., Swianiewicz P., Steyvers K., and Navarro C. (2019). *Patterns of Local Autonomy in Europe*. Cham: Palgrave Macmillan.
Ladner A., Keuffer N., and Bastianen A. (2021). Local Autonomy Index in the EU, Council of Europe and OECD Countries (1990–2020). Release 2.0. Brussels: European Commission.
Ladner, A., Keuffer, N., and Bastianen, A. (2023). Local autonomy around the world: The updated and extended Local Autonomy Index (LAI 2.0). *Regional & Federal Studies*. https://doi.org/10.1080/13597566.2023.2267990.
Laffant, J-J. (Ed.) (2003). *The Principal Agent Model: The Economic Theory of Incentives*. Cheltenham, UK and Northampton, MA, USA: Edward Elgar Publishing.
Lauth, H-J. and Schlenkrich, O. (2021) Democracy Matrix Codebook V.4. www.democracymatrix.com.
Lidström, Á. (1998). The comparative study of local government systems: A research agenda. *Journal of Comparative Policy Analysis: Research and Practice*, 1(1), 97–115.
Lidström, A. (2019). Patterns of asymmetrical divisions of functions at local level in Europe. ECPR General Conference, Wroclaw.
Lippi, A. and Tsekos, T. N. (Eds.) (2019). *Local Public Services in Times of Austerity across Mediterranean Europe*. Cham: Palgrave Macmillan.
Loughlin, J., Hendriks, F., and Lidström, A. (Eds.) (2012). *The Oxford Handbook of Local and Regional Democracy in Europe*. Oxford: Oxford University Press.
Lowi, T. J. (1972). Four systems of policy, politics, and choice. *Public Administration Review*, 32(4), 298–310.
Lyon, A. (2012). *Decentralisation and the Management of Ethnic Conflict: A Case Study of the Republic of Macedonia*. Bradford: University of Bradford.
Magnier, A. (2003). Subsidiarity: Fall or premise of 'local government reforms'. The Italian case. In N. Kersting and A. Vetter (Eds.), *Reforming Local Government in Europe: Closing the Gap between Democracy and Efficiency* (pp. 183–196). Opladen: Leske + Budrich.
Marcou, G. (2010). *Local Competences in Europe. Situation in 2007.* Study of the European Committee on Local and Regional Democracy (CDLR). Strasbourg: Council of Europe.
Mazur, S. (Ed). (2020). *Public Administration in Central Europe: Ideas as Causes of Reforms*. London: Routledge.
Meunier, B. (2006). Les règles relatives aux transferts de compétences entre collectivités publiques. Droit. Université d'Auvergne-Clermont-Ferrand.
Mello, L. de and Tovar Jalles, J. (2024). Natural disasters and intergovernmental relations: More or less decentralisation? *Regional Studies*. https://doi.org/10.1080/00343404.2024.2310116.
Mill, J. S. (1991 [1835]). Considerations on representative government. In J. Gray (Ed.), *John Stuart Mill: On Liberty and Other Essays* (pp. 5–128). Oxford and New York: Oxford University Press.
Mill, J. S. (1994 [1859]). *M. de Tocqueville on Democracy in America, Volume 2.* London: John W. Parker and Son.
Mouritzen, P. E., & Svara, J. H. (2002). Leadership at the Apex: Politicians and Administrators in Western Local Governments. Pittsburgh: University of Pittsburgh Press.

Musgrave, R. A. and Musgrave, P. B. (1976). *Public Finance in Theory and Practice.* New York: McGraw-Hill.

Navarro, C. and Pano, E. (2019). Spanish local government and the austerity plan: In the eye of the perfect storm. In A. Lippi and T. N. Tsekos (Eds.), *Local Public Services in Times of Austerity across Mediterranean Europe* (pp. 95–114). Cham: Palgrave Macmillan.

OECD (2004). Development Evaluation: Lessons Learned on Donor Support to Decentralization and Local Governance. DAC Evaluation Series. Paris: OECD Publishing.

OECD (2013). Investing Together: Working Effectively across Levels of Government. Paris: OECD Publishing. http://dx.doi.org/10.1787/9789264197022-en.

OECD (2017). Governance of Land Use. Paris: OECD Publishing.

OECD (2019). *Making Decentralization Work: A Handbook for Policy-Makers.* Paris: OECD Publishing.

OECD (2022). Regions and Cities at a Glance.https://www.oecd.org/cfe/oecd-regions-and-cities-at-a-glance-26173212.htm.

OECD and KIPF (2016). Fiscal Federalism 2016: Making Decentralization Work. Paris: OECD Publishing.

Oates, W. E. (1972). *Fiscal Federalism.* New York: Harcourt Brace Jovanovich.

Oates, W. E. (1999). An essay on fiscal federalism. *Journal of Economic Literature*, 37(3), 1120–1149.

Oates, W. E. (2005). Toward a second-generation theory of fiscal federalism. *International Tax and Public Finance*, 12, 349–373.

Olson Jr, M. (1969). The principle of 'fiscal equivalence': The division of responsibilities among different levels of government. *American Economic Review*, 59(2), 479–487.

Page, E. (1982). The value of local autonomy. *Local Government Studies*, 8(4), 21–42.

Page, E. (1991). *Localism and Centralism in Europe: The Political and Legal Bases of Local Self-Government.* Oxford: Oxford University Press.

Page, E. and Goldsmith, M. (1987a). Centre and locality: Functions, access and discretion. In E. Page and M. Goldsmith (Eds.), *Central and Local Government Relations: A Comparative Analysis of West European States* (pp. 3–11). London: Sage Publications.

Page, E. and Goldsmith, M. (1987b). *Central and Local Government Relations: A Comparative Analysis of West European Unitary States.* London: Sage Publications.

Page, E. & Goldsmith, M. (Eds.) (2010). *Changing Government Relations in Europe. From Localism to Intergovernmentalism.* London: Routledge.

Palermo, F. (2021). The impact of the pandemic on the Italian regional system. Centralizing or decentralizing effects? In R. Chattopadhyay, F. Knüpling, D. Chebenova, L. Whittington, and P. Gonzalez (Eds.), *Federalism and the Response to COVID-19: A Comparative Analysis* (pp. 104–112). London: Routledge India.

Paquet, M. and R. Schertzer. (2020). COVID-19 as a complex intergovernmental problem. *Canadian Journal of Political Science/Revue Canadienne de Science Politique*, 53, 343–347.

Pasquier, R. (2021). Devolution, functional decentralization or recentralization? Convergence and divergence in the European territorial governance. In M. Callanan and J. Loughlin (Eds.), *A Research Agenda for Regional and Local Government* (pp. 49–62). Cheltenham, UK and Northampton, MA, USA: Edward Elgar Publishing.

Peters, B. G. (2011). Governance responses to the fiscal crisis: Comparative perspectives. *Public Money & Management*, 31(1), 75–80.

Pierre, J. (1990). Assessing local autonomy. In D. S. King and J. Pierre (Eds.), *Challenges to Local Government* (pp. 37–54). London: Sage Publications.

Pratchett, L. (2004). Local autonomy, local democracy and the 'new localism'. *Political Studies*, 52(2), 358–375.

Prud'homme, R. (1994). On the dangers of decentralization. World Bank Policy Research Working Paper.

Prud'homme, R. (1995). The dangers of decentralization. *World Bank Research Observer,* 10, 201–220.

Putnam, R. (1994). *Making Democracy Work: Civic Traditions in Modern Italy.* Princeton: Princeton University Press.

Reddy, P., Nemec, J., & De Vries, M. (2015). The State of Local Government. *Public Policy and Administration, 14*(3), 160–176.

Rodríguez-Pose, A. and Ezcurra, R. (2011). Is fiscal decentralization harmful for economic growth? Evidence from the OECD countries. *Journal of Economic Geography*, 11(4), 619–643.

Scharpf, F. W. (1970). *Demokratietheorie zwischen Utopie und Anpassung.* Konstanz: Universitätsverlag.

Scharpf F. W. (1985). Die Politikverflechtungs-Falle: Europäische Integration und deutscher Föderalismus im Vergleich. *Politische Vierteljahresschrift*, 26(4), 323–356.

Schmidt, V. (2013). Democracy and legitimacy in the European Union revisited: Input, output and 'throughput'. *Political Studies*, 61(1), 2–22.

Schmidt V. and Wood M. (2019). Conceptualizing throughput legitimacy: Procedural mechanisms of accountability, transparency, inclusiveness and openness in EU governance. *Public Administration*, 97(4), 727–740.

Seabright, P. (1996). Accountability and decentralization in government: An incomplete contracts model. *European Economic Review*, 40, 61–89.

Sellers, J. (2005). Re-placing the nation: An agenda for comparative urban politics. *Urban Affairs Review*, 40(4), 419–445.

Sellers, J. (2019). From within to between nations: Subnational comparison across borders. *Perspectives on Politics*, 17(1), 85–105.

Sellers, J. and Lidström, A. (2007). Decentralization, local government, and the welfare state. *Governance: An International Journal of Policy Administration and Institutions*, 20(4), 609–632.

Sellers, J., Lidström, A., and Bae, Y. (2020). *Multilevel Democracy: How Local Institutions and Civil Society Shape the Modern State.* Cambridge: Cambridge University Press.

Sharpe L. J. (1993). The European meso: An appraisal. In L. J. Sharpe (Ed.), *The Rise of Meso Government in Europe* (pp. 1–39). London and Newbury Park, CA: Sage Publications.

Simmons, B. (2010). Treaty compliance and violation. *Annual Review of Political Science*, 13, 273–296.

Smith, T. (1951 [1851]). *Local Self-Government and Centralization.* London: John Chapman.

Smoke, P. (2015). Accountability and service delivery in decentralising environments: Understanding context and strategically advancing reform. In OECD (Ed.), *A Governance Practitioner's Notebook: Alternative Ideas and Approaches.* Paris: OECD.

Standard Eurobarometer STD94: Standard Eurobarometer 94 – Winter 2020–2021 (v1.00) (2021). [Data set]. European Commission, Directorate-General for Communication. http://data.europa.eu/88u/dataset/S2355_94_1_STD94_ENG.
Steenbergen, M. R. and Marks, G. (2007). Evaluating expert judgements. *European Journal of Political Research*, 46(3), 347–366.
Steyvers, K. (2019). Doing comparative research on local politics: At a crossroads between inertia and innovation. *Croatian and Comparative Public Administration*, 19(1), 53–78.
Stoker, G. (2006). Comparative local governance. In R. A. W. Rhodes, S. Binder, and B. Rockman (Eds.), *The Oxford Handbook of Political Institutions* (pp. 497–515). Oxford: Oxford University Press.
Stokstad, S. and Bock Segaard, S. (2013). *Forsvinner det kommunale selvstyret i statlig klagebehandling?* Oslo: Rapport KS 2013/Institutt for samfunnsforskning.
Sweeting, D. (Ed.) (2017). *Directly Elected Mayors in Urban Governance: Impact and Practice*. Bristol: Policy Press.
Swianiewicz, P. (2014). An empirical typology of local government systems in Eastern Europe. *Local Government Studies*, 40(2), 292–311.
Swianiewicz, P. (2020). Recent and contemporary trends in European studies of local government and local politics. In C. Nunes Silva (Ed.), *Contemporary Trends in Local Governance* (pp. 21–38). Cham: Palgrave Macmillan.
Sześciło, D. (2019). Is there a room for local and regional self-government in the illiberal democracy? Struggle over recentralization attempts in Poland. *Studia Iuridica*, 79, 166–179.
Teles, F. (Ed.) (2023). *Handbook on Local and Regional Governance*. Cheltenham, UK and Northampton, MA, USA: Edward Elgar Publishing.
The World Bank (2009). *Local Government Discretion and Accountability: Application of a Local Governance Framework*. Report No. 49059-GLB. Washington, DC: The World Bank.
Tiebout, C. (1956). A pure theory of local expenditures. *Journal of Political Economy*, 64(5), 416–424.
Tocqueville, A. de (1994 [1835]). *Democracy in America*. London: Fontana Press.
Tocqueville, A. de (2000). *Democracy in America*. London: University of Chicago Press.
Transparency International (2020). Corruption Perception Index 2020. https://www.transparency.org/en/cpi/2020.
UCLG (United Cities and Local Governments) (2008). *Decentralization and Local Democracy in the World*. First global report by United Cities and Local Governments.
UN-Habitat (2009). *International Guidelines on Decentralisation and Access to Basic Services for All*. Nairobi: United Nations Human Settlements Programme (UN-HABITAT).
Vetter, A. (2007). *Local Politics: A Resource for Democracy in Western Europe? Local Autonomy, Local Integrative Capacity, and Citizens' Attitudes towards Politics*. Lanham, MD: Lexington Books.
Vetter, A. and Kersting, N. (2003). Reforming local government: Heading for efficiency and democracy. In N. Kersting and A. Vetter (Eds.), *Reforming Local Government in Europe: Closing the Gap between Democracy and Efficiency* (pp. 333–349). Opladen: Leske + Budrich.

Watts, R. L. (2003). Introduction: Comparative research and fiscal federalism. *Regional & Federal Studies*, 13(4), 1–6.
Yilmaz, S., Beris, Y., and Berthet, R. S. (2010). Linking local government discretion and accountability in decentralisation. *Development Policy Review*, 28(3), 259–293.

Index